FIRE SERVICE LAW

FIRE SERVICE LAW

FOR EMERGENCY SERVICE PERSONNEL

4TH EDITION 2005

W.J. Wilkinson, B.S.E., J.D.

ISBN 10:   Softcover   1-4257-4709-4

ISBN 13:   Softcover   978-1-4257-4709-1

This is a work of fiction. Names, characters, places and incidents either are the product of the author's imagination or are used fictitiously, and any resemblance to any actual persons, living or dead, events, or locales is entirely coincidental.

This book was printed in the United States of America.

To order additional copies of this book, contact:
Xlibris Corporation
1-888-795-4274
www.Xlibris.com
Orders@Xlibris.com
36922

CONTENTS

INTRODUCTION

THE SOURCES OF AMERICAN LAW

THE COMMON LAW

It is of critical significance that if one is to engage in the study of any people, their history is an essential element of that pursuit. Who we are, as a nation and a culture, is derivative of who we were, and what forces and events came to shape us, and continue to define us, as the nation that we are today.

Our forefathers, prior to the establishment of our independent and self-governing nation, had a basis for conducting the daily affairs of business and life that had already been established far before landing at Plymouth Rock. It was a compilations of custom, traditions and laws that we know as the *Common Law*. This had come about as a direct result of the Norman Conquest of England in 1066. William the Conqueror, in order to provide for an effective rule over Great Britain (and the tribes of the Angles, Saxons, Celts, Scots, Picts, et al) imposed upon his subjects the unifying force of a system of laws that was common to all.

It was this cohesive system of laws that English subjects, six centuries later, would bring with them, as colonists to the brave new world on the Mayflower. Their authority was in the form of royal charters that allowed them to engage in the industries that provided their ability to survive economically, and develop trades such as the transference of slaves, molasses and rum into viable and profitable businesses. As such, they also made sources of income for the royal coffers in the form of taxes levied upon those profits.

Taxes upon English subjects, or the subjects of any monarchy, were the lifeblood by which the monarch kept up his standard of living, and provided the wherewithal to maintain armies to protect his kingdom from attack, or initiate attack on another sovereign, should that be necessary or desirable. But the subjects of the crown on English soil had access to something that the colonists did not, for practical purposes: a governmental body of the Parliament, which was composed of the House of Lords and the House of Commons. The colonists could ask for a redress of a grievance, but the delay in bringing it even to the attention of the Parliament and or the king, made for a practical lack of representation for them.

In the years after the colonists arrived, their energies were spent in the simple act of survival (made possible by the assistance of the native Americans they encountered) and establishing those first colonies as viable enterprises. It was after they were established and operating successfully that they could begin to turn their attention to the unique problems of the inequities of being lesser privileged subjects of the crown.

George III was probably no more a tyrant than any of the monarchs that had preceded him, and the colonists had not brought any secret conspiracies of revolution with them in the holds of the ships that crossed the Atlantic. They were, for the most part, loyalists to their monarch, notwithstanding that a good portion of them had sought, in addition to economic opportunities, a better life in the form of freedom to worship as they pleased.

Even if they were less than content with their treatment from George III, one of the elemental doctrines that had been established for ages was the fact of life, and English law, that the king could do no wrong, known as *Sovereign Immunity*. It was a complete bar to any redress of any action of the king, and it was accepted that, if the Massachusetts Bay Colony was operating under the authority of a royal charter, that immunity extended to their governmental actions by extension.

The government was a monarchy, and the monarch's legitimacy to the throne was by reason of his (her) heritage, generally the first born male heir of the previous ruler, and the authority was absolute, at least until the noblemen joined forces to establish that they themselves had some rights, memorialized in a document called the Magna Carta.

This was a feudal society, which based the availability of rights on the ownership of land. Since all of the land was under the reign of the King, he could grant an award of land to those who allegiance had been in the form of financial support and or the provision of men to defend the kingdom or attack another and thereby increase it.

Thus there were created by royal grant, lesser rulers of parcels of land in the form of barons, dukes, earls and the like.

Those who had no ownership simply worked the land for their masters and were known as serfs, and remained with the land when the authority over them changed by subsequent awards to those who thereafter won the favor of the king.

Another concept of the Common Law was that one who employed servants or agents to further the business of the master, then upon the negligence of that servant, his master should be held to answer, or be liable for the injuries or damages caused by the negligent servant. This concept was known as *Respondeat Superior*, literally, "Let the Master Answer" (for the negligence of the servant).

This then was the structure that was transported to the colonies in North America, and the essential of land ownership remained as the critical determinant in the establishment of the legal framework that governed *New* York, *New* Jersey, *New* Hampshire, as well as all the rest of these satellite extensions of the crown.

Thus the Common Law served as a template for the government and the orderly conduct of business in the young colonies, and remained a great cohesive mortar in binding them to England. It was their uniqueness from similar organizations on English soil, however, and the common grievances and life they shared on the rugged eastern shores of this new land, that eventually bound them together in stronger ties than those of their distant mother land.

JUDICIAL DECISIONS

For those without the protective cloak of sovereign immunity, who had not acted in furtherance of the king's business, redress could be had at the royal court, and at such lesser courts as the king established to deal with the ever growing need to settle disputes between his subjects and generally keep his peace throughout the kingdom.

When a dispute was resolved, that judicial decision remained in effect as the determination of similar disputes that came before the courts, and was known as *Stare Decisis* (The decision stands).

STATUTORY LAW

Written law that was created for a particular purpose were called *statutes*, passed into law originally and exclusively by the king, then later by the Parliament. An example was the Statute of Frauds (1577) which required that the transference of land must be accompanied by a writing, amongst other things, to be recognized. This too, was part and parcel of the Common Law that was planted in the colonial soil.

ADMINISTRATIVE LAW

Some authors would indicate as a source of our American Law, that which is produced by an Administrative Agency, a specific form of government created by the larger, autonomous one, to perform a specific task or regulate a particular area of commerce or industry. The National Labor Relations Board was created by Congress to oversee fair labor elections, regulate Labor-Management issues, and thereby create a more peaceful environment for worker and employer to function. As such, it becomes a mini-government if you will, with the same basic three powers of the Federal Government: to create law in the form of regulations, to decide disputes and interpret their regulations, and to enforce their regulatory scheme by fines and injunctions.

While the NLRB, FEMA, OSHA and EEOC are the creations of the US Congress, many other agencies are created by state or municipal governments, also with the same powers but limited to the jurisdiction granted by those governments, such as the Illinois Department of Public Health, the Office of the State Fire Marshal, the Illinois Department of Labor, to name but a few. Similarly, the Cook County Recorder's Office, the Greater Metropolitan Water Reclamation District, the Chicago Board of Education, and the Chicago Transit Authority are the type of local agencies we find in every jurisdiction.

But since these are created from the acts of legislatures, federal, state or municipal, they should be kept within the broader classification of Statutory Law for the purposes herein, unless some particular aspect should warrant examination.

THE CONSTITUTION

When the impatience with the lesser citizenship bestowed upon the colonists grew to much more than the grumbling in New England coffeehouses, the taxes continued without abatement and especially without the representation afforded those on English soil, the colonists began to think of themselves as not only unique, but bound together by similar grievances and in a common cause.

By the summer of 1776, the more vocal of their group had convinced enough of even the colonists loyal to the crown, that the only realistic option was severance from the ties of allegiance to England. Jefferson's words resounded with the not only the righteousness of their cause, but a sacred duty to establish a new form of government.

It would seem indeed that providence had some part in this for the colonists were clearly outnumbered by vaster armies of mercenaries and career soldiers, both which much more experience in the warfare of the day. Ill equipped and meager as they were, led by a young general with a good heart but little experience, the logistics of crossing of the Potomac in winter, together with the aggressive march by weak and hungry men toward the encampment of the Hessians, was probably not even considered as a viable threat by the enemy.

The war was won, however, and the new country now had to address the issue of how it would govern itself. It had a template of government from England in the bicameral houses of Parliament, and it had only to properly the balance of power in this new government to avoid any one branch becoming a substitute for the monarch from whom they had just severed all ties.

What was passed in 1787 was a blueprint for that government, a system of governance of this new republic that would be powerful enough to defend its citizens against foreign powers, and yet shackled enough so that it could not oppress the colonies, those governments which gave it life.

THE BALANCE OF POWERS

THE LEGISLATIVE POWER

Article 1, Section 1, vests the legislative power in Congress, (the Senate and the House of Representatives) and in Section 8, grants those specific powers of levying taxes, borrowing money, regulation of commerce, declaring war, maintaining armies and navies, et al. Included are those powers that would be ancillary to the enumerated ones, those that would be "necessary and proper" to carrying out the essential work of Congress. The limitation on this power is found in the Tenth Amendment, in reserving to the states and their people, any rights not delegated to Congress or prohibited to the states.

THE EXECUTIVE POWER

Article II, Section 1 vests the executive power within the President, which includes authority over internal affairs such as the appointment of ambassadors, cabinet members and the justices of the Supreme Court, "with the advice and consent of the Senate." The President has the power to pardon "for offenses against the United States," under Section 2, and Section 7 allows for his disapproval (veto) of an act of Congress. While this power limits Congress, it may override the presidential veto by a two-thirds majority, thus limiting the presidential veto power. Though not specifically set forth, the Executive Privilege has been implicitly accepted as necessary to protect the interests of the U.S., but even this has been curtailed in certain circumstances (*Nixon v Sirica*, 1973).

Article I, Section 2, states that the House of Representatives has the sole power to impeach (bring a formal charge of impeachment), and Section 3 provides that the Senate, presided over by the Chief Justice of the Supreme Court, has the sole power, by a two-thirds majority of those present, to convict.

THE JUDICIAL POWER

Article III vests the judicial authority in "one Supreme Court and such inferior courts as Congress may from time to time ordain and establish." The Article I courts are the Court of Claims, U.S. Tax Court, courts of the District of Columbia and the like.

Jurisdiction.
The Supreme Court has original jurisdiction over all cases in which a state is a party, cases involving ambassadors and such. It has appellate jurisdiction over all cases to which the judicial power extends except as limited by Congress.

The early case of *Marbury v. Madison* (1803) established that the Supreme Court's appellate jurisdiction extended into judicial review of other branches of government, state legislation and state judicial decisions under its authority over "cases arising under the Constitution."

Appeal from Federal Courts:
The Court must review appeal from a federal court when:

1) a federal statute has been held unconstitutional in a civil matter;
2) a state statute is held unconstitutional or in conflict with federal law;
3) an injunction from a 3 judge district court is appealed in a civil matter.

The Court may hear an appeal of any civil or criminal case from a court of appeals. The granting of the appeal is called *Certiorari*.

The Court may hear an appeal requested by a court of appeals. This is called *Certification*.

Appeal from State Courts:
The Court must hear the appeal

1) where a state court held a federal statute invalid, or a state statute challenged as unconstitutional was upheld.

The Court may hear the appeal

1) when the federal statute or treaty is questioned as unconstitutional;
2) when the state statute is challenged as unconstitutional; or
3) where any title, right, privilege or immunity under the Constitution or Federal statutes or treaties is raised in state proceedings.

The state court's decision must be *final*, and the appellant must have exhausted all administrative remedies before certiorari will be granted. Also, there must be an actual *case or controversy* and not a *moot* issue (the Court will not issue advisory opinions), the parties must have *standing* (an actual stake in the outcome), the issues *ripe* (not just theoretical or potential), and there must not be an ability to render a decision *without deciding federal question* (i.e., it can be decided on purely state law).

This then is a basic sketch of the system of American Government and the Constitution as originally set forth was the blueprint for the creation of the new republic, with the limitations and checks that would prevent power from becoming out of balance.

When the colonists also agreed that the individual should be protected from the reach of Federal Government into certain personal rights and privileges, they agreed to the first changes to their defining document of freedom. The first ten of these are known as *The Bill of Rights*.

THE BILL OF RIGHTS

Amendment One. Congress shall make no law respecting an establishment of *religion* or prohibiting the free exercise thereof; or abridging freedom of *speech*, or of the *press*; or the right of the people *peaceably to assemble*, and to petition the government for a redress of their grievances.

Amendment Two. A *well regulated militia*, being necessary to the security of a free State, *the right of the people to keep and bear arms*, shall not be infringed.

Amendment Three. No soldier shall, in time of peace be *quartered in any house*, without the consent of the Owner, nor in time of war, but in a manner prescribed by law.

Amendment Four. The right of the people to be secure in their persons, houses, papers, and effects, against *unreasonable searches and seizures*, shall not be violated, *and no warrants shall issue, but upon probable cause*, supported by Oath or affirmation, and *particularly describing* the place to be searched, and the person or things to be seized.

Amendment Five. No person shall be held to answer for a capital, or otherwise infamous crime, unless on presentment or indictment of a Grand Jury, except in cases arising in the land or naval forces, or in the Militia, when in actual service, in time of War or public danger; nor shall any person be subject for the same offence to be *twice put in jeopardy* of life or limb; nor shall be compelled in any criminal case to be a *witness against himself*, nor be deprived of life, liberty or property, without *due process* of law; nor shall private property be taken for public use, without just compensation.

Amendment Six. In all criminal prosecutions, the accused shall enjoy the right to a *speedy and public trial*, by an *impartial jury* of the State and the district wherein the crime shall have been committed, which district shall have been previously ascertained by law, and to be *informed of the nature and cause of the accusation*, to be confronted with the witnesses against him, to have *compulsory process for obtaining witnesses* in his favor, and to have the *Assistance of Counsel* for his defence.

Amendment Seven. In suits at common law, where the value of the controversy shall exceed twenty dollars, the *right of a trial by jury* shall be preserved, and no fact tried by a jury, shall be otherwise reexamined in any Court of the United States, than according to the rules of the common law.

Amendment Eight. Excessive bail shall not be required, nor excessive fines imposed, *nor cruel and unusual punishment* be inflicted.

Amendment Nine. The enumeration in the Constitution, of certain rights, shall not be construed to deny or disparage others retained by the people.

Amendment Ten. The powers not delegated to the United States by the Constitution, nor prohibited by it to the States, are *reserved to the States* respectively, or to the people.

All of the above summary is for the purpose of providing a key to understanding the principles of law set forth in the cases herein selected, and cannot substitute for a full study of the historical underpinnings of the Common Law, the most current statutes and judicial decisions interpreting them, and finally, the complete text of the Constitution and the defining decisions of the United States Supreme Court, who alone determines the breadth and scope of our most hallowed document.

TORT LAW

The Nature of the Wrong
    Private v. Public
    Standard of Proof
    Prima Facie Case

Classes of Tort
    Intentional
    Negligence
        The standard of Reasonableness
        The Prima Facie Case

Duty	*Horsham v Ft Washington*
Breach	*Johnson v Brown*
Damage	*Johnson v Brown*
Proximate	*Cause*
	Gilbert v New Mexico Construction

Defenses to Negligence
    Contributory Negligence
    Fellow Servant
    Assumption of Risk
        Bartels v Continental Oil
    Doctrine of Rescue
        Walker Hauling v Johnson
    The Fireman's Rule
        Krauth v Geller
        Dini v. Naiditch
    Erosion of the Rule
        Mahoney v Carus Chemical
        Hauboldt v Union Carbide
        Brown Trucking v Flexon Industries
        Furch v General Electric

Immunity: Sovereign to Statutory
Respondeat Superior
Sovereign Immunity
Steitz v Beacon
City of Daytona Beach v Palmer
No Duty   *Jackson v Chicago FF Union, Loc. 2*
Special Duty
Control
Anthony v City of Chicago
Inspections
Cracraft v City of St Louis Park
Andrade v Ellefson

TORT LAW

Public v. Private Wrong

The crime, as we shall examine later, is a *public* wrong as opposed to a *private* wrong. It is society as a whole that is harmed, notwithstanding that there is probably specific, often physical harm to an individual victim. When someone is a defendant in a criminal case, it is that society as a whole that prosecutes him for the harm done to it, e.g., People of the State of Arizona v. Miranda; the United States of America v. Wong Sun Kim; the city of Chicago v. William Smith. The prosecutor, as agent of the governing body (Village Prosecutor, State's Attorney) represents all of us in seeking to convict the defendant of violating a section of the appropriate statute, of committing the act or acts which are prohibited by the code of criminal conduct in his jurisdiction.

A Tort is a *private* wrong; harm done to someone's person or property. This minimalistic definition might also apply to a crime, and it does, but without more falls far short of providing workable understanding of either element of law. The genesis of Tort is in the Common Law, which also had as part of its progeny, crimes and contracts.

While the king could do no wrong, often his subjects did, and when that wrong was such as to disrupt his royal peace, it was a wrong against the entire society, punished by death, imprisonment or fine. If the wrong was a failure to live up to the terms of an agreement had between the parties, most often merchants, tradesmen and the like, remedies were allowed most often in the form of monetary damages. But between the two forms of law were the incidents of harm done to a specific party, causing harm or damage, by the acts of another, that fell short of the societal wrong called a crime, and were not a breach of any agreement.

There developed the body of law called Torts (derived from a French word meaning "wrong" or "twisted"). The tortuous conduct of a defendant, was that which harmed the person or property of the specifically injured party, the petitioner, and if all the elements were proven to the satisfaction of the king's court, there would be an order compensating him for the loss (damages).

The remedy of *injunctions*, orders of the court to cease and desist the tortuous conduct, arose when money damages, the common remedy for breach of contract, was insufficient to compensate the petitioner, or the harm was likely to recur.

The *prima facie* (*"at first sight"*,) case is the minimally required elements of a cause of action, which must be proven to the court; unless these elements are defeated by evidence from the defendant, the plaintiff will have established his prima facie case, and he need go forward with no further proof of his claim. If the prima facie case can be established by a *preponderance of the evidence* (e.g., 51%) then the plaintiff will be awarded monetary damages and/or injunctive relief by the court.

Generally, torts fall into two categories: one is the type of conduct that is intended by the defendant, and the other, more commonly known type, are those acts considered as negligence, resulting from the careless conduct of the defendant.

While the greatest attention in our text, as in the law, will be devoted to elements of negligence and the liability for negligent acts, we should examine some of the kinds of intentional torts that also create a cause of action for damages.

Intentional Torts

Property

1. **Trespass**. Entering upon the land or property of another without permission; the essence of the action is the unlawful entry, not the damages, which are often negligible. Land, as indicated, was the single, most critical factor in rights, and it was unlawful for anyone to interfere with those rights of the landowner.
2. **Conversion**. Unauthorized control over or use of the property of another without his permission.
3. **Nuisance**. The use of one's own property in such a way that it interferes with the rights of others' use of their property, or causes harm to them is considered nuisance. Where property is left in such disrepair, not sufficiently protected to keep persons from being harmed, especially inquisitive children, the doctrine is called *attractive nuisance*.

Personal

1. **Assault**: act or conduct which puts a person in reasonable apprehension of receiving injury; threatening injury with the apparent ability to carry it out; grossly insulting behavior

2. **Battery**: contact with a person of an injurious or insulting nature; striking or other intentional physical contact with a person without their permission.
3. **False Imprisonment**: holding another person against their will without legal justification.
4. **Slander**: orally stating things about someone that are damaging to their reputation, and
   Libel: stating things in print or otherwise publishing statements about someone that damages their reputation or good will.
5. **Intentional Infliction of Mental Distress**: Any action done with the intent to humiliate or cause great stress or distress to another person.

The intentional torts with the most immediate impact for by Fire and EMS personnel are probably those of battery, and to a much lesser extent, trespass and conversion. Generally, statutes in all jurisdictions allow for firefighter to come on the land and premises of property without permission, under the exceptions created even in the Common Law for *licensees/invitees*: persons granted permission by law to come onto property, enter premises, and under critical conditions, exercise such authority over it even unto its destruction, for the greater good of the public.

The law has also developed the fiction of implied consent to deal with the otherwise unpermitted contact with a person's body during the assessment and treatment phases of emergency services. Without it, every checking of pulse, tactile assessment, direct/indirect pressure points or many other phases of routine EMS work would constitute the tort of battery. So the law, as a matter of public policy, creates the legal presumption that anyone who was injured, and unable to give their consent to treatment for reasons of disability, comprehension or the like, would certainly do so to secure treatment for their injuries. Thus their consent is implied, if unable to be actually given.

Negligence

The vast area of Tort law that will be the subject of this text, however, will be the area of Negligence, wherein one has been injured, not by any intentional act of another, but by his failure to do something in a reasonable manner so as to avoid causing such injury. But what does the law, or society, consider as reasonable, since even reasonable people can disagree on just what is reasonable? What conduct should be considered as that which the law should deem to be subject to redress by the person wronged?

Justice Oliver Wendell Holmes, in his treatise, *The Common Law*, addresses the issue of defining the general standard of conduct:

> The rule that the law does, in general, determine liability by blameworthiness, is subject to the limitation that minute differences of character are not allowed for. The law considers, in other words, what would be blameworthy in the average man, the man of ordinary intelligence and prudence and determines liability by that. If we fall below the level in those gifts, it is our misfortune; so much as that we must act at our peril, for the reasons just given. But he who is intelligent and prudent does not act at his peril, in theory of law. On the contrary, it is only when he fails to exercise the foresight of which he is capable, or exercise it with evil intent, that he is answerable for the consequences.

Thus the fictional person against whom we shall measure our conduct is the average man, who acts with reasonable care so as to avoid injuring the property or person of another. This then, is the *Reasonable Man Standard*, and the actions of any one of us would be judged against this standard.

The *intent* of which Justice Holmes spoke will be studied in the area of criminal law (and to some extent where severely negligent actions have the semblance of intent), but for the purpose of our examination of Tort law, the controlling word is *foresight*.

The examination for liability is what was, or should have been, *reasonably* foreseen as a likely result of the conduct or behavior.

In 1928, the New York Court of Appeals decided a case which attempted to apply the reasonably foreseeable harm to the reasonably foreseeable party injured by the harm. Mrs. Palsgraf was standing on a train station near some scales. A passenger was running to catch the train pulling out, and the agents on the train tried to help him aboard, but in doing so, jostled some of his packages, which fell to the ground. The packages contained fireworks, which detonated when they struck the ground, and the force of the detonation tipped the scales which fell on Mrs. Palsgraf. While the jury found that the servants of the railroad were negligent, Justice Cardozo, representing the majority of four justices on the court, found that there was no liability to Mrs. Palsgraf, since there was no negligence toward her, only toward the tardy passenger. The negligence toward him, which was a foreseeable harm, could not be transferred, in effect, to her since the harm to her was not foreseeable. There was a strong dissent by the other three justices, as evidenced by Justice Andrews' argument:

> "Due care is a duty imposed on each of us to protect society from unnecessary danger, not to protect A, B or C alone." (*Palsgraf v. Long Island Railway Co.*, (1928), 248 N.Y. 339, 162 N.E. 99).

The debate on where to draw the line of foreseeability has extended far beyond the divided court of New York in 1928, in many jurisdictions, and there have been many decisions since which have refined the concept of liability along either the majority opinion or that of or the dissent. What might be distilled from this case, however, is an appreciation of the continuum as to how far a court is willing to extend the common law boundaries of foreseeability, and therefore liability.

What is fairly universally accepted is the burden of proof, which the plaintiff must prove to the judge or jury, as the prima facie case of negligence, and the basic elements without which there can be no liability.

Negligence: The Prima Facie Case

A Prima Facie case of negligence is the establishment, by competent evidence of the minimal basic elements of the tort.

1) **Duty**. The first element in proving up our case of negligence is that of duty, the duty to act so as to not cause injuries that are reasonably foreseeable to others. The duty can be that of a general obligation to act with appropriate care in all circumstances, or it may be imposed upon us by a law, such as a statute regulating the speed of automobiles on a highway.

2) **Breach** (of the Duty). When our conduct falls short of that required of reasonable people (driving without watching the road), or violates the statutorily imposed duty (by exceeding the speed limit), we have breached our duty of care and if proven by the plaintiff, will have established the second element of the prima facie case.

3) **Injury** (damages). Even though it is proven clearly that the defendant was negligent, there can be no liability if in fact, no one was injured by the defendant's negligence; i.e., if the plaintiff proves that the

defendant traveled at 80 mph down the highway posted at 55 mph, there is no liability if nothing else happened. Injury or damages to the plaintiff is the third element of the prima facie case of negligence, but the damages need not be physical to be compensable.

4) **Proximate Cause.** The injuries to the plaintiff must have been caused by the breach of defendant's duty to him; without such required causation, if the injuries complained of were not caused by the acts or conduct of the defendant, there will be no liability.

Up until 1981 in Illinois, there was a fifth element which caused some inequitable results. The plaintiff was also required to be free from any *contributory negligence* himself. If he were in any way negligent, recovery was barred, even though all the other elements were proven. Serious inequity resulted when a plaintiff who was 2% negligent, as an example, was denied any recovery for his damages from the acts of a 98% negligent defendant.

In 1981, the Illinois Supreme Court, in the case of *Alvis v. Rebar*, adopted what other jurisdictions had already incorporated: the theory of *comparative negligence*. Thus if our plaintiff were 2% negligent, he could still recover for 98% of his damages from the much more negligent defendant. The remaining 2% would be borne by the plaintiff himself. This resulted in a much more equitable allocation of liability. The plaintiff could still recover, notwithstanding the fact that he had been negligent himself.

Thus the establishment of the prima facie case in tort required the proof of its four elements: duty, breach, damages and proximate cause. The first of the elements required was duty, and at the threshold of the case was the presence or absence of duty. Since tort was a product of the common law, courts would look to see, initially, if there was any duty owed at common law. If there had been none at common law, the case was over.

For governments, that absence of duty was known as Sovereign Immunity, and was insurmountable against governmental defendants unless there had been a waiver by the enactment of statutes allowing for litigation against the governing body.

A clear case of duty is that of the Rules of the Road of various jurisdictions, which place various duties upon all those who drive vehicles upon our highways. While not identical, there are many similarities in the kinds of care imposed, such as speed and directional limitations, safety and lighting equipment, and the general standard of due care towards others on the road.

Right of way and the required yielding to another is set forth in all jurisdictions, with a clear deference to emergency vehicles such as police, fire and ambulances. The first of the cases examines upon whom that duty is placed.

Duty.

From the time of their very first emergency runs, most firefighters should have come to the realization that, while they are certainly often first responders, they are clearly not the only responders.

HORSHAM FIRE CO. NO. 1 v FORT WASHINGTON FIRE CO. NO. 1
Supreme Court of Pennsylvania (1956)
119 A.2d 71

MUSMANNO, Justice.

This case is unique in that it has to do with two fire companies which responded to an alarm to fight the common enemy and ended up by fighting each other. On October 9, 1951, the fire truck of the Horsham Fire Company collided with the fire truck of the Fort Washington Fire Company at the intersection of Welsh Road and Butler Pike in Montgomery County. The Horsham Fire Company sued the Fort Washington Fire Company in trespass and recovered a verdict of $10,331. The defendant moved for a judgment n.o.v. and a new trial. The Court below refused a judgment n.o.v. and granted a new trial. The defendant appealed urging the entering of judgment n.o.v . . . .

In the case at bar the driver of the Fort Washington fire truck drove through a stop sign on Butler Pike at a speed of from 55 to 60 miles per hour into an intersection which he knew to be a dangerous one, aware that drivers approaching from his right on Welsh Road could not see him because of a field of standing corn, as indeed it also shut off his vision of traffic coming from the east on that thoroughfare . . . .

The driver of the Horsham fire truck, although entitled to the same privileges enjoyed by the Fort Washington fire truck, was circumspect in his approach to the perilous intersection. While not ignoring the demands for reasonable dispatch in the fulfillment of his appointed mission to reach the conflagration to which his fire company had been summoned, he adjusted his movement to the circumstances which confronted him. Taking heed of a bus which had stopped on Welsh Road he decelerated his speed to 20 to 25 miles per hour and swung around the bus as he approached Butler Pike. Aware of the stop sign on Butler Pike, which should halt all traffic before crossing Welsh Road, and knowing that he was approaching the intersection from the right, he had reason to assume that the crossing would be clear for him to pass. He could not see the approaching defendant truck because of the field of unharvested corn which screened the lateral view of Butler Pike from his vision, nor could he hear the siren or bell of defendant's truck because of the din made by his own warning, noise-making devices as he hurried on his errand. Suddenly "a big red flash and a blur" loomed before him, and the crash followed. The speed of the defendant truck carried it 81 feet beyond the point of impact, the plaintiff truck drifted 31 feet before it turned over.

If the vehicles involved in this accident had been ordinary pleasure cars or business trucks, it is perhaps unlikely that the defendant would be seeking judgment n.o.v. since the issue of negligence, which was not a complicated one, was properly submitted to the jury which could find, as it undoubtedly did, that the defendant vehicle proceeded into the intersection at an excessive rate of speed after ignoring stop signs. It is urged, however, on behalf of the defendant, that this encounter was not the usual traffic accident since the defendant vehicle was an apparatus enjoying certain immunities under the Motor Vehicle Code.

It is true that fire department cars are not bound by certain prohibitions in the code. Sec. 501(f) of the Motor Vehicle Code, 75 P.S. § 501, provides that "The speed limitation set forth in this section (50 Miles per hour) shall not apply to vehicles, when operated with due regard for safety, . . . to fire department . . . vehicles when travelling in response to a fire alarm."

Section 1016(d) of the code, 75 P.S. §591 (d), declares that this section (requiring stoppage at "'Thru Traffic Stop'" signs) shall not apply to vehicles, when operated with due regard for safety . . . to fire department or fire patrol vehicles responding to a fire alarm."

Section 1013 of The Motor Vehicle Code, 75 P.S. §572, directs that when two vehicles approach an intersection at approximately the same time, "the driver of the vehicle . . . on the left, shall yield the right of way to the vehicle . . . on the right." Section 1014(b), 75 P.S. §573, however, provides an exception to this rule, namely, "The driver of a vehicle upon a highway shall yield the right of way to . . . fire department vehicles."

In view of these legalized immunities in behalf of fire department vehicles from requirements laid down for the ordinary passenger and commercial vehicles by the Code, counsel for the appellant contends that his client cannot be held liable in damages for doing what the law permits. But it is to be noted in this connection that while the law-in view of the vital and urgent missions of fire department vehicles-wisely allows them certain privileges over other vehicles, it does not assign to them absolute dominion on the road. The appellant's fire truck was engaged in a praiseworthy enterprise: it was on its way to extinguish a conflagration, it had the right to proceed through red lights, to surpass speed limits, and to take the right of way over ordinary vehicles. No words can be too laudatory in extolling the merit and sacrifice of members of volunteer fire companies who expend time, money, energies and often health and impairment of body without any recompense except the satisfaction of serving one's community and one's fellow man. The defendant here is a volunteer fire company, but it is to be kept in mind that the plaintiff is *also* a volunteer fire company. Its fire truck was also on its way to a fire, in fact, the same fire which cried for the services of the defendant company. The plaintiff company thus also had the right to discard speed limitations and to pass up stop signs.

It is, of course, regrettable that the vehicles of these estimable organizations should have met in collision. It is unfortunate that the very attribute which sounds the highest praise for fire companies, namely, speed, should have been the very demon that brought about their undoing. The need for celerity of movement on the part of fire engines and fire trucks is not only traditional but objectively demonstrable. The sooner the fire extinguishing apparatus arrives at the conflagration, the less chance there is that human lives and valuable property will be lost in the all-consuming blaze. But speed which is uncontrolled, is capable of wreaking as much havoc and causing as much sorrow as fire itself.

What happens when two vehicles with equally assumed privileges insist on the right of way? The answer was dramatically provided in this case: collision, destruction and disaster. It was providential that, considering the massive weight and size of the two trucks, no one was killed or injured. The most poignant type of regret is that which is based on a misfortune which could have been avoided, and it requires no sapience to conclude that when the paths of two fire engines cross, one of them must stop. This is not only a matter of common sense, but a proposition of imperious self-preservation.

The authors of the Motor Vehicle Code, in providing exemptions for fire vehicles, police cars, and ambulances, obviously intended those exemptions to operate against ordinary non-privileged vehicles, and not as against each other. Certainly they did not plan to set up at street crossings an arena of combat between police motorcycles and ambulances, hook-and-ladder vehicles and police wagons, between fire trucks and fire engines. Where parity is involved, elemental judgment dictates that normal rules must apply. Two police cars as against each other enjoy no privilege under the code. Their common purpose wipes out priority. * * * If two fire trucks arrive simultaneously at intersecting streets, one being confronted with a stop sign and the other with a through highway beacon, the fire truck facing the stop sign should stop to permit the other to proceed. It would be absurd for both vehicles to insist on precedence because they happen to enjoy similar privileges under the code. * * *

Appellant's counsel complains in his brief that to sustain the lower court would mean that the driver of every fire truck "must be prepared to slow down at every intersection to yield the right of way to some other hypothetical fire department vehicle that might just possibly be approaching from his right." But there is nothing on the road that can be less hypothetical than a fire truck. Its massive volume and elongated dimensions, its numerous chariot wheels, ponderous equipment, fiery color, screaming siren, clanging bells and flashing warning lights make it as conspicuous as a herd of trumpeting elephants on a rampage.

Maxon, the defendant's truck driver, knew that Welsh Road and Butler Pike formed a dangerous crossway. He testified that he saw one car proceeding east on Welsh Road before he arrived there. Despite defendant's counsel's argument that it would be impractical for the driver of a fire truck to be prepared to slow down at an intersection, Maxon was actually slowing down to stop at Welsh Road:

"Q. You say you were slowing down? A. I was slowing down, to stop.
"Q. To what? A. To stop.
"Q. To come to a stop. A. That is correct.
"Q. For what reason were you going to bring your truck to a stop. A. I have always figured that no fire is worth getting killed over."

Maxon knew this was a dangerous intersection:

"Q. Well, just tell us what was your intention or your purpose in stopping your truck at the Welsh Road intersection, or intending to stop it? A. Having lived in that section for many years, I know it is a very dangerous intersection. I wouldn't normally go through it without stopping.
"Q. Well, of course 'normally' is a word of some significance. Was this a normal or abnormal situation? A. To me, it was a normal situation. I would have stopped.
"Q. Normal for a fire truck? A. Regardless."

What caused Maxon finally not to stop was the waving of a passenger on the bus which Maxon interpreted as an invitation for him to proceed. But this ambiguous hand waving was a very precarious assurance on which to move into a recognized danger. Maxon did not know the passenger, the passenger was inside the bus and could not be aware of traffic conditions on all sides of the bus. The jury could well have concluded that Maxon's statement that he relied on so vague and unreliable a signal to hurl his 18,000 pound fire truck into an admittedly perilous situation was of itself enough to constitute the recklessness which would make the defendant liable in damages for what happened.

. . . Here we have an entirely novel situation where both vehicles stand in a favored class, and since neither can have an advantage over the other, they must in effect lose their priority rights and be treated as normal vehicles, insofar as rights against each other are concerned.

. . . The object of a fire truck's journey is not merely to make a show of rushing to a fire, but actually to get there. If the driver is to ignore all elements of safety driving at breakneck speed through obviously imperiling hazards, he may not only kill others en route, but he may frustrate the whole object of the mission and not get there at all! . . .

Affirmed.

It is important to note that the umbrella of sovereign immunity, as codified into the statutory immunity provided to fire service, though it was absolute in critical areas, did not shelter the firefighters riding on the public way in their "chariots of fire". On the highway, while there are statutory exemptions afforded to emergency vehicles, there is still the standard of due care required. The reasonable man has become the reasonable firefighter, or at least apparatus driver. An examination of the Illinois statute requiring all vehicles to pull over to the curb and yield to the approaching emergency vehicle, reaffirms this policy in the last sentence:

(b) This section shall not operate to relieve the driver of an authorized emergency vehicle from the duty to drive with due regard for the safety of all persons using the highway.

Breach of the Duty

The plaintiff, (and now respondent) Mr. Brown, was a passenger in a truck wherein the driver was "applying his brakes" as he was proceeding north on Chestnut Street, approaching West Commercial Row in the city of Reno, Nevada. A fire engine came around the corner, with lights and siren in operation, and struck the truck in the truck's lane.

There was case law from other jurisdictions that held that the use of lights and siren meets the duty of care (*Lucas v City of Los Angeles*, 10 Cal.2d 476, 75 P.2d 599,601) and case law that held that more than just lights and siren were required for due care (*Montalto v Fond Du Lac County*, 272 Wis. 552, 76 N.W.2d 279, 282).

The jury held for the respondent (the plaintiff, Brown) and the appeal followed by Johnson, the original defendant fireman, now the appellant.

H.C. JOHNSON *v* OREN BROWN
Supreme Court of Nevada (1959)
345 P.2d 754

McNAMEE, Chief Justice.

Appellant argues that the requirement that he drive "with due regard for the safety of others" is met by his compliance with the conditions that entitle him to exemptions.

There is substantial authority to sustain this view of the appellant.

In the case of Lucas v. City of Los Angeles, 10 Cal.2d 476, 75 P2d 599,601, where a statute similar to the Reno ordinance provided that an authorized emergency vehicle is exempt by law from complying with specified statutes and ordinances regulating the operation of vehicles on public roads, the court held that if such vehicle is responding to an emergency call, is displaying a visible red light from the front, and is sounding a siren, the driver thereof cannot be negligent in violating such regulations in the absence of reckless disregard of the safety of others. With respect to that part of the statute which states that the provisions thereof "shall not relieve the driver * * * from the duty to drive with due regard for the safety of others . . .

There have been jurisdictions that followed the concept that the duty of care on the road was met by the use of audible and visible warning devices, i.e., "lights and siren", but the more equitable doctrine provides that the use of lights and siren are statutorily minimally required, and there is still the requirement that must be met of driving with due care, especially considering that the exemptions already granted increase the possibility and probability of an accident. It should be noted that when the Supreme Court of Nevada was faced with this matter in a case of first impression, they opted to follow those jurisdictions which construed their statutes to mean that the provisions which authorized exemptions from rules of the road did not "relieve the operator of an authorized . . . vehicle from the duty to operate with due regard for the safety of all persons using the highway." *Montalto v. Fond Du Lac County, 272 Wis. 552, 76 N.W.2d 279,282.*

Even though the Nevada Supreme Court could have held with a series of cases from California allowing no recovery for negligence if a driver had met the minimal statutory mandates with lights and siren, they clearly thought the Wisconsin, Maryland and Michigan interpretations of requiring due care of their emergency vehicle drivers better law.

The facts of the case as well, tip the scales in favor of the plaintiff and against the apparatus driver who at a busy time of day for traffic, ignored the stop sign, drove in excess of the speed limit, on the wrong side of the street, and substantially cut the corner of the intersection (recognize anyone?). On his side of the scales were only siren and lights (still flashing?).

Damages (Injury)

A critical element of the Tort is that the party seeking to be compensated have sustained some injury. The injury or damages may in fact be physical, as the injuries resulting from a vehicular accident, or the damages could be economic, such as the loss of the vehicle involved in the same accident, lost time at work, the cost of securing medical treatment.

All of the above are considered compensatory damages, in other words, they involve a loss, and the plaintiff then seeks to recover appropriate compensation for those losses in the form of a money judgment against the defendant.

There are other damages not of a physical nature, such as psychological harm or emotional distress. While courts have been reluctant in awarding such damages, they nevertheless, under certain circumstances and in particular jurisdictions, have recognized them as a compensable loss. Some courts have required that there be some finding of physical injury as a prerequisite to finding such psychological damages, but more awards are being granted as a result of psychiatric testimony regarding the reality of mental disorders.

Often the recovery is allowed where the physical injury is to a member of the immediate family of the party suffering the emotional distress, or when the plaintiff was in the "zone of danger" and could have been injured, but narrowly escaped injury and/or witnessed the traumatic injury to another bystander.

Punitive damages are not normally recovered in general negligence cases, because they are more than what is compensation for injuries sustained. But where the negligence is so gross as to equate with a wanton and wilful negligence, which borders on intentional tort, for which punitive damages may lie, they are often awarded to deter others from such action.

While compensatory damages are mathematically ascertainable by evidence indicating the market value of property such as an automobile, or adding up the medical costs incurred as a result of the injuries, damages for pain and suffering are less quantifiable. In the previous case, while the attorney for the defendant objected to his opponent's mathematical determination of pain and suffering, the appellate court felt he had not overstepped his bounds nor invaded the province of the jury. In his summation on behalf of his client he had merely provided an imaginative approach to this question.

> The argument that I am going to make is obviously distasteful to the defendants' attorney, but it is the only way I can possibly aid you and give you a guide. If you think I am being unfair, you go into the jury room and say so and come to your own conclusion. It is the only way I know how to argue pain and suffering, and I am frank to say that, ladies and gentlemen. As I stated, what is it worth to have your femur violently driven into your pelvis? What is it worth to have your doctor save your life by a tube tapped into your chest? I suggest $5,000 for the initial blow and injury. He was in the hospital for 75 days, but for only 67, approximately, he was in traction and cast.
>
> You have seen the traction and you heard the doctor describe the cast. Now, what is it worth, what is it worth to have the traction pin pushed through your leg? What is it worth to have a cast around your body? What is it worth to be in a prison for 67 days? Would ten cents a minute be unfair? That would be $6 an hour. Consider it yourselves. I will give that ten cents a minute, $6 an hour. You can make up your minds whether you feel that is unfair or not. That would be $144 a day, or counsel can correct me if I am wrong, $9,648 for 67 days.

Proximate Cause

In proving up the Prima Facie case in Tort, it must be remembered that there must be a direct, causal connection between the defendant's breach of a duty owed the plaintiff, and the harm or injury to that plaintiff. The issue of causation is not always as easy as it seems at first to determine; while we can usually establish a sequence of events, the *proximate* cause can be more problematic, especially when the court itself seems confounded.

GILBERT v NEW MEXICO CONSTRUCTION CO.
Supreme Court of New Mexico (1935)
44 P.2d 489

WATSON, Justice.

Appellant was in pursuit of a paving contract with the city. Though informed of the location of the water mains, it so operated its power shovel, in excavating, as to break a main. This occurred at 10:00 A.M. Appellant immediately notified the city, which undertook the necessary repairs. With ordinary diligence the break could have been repaired in two hours. It remained unrepaired until about 6 o'clock P.M.

At about 5:30 P.M. appellee's house caught fire. When discovered, if water pressure had been normal, a garden hose would have been sufficient to extinguish the flames. The firemen, with their equipment, were on the spot within two to five minutes after the discovery of the fire. If the pressure had been normal it would have extinguished the fire without appreciable damage.

To facilitate the repairs, the city water superintendent directed the city engineer to reduce the pressure to twenty pounds, the normal being sixty. The fire fighters, finding the pressure to be insufficient, requested the operator of the pumps for more. He declined to increase it until so ordered by the water superintendent. It was increased later, and the fire extinguished, after damage of $3,700 to appellee's house, shrubbery, trees, lawn and flowers.

The court below found the foregoing facts, and held that the appellant's negligence was the proximate cause of the appellee's injury. It held that the city's negligence was a contributing cause, but that the city was not legally liable to appellee.

. . . It is next contended that the breaking of the pipe was not, in any sense, a cause of the damage. It is claimed that the repairs were complete before the fire alarm was given; that the broken main had ceased to affect the situation; and that the low water pressure was attributable solely to the failure of the city to restore it immediately upon completion of repairs, or at least when the alarm was given. This depends on nice calculation as to the time of events. It attacks the findings that the fire occurred about 5:30 o'clock, and that the repairs were completed at about 6. We doubt if the evidence brought to our attention would warrant disturbing those findings.

It is apparent that the repairs were completed and the fire discovered at about the same time. An attempt to reduce events to an exact and accurately timed sequence would no doubt fail, and does not seem warranted. We think that a few minutes delay by the city in restoring pressure after appellant had made it necessary to reduce it, would not enable us to say, as a matter of law, that the primary negligence had spent its force.

It is also contended that, even with the break unrepaired, sufficient pressure could have been furnished, at slight damage, to have enabled the firemen to accomplish their task. The trial court refused to find that, notwithstanding the break, "the water could have been turned on at . . . the plant when the . . . telephone communication was received from the scene of the fire . . . and sufficient pressure could have been forced to plaintiff's residence to have extinguished the fire." Appellant points to evidence which might have required the court to find that the mere existence of the break would not prevent putting the hydrant pressure to fifty pounds. It is not shown how long, the break existing, it would require to advance pressure from twenty pounds to fifty. After the fire broke out, time was important. Assuming that there is merit in the legal contention, we find no error in refusing the proposed finding.

Appellant's most important and interesting contention is that the breaking of the water main was not the proximate cause of the fire loss. The first aspect of its proposition is that such cause, regardless of any intervening negligence of the city, is but remote.

We find no contention between counsel as to the general rule of proximate cause. So far as the definition goes, all seem content with the round statement. (Cit. om.) "The cause which, in natural and continued sequence, unbroken by any efficient, intervening cause, produced the result complained of, and without which that result would not have occurred.'"

A general survey of the appellant's argument discloses these grounds for asserting the remoteness of this cause: the fire itself was the proximate cause of appellant's loss; appellee had no right to this municipal fire extinguishment sevice capable of supporting an action for interference with it; appellant could not reasonably have anticipated that its act would produce the result so long subsequently.

The first contention we deem so well settled against appellant to require more than citation of some of the decisions. In the leading case the court answered it thus: "The law regards practical distinctions, rather than those that are merely theoretical; and practically, when a man cuts off the hose through which firemen are throwing a stream upon a burning building, and thereupon the building is consumed for want of water to extinguish it, his act is to be regarded as the direct and efficient cause of the injury." (Cit.Om.) . . .

The Supreme Judicial Court of Massachusetts said: "While it is true* * *that there was no obligation on the part of the city to extinguish the fire, it does not follow that the plaintiff was not deprived of anything to which she had a legal right if the defendant obstructed the firemen in getting water from the hydrant. She had a legal right to have firemen get the water if they chose to do so from a supply provided especially for that purpose." . . .

Well aware that the city's immunity extends to the servants or agencies through whom it may afford its fire extinguishment service, we know of no precedent and recognize no principle for invoking that immunity in favor of this paving company. The servant's liability precedes, it is not ordinarily dependent on, the master's liability. If, on the principal of respondeat superior, this was the city's act of negligence, appellant is not aided. It was none the less its own act.

Leaving now this most interesting phase of the case, we pass to the third of the above stated grounds on which it is urged that the negligent act was but a remote cause of the loss; that appellant could not reasonably have anticipated such a result.

Here is stated a recognized test of proximate cause. (Cit.Om.) Undoubtedly, it is a proper inquiry whether appellant anticipated this result or whether it may reasonably be said that it should have been anticipated . . . .

Appellant expresses great concern for the consequences of sustaining this judgment. If appellant may be charged with a reasonable anticipation that the injurious results of its act would obtain for eight hours, why not for a week? Where is the line to be drawn? The answer must be that the line will be drawn where reasonable minds cannot differ . . . .

The other aspect of appellant's contention on proximate cause is that, even if its act could proximately have caused the injury, it did not in this case, because the chain of causation was broken, by the intervening negligent delay of the city in making repairs or in restoring pressure after completion of the repairs.

It is no doubt true that the injury to appellee might have been avoided by greater diligence or better directed effort on the part of the city. That does not in our opinion interrupt the natural and continued sequence of the original force. The city's negligence was passive merely. (Cit.Om.) It was not independent. The necessity for it to act at all arose wholly from appellant's act. In reason, one who sets a harmful force in motion should not be heard to defend against liability by the claim that another than the injured party might have prevented the injurious result by an active and timely intervention. The negligence of physician, surgeon or nurse may intervene to aggravate an injury or make it fatal. That will not sever the chain of casualty leading to him who made the treatment necessary. (Cit.Om.) And if it could be questioned whether the city's negligence, being passive, is a cause set in motion by the original wrongdoing, the intervening cause may as readily be given an active character by conceiving it the act of the city in reducing the water pressure . . . .

We do not see how appellant can thus rid itself, as a matter of law, of the primary liability. Having broken the main, damaged the city's property, and endangered appellee's, we cannot say that appellant has no concern or duty or liability with respect to the time or manner of restoring the main to service. If the city were not under a legal exemption, its negligence would be a concurring cause, we think. We do not consider that its nonliability changes the situation.

Aetna Insurance Co. v Boon, 95 U.S. 117, 130, 24 L.Ed. 395, is a fruitful source in this connection. Mr. Justice Strong there says: "The proximate cause is the efficient cause, the one that necessarily sets the other causes in operation. The causes that are merely incidental or instruments of a superior or controlling agency are not the proximate causes and the responsible ones, though they may be nearer in time to the result. It is only when the causes are independent of each other that the nearest is, of course, to be charged with the disaster."

And he quotes thus from a leading case (Cit.Om.): "The inquiry must always be whether there was any immediate cause disconnected from the primary fault, and self-operating, which produced the injury . . ."

Before leaving proximate cause, another matter should perhaps be mentioned. The findings disclose that the city's system of mains was equipped with shut-off valves, and that on the occasion in question they were found useless from corrosion, due to the city's negligence. Except for this, we take it, the effects of the break would have been so localized that in other places, including the situs of the fire, water pressure would have been maintained.

Appellant makes no use of these facts in argument other than as partly explanatory of the delay in making repairs and of the necessity of reducing pressure throughout the city. We readily perceive, however, that these facts, in connection with others not shown, might have been of importance in the case, at least in the trial court. If it had been shown, either that appellant knew of the shut-off equipment, or that such equipment was in universal or general use, it could more forcefully have urged that the inquiry occurring eight hours later. and in a different part of the city, was not reasonably to have been anticipated.

The judgment will be affirmed, and the cause remanded. It is so ordered.

*   *   *

On Motion for Rehearing.
WATSON, Justice.

The motion for rehearing is denied. We take advantage of the opportunity to add a word of explanation.

In concluding against the contention that the city's negligence broke the chain of causality leading to appellant's negligence so as to render the latter but the remote cause of the injury, we may have placed more emphasis than we intended upon the passive character of the city's negligence. We are aware of some situations in which nonaction is held to be an intervening cause.

The real basis of decision is that the city's negligence was not an independent cause. It was the primary fault, and it alone, that called for action on the part of the city. Its failure to act or to act in time was not a self-operating cause, and it was directly connected with the force previously set in motion.

The principle is quite different where a railroad company fails to perform its duty to inspect a car delivered to it for transportation, and an injury results from a defect which proper inspection would have discovered. There the passive negligence is independent of the original fault which occasioned the defect and serves as an intervening and the proximate cause. It is cases in this class on which the appellant has relied.

Defenses

Contributory Negligence: *The once absolute defense*

As previously indicated, in many jurisdictions, the plaintiff who successfully proved up all the elements of the prima facie case of tort, nevertheless could be defeated by defendant's showing (who now bore the burden of proof to avoid judgment against him) that the plaintiff was himself part of the cause of his own damages, i.e., that he was contributorily negligent. The amount of the plaintiff's negligence was not material, only the fact that it existed. Thus, the plaintiff who was two per cent negligent, if that were shown, would receive no compensation from the overwhelmingly (98%) negligent defendant. As one might imagine, insurance companies and defense counsel were thus armed with a powerful, albeit unfair weapon from the common law, both as antiquated and as effective as the mace.

Assumption of Risk

An effective form of Contributory Negligence was used against plaintiffs who were aware of the possibilities of injury to themselves should they place themselves in an area where it was reasonable to assume that there was a likelihood of injury.

There is often a great deal of confusion with regard to the difference between contributory negligence and assumption of risk, and the distinction is often more legalistic than practical. The Second Restatement of Torts has utilized an example which attempts to delineate the difference, with limited success. Should a person crossing a street, jaywalk at the middle instead of at the crosswalk, he does not assume the risk of being struck by an oncoming car, but he is clearly contributorily negligent. The fan at the baseball park assumes the risk of being conked with a fly ball, notwithstanding the fact that he has done nothing contributorily negligent himself; amusement parks post warnings as to the risks of riding particularly exciting rides; and skiers of any ability are both realistically and legally assuming risks of potential injury.

The general types of assumption of risk have been (a) in the area of contract law, involving an agreement whereby one of the parties acknowledges and agrees to assume that very risk, and (b) where the risk is understood as inherent in the project or contract of employment (a salvage diver or a demolition expert) and more or less "goes with the territory".

Finally, we all assume risks in being sports fans, skiers amusement park patrons and golfers of all kinds and ability. If one doesn't want to assume the risk, don't participate, or as Justice Cardozo said: "The timorous may stay at home."

The Fellow Servant rule

The third common law defense against liability was the doctrine that a servant who was injured at work by the negligence of another servant, could not claim damages from the master, or employer. This was the *fellow servant rule*, but since it was in actuality a defense utilized by employers, it will be discussed in the chapter on employment law. For purposes at this juncture, it will serve to complete the trio of defenses to liability; or, the common law witches of Macbeth: *Contributory Negligence and/or Assumption of Risk, the fireman's rule and the fellow servant rule.*

It must be remembered that tort law was a creature of the common law, and the common law was from a system that based rights and responsibilities on the parties' relationship to the land. Those who owned land were favored, to say the least, and the doctrine of assumption of risk was uniquely designed to relieve them from responsibility for injuries to those who came upon their land. Its blanket protection led to several gross miscarriages of justice, and consequently, the judicial refining of the common law doctrine.

Nowhere was the defense of assumption of risk used more effectively as a bar to recovery for injuries than against people who by reason of their occupations, took risks of which even those not in the occupation were acutely aware. Coal miners, police officers, rodeo cowboys, and handlers of dynamite have assumed the risks that "went with the territory", but many jurisdictions struggled with the result where there had been serious negligence shown on the part of the defendants and yet this defense allowed them to escape any liability to often severely injured plaintiffs.

Even when several jurisdictions had eroded the defense with decisions that held it to be grossly unjust and against public policy, it had remained alive and well, into the sweltering summer of 1959, in Kansas City, Mo.

On the morning of August 18, 1959, a tank truck driver employed by Continental Oil Co., was filling his tank truck from tank two and tank four of four large storage tanks, with regular and premium gasoline respectively. The other two tanks contained kerosene and regular gasoline.

Another tank driver had climbed up onto the truck to show him his new lighter, and (not surprisingly), flames flashed suddenly from the fifth compartment on the truck. The first driver tried, but was only successful in shutting off one of the storage tanks hoses, the other continued supplying gasoline to the spreading fire below the truck.

Firemen responded and sought to contain the spread of the fire from the highway adjacent the storage facility.

The firemen fought with multiple hose lines in a defensive strategy. One of the tanks ruptured about 9:15, followed shortly by the second and third tanks. The fourth tank rocketed into the street, overtaking five of the firemen and one bystander with the resulting fireball.

The plaintiffs, the four minor children and widow of Captain Bartels, had won judgment of $25,000.00 in the lower courts, in their wrongful death claim against Continental Oil Co., and the doctrine of assumption of risk was still a valid defense and one which the appellant oil company raised confidently before the Supreme Court in Missouri.

BARTELS v. CONTINENTAL OIL COMPANY
384 S.W. 2d 667
Supreme Court of Missouri (1964)

BARRETT, Commissioner.

. . . It is not necessary to a disposition of this case to enter upon an extended discussion of the general rules or to determine Bartels' status . . . . (A)nd upon the merits of the cause, there are no precisely applicable and governing Kansas cases.

Under these general rules, an experienced fire captain would of course accept the presence of kerosene and gasoline as a known hazard of fire in a gasoline storage facility. (Cit.Om.) But the law does not compel firemen in fighting a fire to assume all possible lurking hazards and risks; (and) it may not be said that a "fireman has no protective rights whatever." (Cit.Om.) . . .

". . . Although firemen assume the usual risks incident to their entry to premises made dangerous by the destructive effect of fire, there is no valid reason why they should be required to assume the extraordinary risk of hidden perils of which they might easily be warned." (Cit.Om.)

Continental's four storage tanks, constructed of quarter-inch steel, were installed in 1924. They were 30 feet long, eleven feet in diameter, with flat ends, and when installed as well 35 years later "were fitted with two-inch pressure valves." Originally, the tanks were installed perpendicularly but in 1958 Continental Oil Company dismantled the storage facilities, removed the two-inch vents, and installed the four tanks horizontally on the concrete saddles. But in changing or replacing the installation Continental again placed two-inch vents on the tops of the storage tanks. And in response to interrogatories and "requests for admissions" Continental stated that "four tanks was (sic) vented only by a single A.Y. McDonald 2-inch plate 925 combination gauge hatch and P & R valve, known as a 'breather valve.' * * * that these said four tanks had no vent or mechanism designed to relieve pressure (such as might occur during a fire) other than what relief was provided by the single 2-inch diameter breather valve on each tank." The appellant has made unnecessary further recitation of the facts in connection with these valves because in its brief there are further concessions; (t)he four tanks in question were vented with 2" pressure and relief valves, which were admittedly (and obviously) not adequate to keep these tanks from rupturing; and, "we will concede for the purpose of that question only (viewing the record favorably to the respondents), without admitting it, that by reason of the size of the vents, defendant did not maintain the premises in a reasonably safe condition, and that that was the cause of the ruptures."

In addition to these admissions, the Chief of the Fire Prevention Division of the Kansas City, Missouri Fire Department, who was present while the fire was in progress and when tank number four rocketed, and afterwards made an investigation, testified that the reason that the tanks ruptured was that "(t)he vents were too small."

He testified that the Flammable Liquids Code required "5-1/2 inches of emergency venting." An expert witness, "a protection engineer specializing in petroleum hazards," referred to all the literature connected with the petroleum industry (with which Continental was familair) and in connection with his years of experience in the industry, testified that for petroleum storage tanks of 18,000 to 25,000 gallon capacity "a free circular opening of 5-1/2 inches in diameter" was required. As he testifies on both direct and cross examination this witness gave the formulas and made the computations as to the "normal safety operating pressures of a tank" as well as the pressures built up in a storage tank during a fire. He testified that tank number four rocketed because the two-inch vent was not large enough to take care of the vapor generated by the fire. And, he said, "I can say without any worry at all that no tank that has been equipped with the vent of the size specified in these suggested standards (5-1/2 inches) has ever rocketed." The appellant's expert, a professor of chemical engineering at Kansas University, was of the opinion that a 5-1/2 inch vent would not have prevented the tank from rocketing; but even this witness was of the opinion that a 7-1/2 inch vent "would have been sufficient to vent all the vapor that was formed" in this fire and would have prevented the rocketing of tank number four.

And upon this particular phase of the case, in its answers to interrogatories and in its counsel's opening statement, there were these additional admissions: "that Continental Oil Company and Continental Oil Company officials, the officials of my clients, knew at the time of this casualty that a two-inch vent was small enough that there was more apt to be a rupture in the event of an exposure fire * * *. And I want to tell you here at the outset that there is no real issue whatever. These were old-fashioned tanks. The two-inch vents in these tanks were smaller than was recommended by the literature, by the National Fire Protection Association and the Association of Petroleum Industries * * *." And further of knowledge by the industry he said, "Our company people * * * read the literature, * * * their safety director belonged to some of the these organizations, and was on committees, and so they did know full well long before 1959 that a larger emergency vent would be safer."

While Bartels was an experienced fireman and was therefore necessarily aware of some of the hazards of petroleum products fires, there is no fact or circumstance indicative of any knowledge on his part that these particular storage tanks were equipped with inadequate safety vents. And as the appellant says in its brief "(a)lthough the men on the line knew that the number four tank would probably rupture (since the three other tanks had ruptured), they did not know the tank would rocket in the freakish manner in which it did. They had never seen a tank act like that. The action of this particular tank was entirely unpredictable." Also aerial photographs taken while the fire was in progress and before tank number four rocketed, as well as the testimony of witnesses, reveal that it was not possible through the enormous black smoke clouds and flames that firemen or anyone else could or did see the two-inch valves on the tanks, much less appreciate their danger. The fire prevention chief and other firemen testified that they did not know the size of the safety valves on the tanks. Six of Continental's employees, including its bulk plant supervisor, were present prior to and during the course of the fire and of course there were no warnings in any manner to the firemen that the tanks were equipped with the inadequate two-inch vents . . . . Some of the firemen heard a "hissing sound" before tank number four rocketed but others heard no such sound.

Further and explicit details could be recited and permissible inferences indicated, it is sufficient, however, to say that in these particularly detailed circumstances the evidence favorable to the plaintiffs supports the finding of a known hidden danger of which there was no warning whatever, a hazard that in any and all events Bartels as a fireman was not bound to accept as a usual peril of his profession. In these circumstances, reasonable minds could differ and Continental was not for any of the reasons here advanced entitled to a directed verdict.

Penetrating the defense: Rescue

The Missouri Court managed to avoid the harsh effect of the application of the defense of assumption of risk and effect justice by a judicial interpretation that the risk, if assumed at all, must be known. Other courts developed a doctrine that accepted the premise that the plaintiff had assumed the risk, but reasoned that he assumed the risks only because of the defendant's initial negligence in causing the fire. Since that necessitated the plaintiff's being there at all, by inviting the response of emergency personnel, there would be no lessening of liability, even if the first responders were themselves negligent. This was the doctrine of *rescue* and, founded in the concept of reasonable foreseeability, defeated the defendant's defense of assumption of risk.

Rescue was used even where the party responding was not one clearly expected to respond, or was a volunteer, in the more liberal and equitable jurisdictions. The most significant decisions were handed down dealing with bulk oil tank storage fires, and might possibly have been driven by the desire of the court to place responsibility for the injuries upon those who could most afford it, as a matter of public policy.

Given the fact that oil had been (and continues to be) a nationally 'most favored' enterprize whose profits increased geometrically, and the reluctance of courts to allow them to escape from responsibility for the full extent of the damage from their acts of negligence, it seemed as though the earlier courts were not in error in lying the blame, legally, at the doorstep of the growing industrial giants.

When a fire was raging out of control in a bulk petroleum storage plant, the chief of the fire responding jurisdiction requested help via the Georgia State Police for volunteers to help bring it under control. Among those firefighters who came to assist the chief was the plaintiff, an experienced firefighter who nevertheless clearly answered the call voluntarily.

Assumption of risk, with some interesting applications, was what the Georgia Trial Court dealt with in finding liability in the case, and the Appellate Court of Georgia affirmed the lower court's reasoning and result.

WALKER HAULING CO. v JOHNSON
139 S.E.2d 496
Court of Appeals of Georgia (1964)

The allegation that the plaintiff was a "skilled firefighter" is not reasonably susceptible to the construction that he was a "fireman", volunteer or otherwise. True, pleadings must be construed against pleader on demurrer but the rule does not require strained or unreasonable or illogical constructions. Proof that one is a skilled fireman would not alone authorize a finding that he was a fireman. Likewise, an allegation that the Fire Chief of Manchester, GA, asked for volunteers to fight the fire is not reasonably susceptible to the construction that the plaintiff was a volunteer fireman of the city of Manchester. But even if we are wrong in the above conclusions a volunteer fireman who receives no remuneration is even more entitled to the benefits of the rescue doctrine than one who is less experienced and who would more likely assume an unreasonable or foolhardy risk. To reduce the ranks of rescuers to the less competent would be top contradict and weaken the application and consequences of one of the most advanced doctrines evolved by the conscience of mankind.

The allegations, that the defendants' negligence was the proximate cause of the explosion and fire which caused the plaintiff's injuries and that the plaintiff was free of contributory negligence, raised issues of negligence that a jury must resolve. There is no issue involved as to assumption of risk, since the doctrine of rescue necessarily contemplates an assumption of risk inherent in the peril created by the defendants' negligence and allows for recovery for injuries thereby incurred, for the reason that the defendants were charged with the foreseeability of their negligence attracting rescuers to assume risks . . .

The defense of Assumption of Risk was but part of the Common Law heritage in the area of torts, and if one remembers that the entire feudal system was based upon the ownership of land as the delineating hallmark of status, and therefore rights, the following related doctrines are but the logical extension of protection of the rights of the landowner.

The first element of tort is the existence of a duty, and it is here that the common law provided a duty that was based not entirely upon foreseeability of harm, but upon the status of the person that came upon the land.

To the person who came upon another's land without any right whatsoever, there was no duty whatsoever owed. Thus if there were hazards on the land caused by the negligence of the land owner, there was absolutely no duty of care owed to the trespasser, and if he were injured, even through no fault of his own, he had no recourse against the landowner. The trespass being a violation against the owner's rights in the land, no action could be successfully maintained for injuries, no matter how severe or unavoidable (since they might be avoided by not committing the trespass).

There were, however, others who came upon the land, either at the express request of the owner or at least at his implied request or permission. The distinction was whether or not there was any benefit to be derived by the landowner.

Those who were permitted to come on the land, or into the premises as a result of an implied permission were those who were some public officials, salesmen, and other type visitors whose presence was tolerated, but not really welcomed. These were known as licensees, and the landowner owed them some duty of care although it was fairly limited to the duty to refrain from grossly negligent conduct. In other words, for a licensee to recover against a landowner, the licensee would have to prove that the landowner was guilty of wanton and wilful, or gross negligence toward him. Ordinary negligence was not enough to allow recovery.

The last class of common law persons upon the lands of another were called invitees. These were people that brought benefit to the landowner by reason of their coming onto his land or into his premises. Such people were mail carriers, utility workers, and although the benefit might be arguable, tax collectors. To these, the land owner owed the greatest of care, and thus could be held to answer for damages if guilty of ordinary negligence.

The Fireman's Rule

Based upon the above and foregoing, what would be the likely classification for firemen? Unfortunately, illogically, it was widely held that they were licensees, and this concept, known as the firemen's rule, prevented recovery from injuries on the land or in the premises of another who had been clearly, though not wantonly and wilfully negligent. It was the majority doctrine, as late as 1960, when the matter came before the Supreme Courts of New Jersey and Illinois. The facts of the New Jersey case had enough elements of the common law defenses present for the court to hold consistent with the majority line of precedent, but a Justice who looked beyond the dusty common law that had relegated both firemen and women to a lesser class of citizen, saw an opportunity to what too few courts had done: effect justice.

A fire company had responded to a house under construction, and found that a salamander, used by the plasterers to help the plaster dry, had caused neighbors to believe that there was a fire within. The following day (another platoon) the same false alarm occurred, and, two days later, with the plaintiff on duty again, the company responded once more.

This time, on the balcony of the second floor which was filled with smoke, and obscured the stairs, the fireman fell and was injured. A jury held for the plaintiff fireman, but the decision was reversed by the Appellate Court, and the appeal followed.

KRAUTH v GELLER
Supreme Court of New Jersey (1960)
157 A.2d 129

WEINTRAUB, C.J.

Much has been written with respect to the duty owed to and the status of a fireman who enters private property pursuant to his public employment. He is not a trespasser, for he enters pursuant to public right. Although it is frequently said he is a licensee rather than an invitee, it has been corrected observed that he falls within neither category, for his entry does not depend upon permission of the owner or occupier, nor may they deny him admittance. Hence his situation does not fit comfortably within traditional concepts. * * *

In what circumstances should the owner or occupier respond to the injured fireman? That the misfortune herein experienced by a fireman was well within the range of foreseeability cannot be disputed. But liability is not always coextensive with foreseeability of harm. The question ultimately is one of public policy, and the answer must be distilled from the relevant factors involved upon an inquiry into what is fair and just. * * *

It is quite generally agreed that the owner or occupier is not liable to a paid fireman for negligence with respect to the creation of a fire. The rationale of the prevailing rule is sometimes asserted in terms of "assumption of risk," used doubtless in the so-called "primary" sense of the term, and meaning that the defendant did not breach a duty owed, rather than that the fireman was guilty of contributory fault in responding to his public duty.

Stated affirmatively, what is meant is that it is the fireman's business to deal with that very hazard and hence, perhaps by analogy to the contractor engaged as an expert to remedy dangerous situations, he cannot complain of negligence in the creation of the very occasion for his engagement. In terms of duty, it may be said that there is none owed the fireman to exercise care so as to not require the special services for which he is trained and paid. Probably most fires are attributable to negligence, and in the final analysis the policy decision is that it would be too burdensome to charge all who cause or negligently fail to prevent fires with the injuries suffered by the expert retained with public funds to deal with those inevitable, although negligently created occurrences. Hence, for that risk, the fireman should receive appropriate compensation from the public he serves, both in the pay which reflects the hazard and in workmen's compensation benefits for the inherent risks of the calling.

Although there is virtual unanimity with respect to nonliability for negligence as to the creation of a fire, there is appreciable authority which would impose liability upon the land occupier for negligence with respect to conditions creating undue risk of injury beyond those inevitably involved in firefighting. Thus it has been held that an injured fireman may recover if the injurious hazard was created in violation of statute or ordinance. So he also has prevailed if the occupier failed to utilize an available opportunity to warn him of a hidden peril. And the land occupier has been held where he failed to exercise due care with respect to the condition of places intended as a means of access by contemplated visitors. (Cit. Omitted)

The present case does not fall within any of the exceptions, if such they may be called, outlined in the paragraph above. Defendant was the owner and builder of a one family home under construction at the time of the occurrence. While proceeding along an interior balcony and meaning to descend the stairs, plaintiff mistook layers of smoke for them and fell. Neither the balcony nor the stairs were protected by a railing-the construction simply had not reached that stage. No breach of duty could be found with respect to the premises. And the defendant not being on the scene, there was no culpable failure to seize an opportunity to warn of a hidden danger. In fact, plaintiff, who had been on the premises a few days before the accident, admitted that he was fully aware of the precise stage of the construction of the balcony and the stairs.

What plaintiff seeks is an inroad upon the basic rule that the occupier is not liable to a fireman for the creation of a fire . . . .

We are not concerned with the liability to a fireman of an arsonist or one who deliberately induces a false alarm. Rather we are asked to hold that "wanton" conduct resulting in a fire and consequent alarm will suffice. Wantonness is not too precise a concept. It is something less than intentional hurt and, so viewed, it is an advanced degree of negligent misconduct. In the context of the policy considerations which underlie the rule of nonliability for negligence with respect to the origination of a fire, it is debatable whether or not degrees of culpability are at all pertinent.

At any rate, we need not decide the question since we can see no basis for a claim of wanton misconduct as the term is ordinarily defined. To warrant that characterization, the act or omission to discharge a duty must be intentional, and coupled with a consciousness, actual or imputed, of a high degree of probability that harm, here to a fireman, will ensue. Plaintiff does not suggest that the incidents of March 1 or March 2 fall within this area. Rather he claims a third episode crosses the line. Three such occurrences within five days evoke exasperation, but, however indicative of lack of care, they do not reveal a purpose to cause a conflagration or to attract the fire department. And although injury to a fireman is surely foreseeable, and despite the rather freak circumstance that layers of smoke simulated a stairway, yet there was no evidence of consciousness, actual or imputable, of a high degree of probability that that harm would befall a fireman. In fact, on the first two occasions none resulted although the physical scene was identical.

We think it would be artificial to squeeze the situation within the category of wanton conduct. Rather, in proper perspective, the question is whether the land occupier should be held liable for a second or third act of carelessness. If the time interval had been greater, it would be more apparent that the issue is the one just stated, and the sense of exasperation to which we just referred would be less pronounced or absent. But if the prevailing rule of nonliability to a fireman with respect to the origination of the occasion for his work is sound, and we are not persuaded otherwise, we think it unwise to attempt to substitute, or to qualify it with, a formula in which the factors of number and time intervals will somehow be decisive.

There being no suggestion that the plaintiff would fare any better on retrial, the judgment of the Appellate Division directing the entry of judgment is affirmed. No costs.

DINI v. NAIDITCH
170 N.E.2d 881 (1960)

BRISTOW, Justice.

It also appears from the testimony of residents of the hotel that there were oil drums converted into open garbage cans in the hotel corridors, which were emptied only two or three times a week, that paper and other waste was piled in the corridors beside the cans, that the walls were cracked and leaked through the roof into the fourth floor hallway, and that the janitor, Jimmy Sato, was "always drunk" but retained despite complaints. It also appears from the record that prior to the fire, defendant's attention had been called to nine separate violations of city ordinances within the building, although there is some controversy as to the findings of a former building inspector who testified for defendant.

With reference to the condition of the premises on the night of the fire, one of the residents testified that two garbage cans on the first floor of the hotel were full and overflowing, and that paper was piled about a foot high on the floor. Another resident, who returned home about 11 P.M., said that three or four garbage cans in his section of the fourth floor were full, with paper piled around the cans so that he had to "cross around." According to firemen who fought the blaze, they could see rubbish in the hotel corridor when they reached the second floor of the building, as well as trash and litter on the stairs. Moreover, there were no fire doors, according to the testimony of the deputy fire marshal who was on the premises during the fire and made a minute inspection after the fire, and that of the chief building inspector, and of the division fire marshal who was also inside the building during the fire and directed the fighting of the blaze. Nor were there any fire extinguishers of any kind in the hotel, according to the original admission of Naiditch and the testimony of residents who had lived there for three or four years, and that of the police detective who examined the premises after the fire.

According to the fire battalion chief, the fire was located in the stairway at the Green Street entrance, blocking the exit. He therefore ordered an engine company up the inside of the stairway to cool the fire off in order to effect rescue operations. Fire captain Duller, and firemen Smith, Collins and Dini, who was carrying a hose on his shoulder, entered the building through the Green Street entrance, and proceeded up the stairs to the second floor landing, where they could hear the roar of the fire above. Collins was sent for a smaller hose, and Dini was left on the landing to couple the smaller hose into a shut-off pipe, while Duller and Smith started up to the third floor where they could see the fire raging above then. At that moment, and without any warning, the entire stairway collapsed and fell into a heap at the firs floor level. Captain Duller was buried in the burning debris and his body was not recovered until the following day. Smith, who escaped, testified that something hit him on the head and drove him through the stairs onto the area below. Dini was pinned in a pile of burning wood, but extricated himself with great difficulty, and made his way out in flames which he extinguished by jumping into a puddle of water at the curbing.

Dini was so severely burned that his recovery was in doubt for two months. He suffered third degree burns on his scalp, face, neck, chest, arms, left leg and knee. Both outer ears were almost completely burned off, as were his nose, lips and eyelids. He also suffered severe burns inside his mouth and throat, which not only made breathing difficult, and swallowing and eating impossible, but interfered with the administration of anesthesia. When the burned skin sloughed off, leaving raw areas, it was necessary, in order to prevent infection, to make some thirteen skin grafts from other areas of his body. That phase of his hospitalization lasted until August 13, 1955; and from October 13, 1955, to February 25, 1959, Dini underwent some fifty-nine additional operations for skin grafting and for the reconstruction of eyelids, and ears, and the removal of scar tissue.

His injuries are permanent insofar as loss of motion and flexion in the affected members is concerned, and insofar as they affect his appearance. Moreover, since March of 1956, except for periods of hospitalization, Dini has worked only approximately three hours a day in the Fire Prevention Bureau operating a typewriter, with the resulting loss of income.

Captain Duller was 54 years of age at the time of his death in the fire. He had been married some 21 years, and left surviving a widow, an 18-year-old son, and a 16-year-old daughter.

On the basis of substantially the foregoing facts, the jury returned the verdicts for plaintiffs Dini and Duller, as hereinbefore noted, and the superior court entered judgment notwithstanding the verdict on the ground that there was no basis of liability, since the fire ordinances violated by the defendants were not enacted for the benefit of the firemen. Moreover, the court entered summary judgment dismissing the complaint of Elizabeth Dini on the ground that a wife had no cause of action for loss of consortium resulting from the negligent injury of her husband.

In reviewing this cause, we shall consider first the claims of Gino Dini and administratrix Lillian Duller, which involve the issue of landowners' liability to firemen for the negligent maintenance of the premises. We believe that this question, considered last by this court in 1892, should properly be reexamined in its entirety.

It must be recognized at the outset that the English common law, from which our law is derived, was part and parcel of a social system in which the landowners were the backbone, and that it was inevitable that in such a legal climate supreme importance would be attached to proprietary interests. (Cit. Om.) It was the feudal conception that the landowner was sovereign within his own boundaries that gave birth to the rule that the only duty a landowner owed a licensee was not to wilfully or wantonly injure him. (Cit. Om.) It was, then, hardly a "giant step" to give the label of "licensee" to a member of the fire department who, in an emergency, enters the premises in the discharge of his duty, and to hold, as the early cases did, that the owner or occupant owed the fireman no greater duty than to refrain from infliction of wilful or intentional injury. (Cit. Om.)

However, the history of the law on the subject of landowners and "licensees" shows a tendency to whittle away a rule which no longer conforms to public opinion. As Bohlen points out, "Like so many cases in which a barbaric formula has been retained, its content has been so modified by interpretation as to remove much of its humanity." 50 Harv.L.Rev. 725,735. Thus, to avoid extending what has been deemed a "harsh rule" (Cit. Om.); courts have held that firemen were entitled to be warned of "hidden dangers" or "unusual hazards" known to the landowner or occupant. (Cit. Om.)

Other courts have avoided the harsh rule by finding from slight variations of circumstances that the injured fireman was an "invitee" (Cit. Om.); or a "business visitor" to whom the landowner owed a duty of reasonable care to keep the premises safe. (Cit. Om.)

Still other courts, as well as legal scholars, have forthrightly rejected the label of "licensee" with its concomitant set of rights and duties for firemen. (Cit. Om.)

. . .

In reviewing the law on this issue, we note further that this legal fiction that firemen are licensees to whom no duty of reasonable care is owed is without any logical foundation. (Cit. Om.)

It is highly illogical to say that a firemen who enters the premises quite independently of either invitation or consent *cannot be an invitee* because there has been no invitation, but *can be a licensee* even though there has been no permission. The lack of logic is even more patent when we realize that the courts have not applied the term "licensee" to other types of public employees required to come on another's premises in the performance of their duties and to whom the duty of reasonable care is owed. If benefit to the landowner is the decisive factor, it is difficult to perceive why a fireman is not entitled to that duty of care, or how the landowner derives a greater benefit from the visit of other public officials, such as postmen, water meter readers and revenue inspectors, than from the fireman who comes to prevent the destruction of his property. 35 Mich.L.Rev. 1161.

Consequently, it is our opinion that since the common-law rule labelling firemen as licensees is but an illogical anachronism, originating in a vastly different social order, and pock-marked by judicial refinements, it should not be perpetuated in the name of "stare decisis." That doctrine does not confine our courts to the "Calf Path," nor to any rule currently enjoying a numerical superiority of adherents. "Stare decisis" ought not to be the excuse for decision where reason is lacking. (Cit. Om.)

. . .

Inasmuch as firemen obviously confer on landowners economic and other benefits which are a recognized basis for imposing the common law duty of reasonable care (Restatement, Torts,:343a; Harper, Torts, :96; Prosser, 26 Minn. L.Rev. 573,574; 35 Mich.L.Rev. 1161), we would agree with the court in the Meiers case, and with its adherents, that an action should lie against a landowner for failure to exercise reasonable care in the maintenance of his property resulting in the injury or death of a fireman rightfully on the premises, fighting the fire at a place where he might reasonably be expected to be.

This interpretation does not run counter to any imposing body of legal precedent in this jurisdiction. As hereinbefore noted, this court has only considered the problem once, and that was in 1892 in Gibson v. Leonard, 143 Ill. 182, 32 N.E. 182, 17 L.R.A. 588. A careful reading of that case, however, indicates that the court did not analyze the common-law status of firemen, but was concerned primarily with whether a volunteer member of a fire insurance patrol, injured by a defective elevator counterweight in the basement of a building, was entitled to the protection of a particular safety ordinance. Nevertheless, for the clarification of the law, insofar as any language contained therein might be inconsistent with our interpretation of the common law in this case, it must be deemed to be overruled, along with any appellate Court cases following the archaic lisensee (sic) concept. (Cit. Om.)

. . .

Plaintiffs have called our attention to defendants' violation of certain provisions of the municipal code of Chicago requiring, for structures such as the Green Mill Hotel, enclosed stairwells (sec. 62-3.2); fire doors (63-3.6); fire extinguishers (64-4.1); and specifying that oil rags and waste shall be kept during the day in approved waste cans of heavy galvanized iron with self-closing covers, and shall be removed at night, and that rubbish shall not be allowed to accumulate in any part of any building (90-25). These ordinances further provide that, "It shall be unlawful to continue the use of or occupy any structure or place which does not comply with these provisions of this code *which are intended to prevent a disastrous fire or loss of life in case of fire*, until the changes, alterations or repairs or requirements found necessary to place the building in a safe condition have been made." (Sec. 90-3.) (Italics ours.)

Defendants, however, argue that firemen are not within the purview of these ordinances, and that, therefore, plaintiffs cannot predicate liability thereon. In support of that contention, defendants cite the aforementioned Gibson case, 143 Ill. 182, 32 N.E. 182. Recovery was denied in that case on the ground that the ordinance on which the fireman based his claim specified that it was designed to insure against injury to a specified class-employees of the building; hence, the court reasoned that a volunteer fireman was not within that class for whose protection the ordinance was passed . . . . "But here, in section 1074 of the ordinances of Chicago, *instead of general language, such as was used in the statute considered in* Parker v. Barnard, is found language which shows, in express terms that the ordinance was intended only for the protection and benefit of employees in factories, workshops, and other places or structures where machinery is employed." (Italics ours.)

In the light of that precise statement in the Gibson case, differentiating it, in effect, from the case at bar where the safety ordinance is general in its terms and has the avowed purpose of preventing loss of life in case of fire, regardless of whose life it may be, we can hardly find the Gibson case to be a determinative precedent for the denial of this action. On the contrary, the entire implication of that case is that the ordinances herein, being general in terms, might properly include firemen within their protection.

Such an interpretation, moreover, would be consistent with the case law, both in Illinois and in other States . . . . "it is a reasonable construction to hold that it was passed for the benefit of all persons lawfully on the premises." (Cit. Om.) Similarly, . . . "* * * we have in this case a direct violation of ordinances which were enacted for the benefit of firemen as well as guests in the hotels; at least firemen entering the premises had a right to assume that the law in this particular had been complied with." . . . (Cit. Om.)

We have already noted that there was some evidence from which the jury could reasonably find that defendants were in fact guilty of violating these ordinances and that such violations proximately caused the injuries of plaintiff Dini and the death of Captain Duller. Therefore, it was reversible error for the trial court to enter judgment notwithstanding the verdict with respect to these claims.

In considering next the issue of whether plaintiff Elizabeth Dini may assert an action for loss of consortium due to the negligent injury of her husband, we note that this question has been considered in this jurisdiction in only a single Appellate Court case, decided in 1913 (Patelski v. Snyder, 179 Ill. App. 24), . . . (T)herefore, inasmuch as this question is not overladen with Illinois precedents and is essentially one of first impression for this court, we shall review the origin of the common law rule, examine its application by the courts of other jurisdictions and the reasons advanced for its retention or rejection. The common law rule . . . was promulgated at a period in history when all the wife's personal property, money and chattels of every description became her husband's upon marriage. She could neither contract, nor bring action of any kind. Husband and wife were one, and "he was that one." (Cit. Om.)

. . . He had a right of action for injury to her grounded on the theory that she was his servant. However, should the husband be injured, the wife, being a legal non-entity (1 Blackstone, Commentaries, 442), could bring no action. A servant could hardly sue for the loss of services of the master. 3 Blackstone, Commentaries, 142, 143.

. . . "This, then, is the soil in which the doctrine took root; the abject subservience of the wife to husband, her legal non-existence, her degraded position as a combination vessel, chattel, and household drudge whose obedience might be enforced by personal chastisement." (Cit. Om.)

. . . Other courts concede either expressly or impliedly the inadequacy of the common law rule denying the wife an action for the loss of consortium for the negligent injury of her husband, but insist that the remedy lies with the legislature. (Cit. Om.) We disagree. Inasmuch as the obstacles to the wife's action were "judge invented," there is no conceivable reason why they cannot be "judge destroyed." (Cit. Om.) We find no wisdom in abdicating to the legislature our essential function of re-evaluating common-law concepts in the light of present day realities. Nor do we find judicial sagacity in continually looking backward and parroting the words and analyses of other courts so as to embalm for posterity the legal concepts of the past.

. . . As Justice Cardozo aptly stated: "Social, political and legal reforms have changed the relation between the sexes and put woman and man upon a plane of equality. Decisions founded upon the assumption of a by-gone inequality are unrelated to present day realities, and ought not to be permitted to prescribe a rule of life." Cardozo, The Growth of the Law, pp. 105, 106.

. . . Therefore, the complaint of Elizabeth Dini seeking damages for the loss of consortium of her husband due to the injuries he sustained as a result of defendants' negligence, properly sets forth a basis of liability which the law must recognize. It was error for the trial court to enter summary judgment dismissing her complaint . . . .

In accordance with our analysis, the judgments entered in these claims should be reversed, with directions to adjudicate the complaint of plaintiff Elizabeth Dini, and to reinstate the jury verdicts in favor of plaintiffs Geno Dini and Lillian Duller.

Continued Erosion of the Fireman's Rule

A firefighter who had been injured by the collapse of a wall at a chemical plant fire had sued both the owner of the plant and the manufacturer of the chemical for negligence.

At the trial court, the defendants prevailed, the court ruling against their liability on the basis of the fireman's rule, as did the appellate court. The policy behind the rule was that negligent fires were exactly the type of fires that a fireman should expect to encounter, and to hold defendants liable for their negligence would be too burdensome to the public at large, especially when they had hired the fire "experts" to fight these kinds of blazes.

On appeal to the New Jersey Supreme Court, Mahoney asked the Court to reexamine the impact of the fireman's rule on plaintiffs, like himself, who had been injured by another's negligence in manufacturing such lethal chemicals.

Note the difference in the approach of the courts to the situations and how they distinguish their facts from similar cases to achieve an opposite result. It should be remembered, that such distinguishing is the only means that a court can utilize to avoid following the already decided precedent (other than overruling the earlier case), and in these jurisdictions, that precedent is that the firemen's rule will provide immunity for the landowner or occupier when a fireman is injured fighting a fire caused by the negligence of that landowner.

It is also important to note that, in the quarter century since the well-reasoned *Dini v Naiditch*, a powerful legal defense tool is still the firemen's rule, denying recovery to firefighters who would not have been injured but for the negligence of a defendant, who himself wholly avoids any liability.

The following cases address the same issue, as well as others, from various perspectives, each making its own determination based on those perspectives. Among the issues we find addressed by the court(s):

* products liability
* wanton and willful negligence
* origin and cause of the fire
* health and safety legislation
* duty to warn of hazards
* comparative negligence
* assumption of risk

The following case came before the same state supreme court in whose jurisdiction the Krauth v Geller still stood as precedent, but there were some critical differences between the firefighter in the earlier case and the following one. There were also some very critical differences in the defendants, and the proximate cause of the firefighter's injuries.

MAHONEY v CARUS CHEMICAL CO., INC.
Supreme Court of New Jersey (1986)
510 A.2d 4

STEIN, J.

Plaintiff Thomas P. Mahoney was a volunteer firefighter with the Highland Chemical Engine Company of Pitman, New Jersey. On June 19, 1978, duty called him to the scene of a fire at the Inversand Company chemical plant in Sewell, New Jersey. Based on his prior knowledge of the Inversand business, he knew the fire to be chemical in nature. He concedes that he understood the severe risk of entering a building engulfed by a chemical fire, including the risk of the structure falling. While straddling the threshold of the burning building, a structural wall collapsed on him, trapping him inside the building and causing his injuries. He sued Inversand, Inversand's parent, Hungerford & Terry, Inc., and Carus Chemical Company, Inc. (Carus), the Illinois corporation that supplied Inversand with the highly combustible substance that allegedly caused the fire.

The trial court, relying on the "fireman's rule," *Krauth v Geller*, 31 N.J. 270, 157 A.2d 129 (1960), granted summary judgment in favor of all defendants. The Appellate Division affirmed. We granted plaintiff's petition for certification.

Our principal focus is his claim against Carus. The gravamen of that claim, as disclosed by the complaint and documents obtained during discovery, is that the fire at the Inversand warehouse spontaneously ignited in one of a shipment of fiber-paper drums containing potassium permanganate powder (brand name "Cairox") manufactured by Carus and received by Inversand approximately two hours before the fire; that Carus, based on a series of similar fires, knew that the shipment or storage of Cairox in fiber-paper drums created a significant danger of spontaneous ignition; that the risk of spontaneous ignition of Cairox in fiber-paper drums was so substantial that Carus, in internal memoranda and in a communication to customers a month before the Inversand fire, had announced its decision to replace the fiber-paper drums with metal containers; that the shipment to Inversand included 86 metal drums of Cairox, none of which burned, and 100 fiber-paper drums, virtually all of which burned; and that Carus had continued to ship Cairox in fiber-paper drums in order to exhaust its supply of such drums before making the switch to metal containers.

Potassium permanganate's hazardous properties were confirmed by plaintiff's consulting engineer in a report that was part of the trial court record:

Potassium permanganate belongs to a class of chemical compounds known as inorganic oxidizers. These oxygen-rich compounds accelerate the burning of combustible materials. KNnO4(sic) (potassium permanganate) is one of the compounds used to promote and accelerate the burning of solid propellants. KMnO4 invariably intensifies the burning of combustible materials by acting as a "chemical supercharger". The speed of its reactivity is exponential with rising temperatures. In NFPA's Fire Protection Guide on Hazardous Materials (3rd ed.), it is recognized that KMnO4 reacts violently when mixed or combined with combustible materials.

According to plaintiff, Carus did not ship potassium permanganate in fiber-paper drums until December, 1975. Carus allegedly considered using fiber drums in 1965, but rejected the idea because it recognized that "(t)here is a greater potential fire hazard when fiber is used in place of metal as a container." It is uncontroverted, however, that late in 1975 Carus began using fiber-paper drums to ship potassium permanganate. Plaintiff alleges that this was an economic decision predicated on Carus' estimate that it could save $35,000 annually by using the less expensive, fiber-paper drums. Plaintiff also alleges that Carus recognized the increased hazard to its own premises when it acknowledged that "(i)t is most likely that we would have to install a sprinkler system in the Cairox warehouse if we switch to fibre containers." It is also uncontroverted that the bottom and sides of the fiber drums used for shipping potassium permanganate were "combustible," and in its answers to interrogatories, Carus conceded that potassium permanganate "increases (the) flammability of combustible materials" and "should be kept away from certain combustible materials."

An internal Carus memorandum entitled "Reported Fires Involving Cairox in Fiber Drums" was also part of the trial court record. This document revealed that beginning in February, 1976, two months after Carus initiated the shipment of potassium permanganate in fiber drums, a series of spontaneous, unexplained fires occurred at various Cairox storage locations causing partial or total destruction of the fiber drums as well as considerable damage to surrounding property.

Plaintiff alleges that after the seventh fire in August, 1978, Carus discontinued the use of fiber drums and that there have been no reported incidents of such fires since then. Carus concedes that it decided to discontinue the use of fiber drums after a fire at the Bethlehem Steel Company on April 10, 1978. An internal Carus marketing memorandum dated April 17, 1978, confirms this decision: "As a result of a series of fires involving Cairox in fiber drums, we have decided to eliminate the use of fiber drums and revert to all metal drums." On May 5, 1978, Carus communicated this decision to its customers in writing, informing them that this change would result in a cost increase of 1.5¢ per pound to be passed on to them. Carus justified its decision as follows:

> As you know, some time ago we switched our packaging from metal drums to fiber drums. Whether by coincidence or not, there has been a higher rate of incidents of fires involving our chemical since we have been packaging in fiber drums than before when we packaged in metal drums. Accordingly, in order to minimize the fire risks, we are again switching to metal drums.

Carus shipped 31,460 pounds of potassium permanganate to Inversand on June 13, 1978. Notwithstanding its announced change of policy regarding the use of fiber drums, approximately 22,000 pounds were shipped in 100 fiber drums. The balance was shipped in 86 metal drums. The shipment arrived at the Inversand warehouse at about 11:30 a.m. on June 19, 1978. At approximately 12:45 p.m., an Inversand employee noticed pink smoke coming out of a Cairox fiber drum that was stored inside the warehouse.

*   *   *

The *Krauth* Court considered but did not decide whether the bar of the fireman's rule would immunize from liability one whose conduct was more culpable than ordinary negligence. The opinion implies that an arsonist or one who reports a false alarm would not enjoy immunity.

The opinion appears to acknowledge that the policy considerations underlying the rule could not justify an immunity that would protect the intentional wrongdoer. The premise that the fireman's rule should not immunize the intentional wrongdoer is generally supported (Cit. Om.)

. . . When a fire is intentionally set, the rationale for immunity breaks down. Common experience indicates that the vast majority of fires are not the product of intentional misconduct. Therefore, exposing the wrongdoer to liability will not place a burden generally upon the public, but only upon those whose deliberate conduct warrants the denial of immunity. Moreover, recognition of moral fault as a component of public policy is a common principle of tort law. (Cit.Om.)

. . . Many of the same considerations apply when the hazards to which the firemen or policemen are exposed are caused not intentionally but by willful and wanton misconduct. This court has consistently recognized the importance of the distinction between willful and wanton conduct and ordinary negligence. (Cit.Om.) Our concept of willful and wanton conduct has been expressed in these terms:

> (I)t must appear that the defendant with knowledge of existing conditions, and conscious from such knowledge that injury will likely or probably result from his conduct, and with reckless indifference to the consequences, consciously and intentionally does some wrongful act or omits to discharge some duty which produces the injurious result. (McLaughlin v Rova Farms, Inc., supra, 56 N.J. at 305, 266 A.2d 284)

The difference between an intentional act and willful and wanton misconduct is merely one of degree. For an act to be intentional, the actor must intend the harm or realize with substantial certainty that harm is likely to result. For an act to constitute willful and wanton misconduct, the act must be intended, but not the resulting harm; the actor need only "realize * * *that there is a strong probability that harm may result." Restatement (Second) of Torts § 500(f); Prosser and Keeton.

. . . In the context of other immunity doctrines, this Court has found willful and wanton misconduct to constitute an appropriate exception to the general rule of immunity For example, in the area of parental immunity, . . . (I)n the field of charitable immunity . . . (I)n the field of sovereign immunity . . . (Cit.Om.)

The arguments against excluding hazards caused by willful and wanton misconduct from the protection of the fireman's rule are self-evident. First, it is contended that the hazard encountered by the fireman is no different when it is caused by an act constituting ordinary negligence from what it is when the act creating the hazard constituted willful and wanton misconduct. The argument is premised on the assumption that the immunity is correlative with the risk, and if the risk is the same, the conduct that created the risk should not determine whether the immunity should be available to the wrongdoer.

But as Chief Justice Weintraub pointed out in Krauth v Geller, supra, 31 N.J. 270, 157 A.2d 129, the nature of the risk confronted by the firemen or policemen is only part of the public policy equation. The other part derives from the Court's observation that "most fires are attributable to negligence," and "it would be too burdensome to charge all those who carelessly cause * * * fires with the injuries suffered by the expert retained with public funds to deal with (them)." Id at 274, 157 A.2d 129. It follows that in the extreme case in which the hazard is not created by ordinary negligence but by conduct decidedly more culpable-either intentional acts, or willful and wanton misconduct-the public policy balance that supports immunity in case of ordinary negligence has been fundamentally altered. The risk may be the same but the conduct is extraordinarily culpable. In such cases, as a matter of fairness, deterrence, and sound public policy, the burden sought to be avoided by the fireman's rule for the ordinary citizen who commits ordinary negligence should be visited upon the extraordinary wrongdoer.

. . . Finally, it is contended that the difficulty of distinguishing ordinary negligence from willful and wanton misconduct will impose an unreasonable burden upon the trial courts and lead to unnecessary and frivolous claims. This Court has frequently encountered and rejected analogous warnings directed at modifications of tort law. (Cit.Om.)

Accordingly, we hold that the immunity of the fireman's rule does not extend to one whose willfull and wanton misconduct created the hazard that caused injury to the fireman or policeman.

Two years later, the New Jersey Supreme Court had occasion to deal with yet another injured firefighter, yet there were even more differences that the Krauth case, or even the Mahoney case, that went to the very nature of the fire, and it was enough for the court to distinguish their holding from Krauth once more.

While the common law Firemen's Rule remained the law in New Jersey, as well as several other jurisdictions, it was clear that its application was to landowners who had committed ordinary negligence in starting a fire on their own property.

BROWN TRUCKING v FLEXON INDUSTRIES
Supreme Court of New Jersey (1988)
552 A.2d 1026

MENZA, J.S.C.

Plaintiffs are firemen who were injured as a result of the inhalation of noxious chemical fumes during the course of extinguishing a fire caused by an arsonist at defendant's premises. The premises stored combustible chemicals and contained a sprinkler system which was faulty and which violated both a local ordinance and a statute. Defendant was fully aware of this fact prior to the fire. The arsonist had gained entry into the premises through a door which the defendant knew was unlocked. Plaintiffs contend that these facts constitute willful and wanton conduct for which the defendant must respond to plaintiffs in damages.

This court disagrees. Neither the stored chemicals nor the faulty sprinkler system had anything to do with the intentional act of the arsonist in starting the fire. Nor have plaintiffs been able to point to any facts which would indicate that defendant was aware of prior entries into the building or of surrounding buildings to show that defendant was able to foresee the act of the arsonist. (Cit.Om.) There has been, therefore, no showing by plaintiffs that defendant's conduct was willful and wanton so as to take it out of the application of the fireman's rule.

Plaintiffs also argue, however, that irrespective of the question of negligence with regard to the creation of the fire, defendant's conduct in storing combustible material, and his knowing maintenance of a faulty sprinkler system, was an independent act of negligence which subjected plaintiffs to an undue risk of injury for which he must respond to plaintiffs in damages.

The fireman's rule does not excuse an owner from liability where he is guilty of misconduct which is independent of the causes which started the fire, and which creates an undue risk of injury beyond those normally assumed by a firefighter.

. . . However, the mere fact that combustible material was stored in the premises without a showing that its storage was somehow dangerous (i.e., illegally stored, improperly packaged, etc.,) is not in itself negligence.

With regard to the sprinkler system, it is clear that it was faulty and violated the municipal fire code, which requires that fire protection equipment must be maintained in an operative condition, and the statute, NJSA 34:6A-4, which requires that an owner protect his employees against the origin and spread of fire.

. . . There is nothing in the Plainfield ordinance which in any way hints at the fact that a fire sprinkler system must be maintained for the benefit of the firemen called to the premises to fight a fire. As a matter of fact, there is every indication that the purpose of the ordinance is to provide protection only for those persons who occupy or otherwise utilize the premises.

The focus of the statute, NJSA 34:6A-4, is clear. It is a section of the "Worker Health and Safety Act," and is specifically directed at insuring the well being of an employee by imposing a duty on "every employer . . . to . . . furnish a place of employment which shall be reasonably safe and healthful to employees." NJSA 34:6A-3. Rules of statutory construction hold that where a statute or ordinance specifically mentions a class of persons covered, exclusion of other classes is thereby implied. (Cit.Om.)

Since neither the statute nor the ordinance is intended for the protection of firemen who come upon the premises for the purpose of fighting a fire, no statutory duty was owed by defendant to plaintiffs to maintain an adequate sprinkler system.

. . . There is, however, a common law duty of care that an owner owes to persons who enter upon his land, independent of any statutory duty which may exist. In the case of public officers, the duty that is owed is the duty of reasonable care owed to an invitee.

. . . Thus, a fireman who enters a property for a purpose other than to fight a fire may be doing so at the expressed or implied invitation of the owner, and is therefore, an invitee to whom there is owed a duty of reasonable care. (Cit.Om.) A fireman who enters a property for the purpose of fighting a fire, however, cannot be said to have entered on the business of the owner, and thus, upon his implied or express invitation. He is, therefore, not an invitee. On the other hand, he is not a licensee, because he enters the land not for his own purpose, but for the purpose of extinguishing a fire which is in the interest of the owner and the public. His status is, therefore, a hybrid one, which does not fit neatly in any of the two classifications.

. . . Although the firemen's status is unique, the bulk of the authority holds that the duty which is owed to a fireman who enters the property for the purpose of fighting a fire is that which is owed to a licensee. (Cit.Om.)

. . . Considering a fireman as a licensee, for the purpose of determining the scope of duty owed to him, effects a proper balance between the hazards he normally assumes and anticipates as incidental to his business of fighting fires and those that result from willful and wanton misconduct and hidden defects or peril. The failure to properly maintain a sprinkler system, while negligent, is not the type of conduct which might accurately be characterized as willful and wanton. Nor can it be considered a hidden defect or peril. There are certain risks inherent in firefighting. Smoke and flames are part of those risks. The purpose of a sprinkler system is to extinguish a fire or prevent it from spreading. A defective system permits the fire to burn, the very risk the fireman assumes in fighting a fire.

. . . Defendant's negligence in failing to properly maintain his sprinkler system did not reach the level required to breach a duty owed to a licensee. Under the circumstances, since there is no breach of duty on the defendant's part, he cannot be held responsible for his negligence.

In summary, this court concludes that defendant's conduct was not willful and wanton with regard to the creation of the fire. The court also concludes that, since neither the Plainfield ordinance nor the statute create a duty owed to plaintiffs by defendant, their violations impose no liability upon defendant. Finally, this court concludes that the common law duty owed by defendant to plaintiffs was that of the duty owed to a licensee, and since the faulty sprinkler system constituted, at best, an act of ordinary negligence, defendant is not liable to plaintiffs.

MOTION GRANTED.

FURCH v GENERAL ELECTRIC CO., et al.
Supreme Court, Appellate Division, New York (1988)
142 A.2d 8

MAHONEY, P.J.

The firefighters argue that the common law "firemen's rule" is inapplicable since BEC (the electrical contractor) was not an owner or occupant of the office building at the time of the fire. While there is language in the *Santangelo* decision to support this argument (*id.*), the holding in *Santangelo* casts considerable doubt on such a limitation. The court's discussion of the "fireman's rule" was a preamble to recognition that rule extends to police officers and bars recovery against a defendant who neither owned nor occupied the premises where the police officers were injured, but whose negligence allegedly created the occasion for their services (Cit.Om.) Limiting the "fireman's rule" to the owners and occupiers of the premises where the inuury occurred would, in effect, revive the discredited premises-based rationale for the rule. Rather, looking to the risk-based rationale and the more important policy considerations upon which the rule is grounded, we conclude that the "fireman's rule" is applicable to any person whose negligence creates the occasion for the firefighter's services and thereby exposes him to the hazards normally associated with the performance of firemanic duties. (Cit.Om.)

Application of this general principle to the case at bar establishes that, irrespective of whether BEC was an owner or occupier of the premises, the "fireman's rule" is inapplicable to the negligence causes of action. The theory of recovery is not limited to a claim that BEC's negligence caused a fire in the office building. Plaintiffs also claim that BEC's negligence in installing the electrical system permitted the release and venting of toxic substances that could be released and spread throughout the building in the event of a fire. This negligence is sufficiently separate and apart from the negligence which occasioned the emergency for which the plaintiffs were summoned to bar application of the "fireman's rule". (Cit.Om.)

Experience tells us that the risk of exposure to toxic substances is an unfortunate consequence of modern technology, one that is becoming all too common. Nonetheless, neither the risk based rationale for the fireman's rule nor the policy considerations upon which it is based supports an application of the rule which would absolve a party from liability for negligently exposing firefighters and other emergency personnel to toxic substances where, as here, the alleged negligence is independent of that which created the need for their services and the emergency personnel have no reason to believe that exposure to toxic substances is a risk inherent in the emergency. To be contrasted is the situation where the emergency itself patently involves the risk of exposure to toxic substances (Cit.Om.)

. . . Turning to the causes of action asserted by the firefighters based upon General Municipal Law § 205-a, we conclude that the Supreme Court erred in denying BEC's motion for dismissal. The statute creates a cause of action in favor of firefighters injured as a result of the failure to comply with the requirements of some statute, ordinance or rule pertaining to the maintenance and safety of the premises. BEC contends that the liability imposed by General Municipal Law § 205-a is limited to property owners or those in control of the premises. Both the First and the Second Departments have construed the statute as inapplicable to person who are neither owners nor in control of the property involved in the firefighting operation. (Cit.Om.) The statute, on the other hand, clearly refers to "any person or persons", without any limitation based upon ownership or control (General Municipal Law § 205-a); since the statute was enacted to ameliorate the harsh effect of the "fireman's rule" (Cit.Om.), a construction of the statute which fashions such a premises-oriented limitation appears to be inconsistent with our conclusion that the "fireman's rule" contains no such limitation.

We see no need to resolve the issue, however, since the statute contains an express limitation which precludes imposition of liability on BEC. Pursuant to the statute, liability for injuries to a firefighter caused by neglect, omission or willful or culpable negligence in failing to comply with the requirement of certain statutes, ordinances or rules is imposed only upon "the person or persons guilty of said neglect, omission, willful or culpable negligence *at the time of such injury*" (General Municipal Law §205-a (emphasis supplied)). The complaints and the motion papers in the record allege that BEC failed to comply with certain code requirements during the course of its participation in the construction of the building. Since this construction was completed some eight years before the firefighters were injured, it is clear that BEC was not "guilty of said neglect, omission, willful or culpable negligence at the time of such injury", as required by General Municipal Law §205-a. Accordingly, said firefighters statutory causes of action should be dismissed.

Illinois Firemen's Rule Cases

Dini v. Naiditch, 20 Ill. 2d 406, 170 N.E.2d 881 (1960)

Horcher v. Geurin, 94 Ill. App. 2d 244 (1968)

Erickson v. Toledo, Peoria & Western R.R., 21 Ill. App. 3d 546 (1974)

Washington v. Atlantic Richfield Co., 66 Ill. 2d 103 (1976)

Luetje v. Corsini, 126 Ill. App. 3d 74 (1984)

Coglianese v. Mark Twain Ltd., Partnership, 171 Ill. App. 3d 1 (1988)

Briones v. Mobil Oil Corp., Ill. App. 3d 41 (1986)

Horn v. Urban Investment & Development Co. 166 Ill. App. 3d 62 (1988)

Hedburg v. Mendino, 218 Ill. App. 3d 1087 (1991)

McShane v. Chicago Investment Corp., 235 Ill. App. 3d 860 (1992)

Harris v. Chicago Housing Authority., 235 Ill. App. 3d 276 (1992)

Vroegh v. J&M Forklift, 165 Ill 2d 523 (1995)

Zimmerman v. Fasco Mills Co., 302 Ill. App. 3d 308 (1998)

HAUBOLDT v UNION CARBIDE CORP.
Supreme Court of Wisconsin (1991)
467 N.W.2d 508

CALLOW, Justice.

On the morning of January 8, 1983, a woodburning furnace which Coleman used to heat his garage started a fire. The fire ignited spilled gasoline and spread, causing other containers of flammable substances to explode. Ultimately, the fire reached the tanks, causing the oxygen tank to release its contents, and causing the acetylene tank manufactured by Union Carbide to explode.

Ruth Coleman called the Brookfield Fire Department after the fire started but before the acetylene tank exploded. Police officers responding to the call asked Coleman if there were sealed containers or other items in the garage that might explode. Coleman responded that, "there was some paint thinner and a gas tank." Shortly after this, the fire department arrived to fight the fire. Coleman did not tell the firefighters about the acetylene tank in the garage.

As the firefighters attempted to extinguish the fire with water, the acetylene tank exploded, hurling Hauboldt forty-two feet through the air and into a parked car. This collision injured Hauboldt's back, neck and shoulder.

The acetylene tank was equipped with safety devices (fusible plugs) designed to melt in the event of a fire, to allow the tank to release its acetylene gas before it exploded. The tank's design had been tested, and was consistent with government standards.

Hauboldt sued Union Carbide and its agents on the grounds that the acetylene tank was negligently manufactured and was inherently dangerous, making Union Carbide strictly liable for Hauboldt's injuries. Employers (Insurance of Wausau) was impleaded as a plaintiff because it had made medical and disability payments to Hauboldt pursuant the worker's compensation laws of Wisconsin, and was entitled to reimbursement under sec. 102.29 Stats. Union Carbide filed a third party action against the Colemans, claiming contribution or indemnification on the basis of their negligent use and storage of the acetylene tank.

. . . The jury found Union Carbide 88 percent causally negligent, finding that the tank was defective and unreasonably dangerous when it left Union Carbide, and that Union Carbide was causally negligent in designing or manufacturing the tank and in failing to warn of the explosive nature of the tank. The jury found Coleman 12 percent causally negligent for his failure to warn the firefighters of the presence of the tank. The jury assessed damages against Union Carbide for $1,011,000 for injuries to Hauboldt and $25,000 for loss of consortium for his wife.

. . . We addressed this issue of ordinary care in *Wright v Coleman*, 148 Wis.2d 897, 436 N.W.2d 864 (1989), a case which arose from the same fire as this case. In *Wright*, we stated that the general rule of negligence was as we stated in *Clark* and *Antoniewicz*: the landowner or occupier is negligent when he or she fails to warn, if under the circumstances, it would be reasonable to warn. (Cit.Om.) We did not limit liability for a failure to warn as a matter of public policy. We stated that the exception is *Hass*, where we held that a firefighter may not recover from a landowner or occupier who has been negligent only in starting or failing to curtail the fire. This is Wisconsin's version of the fireman's rule."

. . . In *Clark*, we were unable to find public policy considerations sufficient to justify expanding this exception to expose firefighters to the added risks of hidden hazards known to the landowner. (Cit.Om.) Likewise, in *Wright*, we refused to limit the landowner's or occupier's duty to warn only of hidden hazards, if a reasonable person in the circumstances would have done so. (Cit. Om.) The history of the firefighter's rule illustrates the fact that we have addressed the rule as an exception to the general duty of care law. While in *Hass*, we discerned adequate policy reasons for creating an exception to the general rules, we were unable to find justification for expanding the exception to cover the situations described in *Clark* and *Wright*. For the same reason, we will not expand the firefighter's rule to cover manufacturers whose defective product directly causes injury to firefighters during the course of a fire, when the danger caused by the defective product is not reasonably apparent to them, or a risk anticipated by them.

Union Carbide argues that the exception should be applicable to a manufacturer whose product starts or contributes to a fire. Union Carbide contends that there should not be an arbitrary distinction drawn between landowners and manufacturers under such circumstances. Union Carbide analogizes this case to cases from other jurisdictions to support its proposition that it should be protected by the firefighter's rule. (Cit. Om.)

In this case, the manufacturer's defective product did not merely start or contribute to a fire. Although we have framed the firefighter's rule as protecting landowners and occupiers, the fact that Union Carbide was not a landowner or occupier does not determine this case. In this case, the firefighter was directly injured by the unexpected explosion of a defective acetylene tank, not by fire or structural damage incidentally resulting from this explosion. The firefighter was injured by an event that he did not have an opportunity to prepare for. In this sense, the firefighter was in the same position as any other individual injured by a defective product. It is not logical to expand the firefighter's rule to immunize product manufacturers simply because the defective product happens to injure a firefighter in the course of a fire, where the danger caused by the defective product is not reasonably apparent to the firefighter, or anticipated by the firefighter.

None of the public policies served by the firefighter's rule would be served by an extension of the firefighter's rule to cover manufacturers in this situation. This rationale does not apply to manufacturers of defective products which directly injure firefighters who are not prepared for the danger the defective product presents. Imposing liability where a product, because of a defectively designed or manufactured safety device, explodes in a fire and injures a firefighter is no different from imposing liability for injuries caused by other defective products. The burden on the manufacturer is the same.

Union Carbide argues that to allow recovery against manufacturers would also permit the law of negligence to "enter a field that has no sensible or just stopping point." Id. Union Carbide contends that allowing recovery in this situation would predicate immunity from liability on fortuitous circumstances such as whether the product manufacturer owns the property where the accident occurs. On the contrary, holding Union Carbide liable under these circumstances (where Union Carbide is not the landowner and its defective product directly causes the injury) actually preserves the sensible and just stopping point we have established through our earlier cases. Allowing Union Carbide to be protected by the firefighter's rule in this situation would open the door to expansive immunity from liability for manufacturers whose defective products injure firefighters while they fight a fire in the vicinity of the product, unaware of the danger posed by the defective product. This was not the intent of the firefighter's rule.

. . . Firefighters are hired to fight fires, not confront defective acetylene tanks.

. . . On the contrary, the policy to be promoted by strict liability is the protection of otherwise defenseless victims of defectively manufactured products. (Cit. Om.) The purpose of strict products liability is to insure that the cost of injuries resulting from the use of a defective product are borne by the manufacturer who placed the defective product on the market, rather than by the injured person. (Cit.Om.) As in the products liability cases generally, Union Carbide is in the best position to identify and correct defects in its manufactured products. Rather than furthering these policy goals, providing immunity to Union Carbide under these circumstances would frustrate these goals.

Immunity

Common Law: Sovereign Immunity

The immunity that applied to insulate the monarchy at Common Law was grounded in the belief, at least of the king and his most loyal subjects, that "the king can do no wrong" and was made a part of judicial precedent in the case of *Russell v. Men of Devon,* 100 Eng.Rptr.359 (1788). Other beliefs that grew into the doctrine were that public employees should be immune from liability for their exercise of discretion; public funds should not be subject to attachment from tort judgments and the like, and the decisions of the government should be reviewed only by voters, instead of by judges.

Sovereign Immunity, just as much of the common law, found fertile soil in the colonies and was adhered to through the development of the new nation. The sovereign had become the state as the body of government whose actions were not subject to liability in tort. Thus *governmental* immunity replaced that of the monarch.

The immunity underwent some refinements, however, that neither were consistent among the jurisdictions nor was logic always the driving force behind the decisions.

Quasi-municpal corporations, such as counties, townships, towns and special districts were considered as extensions of the state and therefore granted the state's immunity from liability for its actions and negligence.

Municipal corporations, on the other hand, such as cities, villages and boroughs, were considered to have a more private than public character, and were generally created by the will, or at least with the consent of the people of that jurisdiction. Thus they were not cloaked with the state's immunity, since they were not the agents of the state.

While such distinctions served to allocate liability based upon the status of the governing body, problems arose where the clearly municipal corporation was doing the work of the state, and there then developed the further refinement that held where the municipality was engaged in purely *governmental* functions carrying out simply ministerial functions for the state, it retained the governmental immunity. However, when it was engaged in a *proprietary* function, one which benefited the village or city directly, then it was on its own, and could be sued and be caused to pay damages for the negligence of its agents.

Over the years, the extent of immunity in many jurisdictions became more clearly delineated, not from court decisions, but from statutes which allowed for claims against the municipality and by statutes which clearly set forth the immunities for certain actions. One of the first jurisdictions to struggle with the governmental-proprietary dichotomy was the highest court in the state of New York, just after the fourth anniversary of Pearl Harbor.

STEITZ v CITY OF BEACON
Court of Appeals of New York (1945)
64 N.E.2d 704

THATCHER, Judge.

This action is brought to recover damages as a result of a fire which occurred in the city of Beacon on December 26, 1942. Under section 24 of that city's charter (L.1913, ch. 539, as amended by L.1920, ch. 171, §6) the city "may construct and operate a system of waterworks," and the same section provides that "it shall maintain a police, fire, school and poor departments."

. . . It is alleged that the fire broke out of the(se) premises and that plaintiffs' property was destroyed by the carelessness and negligence of the city in failing to create and maintain a fire department, including fire equipment and protection for the benefit of plaintiffs' property and the properties of others located nearby. It is also alleged that the city negligently failed to keep in repair the pressure and flow regulating valve located near the plaintiffs' property and that it negligently operated a certain manually operated valve, and that by reason of such negligence an insufficient quantity of water was provided to combat effectively the fire in question. Plaintiffs' freedom from contributory negligence and damages in the sum of $27,900 are also alleged and the plaintiffs demand judgment for that amount.

The waiver of sovereign immunity by section 8 (formerly 12-a) of the Court of Claims Act has rendered the defendant municipality liable, equally with individuals and private corporations, for the wrongs of its employees. In each case, however, liability must be "determined in accordance with the same rules of law as applied in the supreme court against individuals and corporations." Accordingly the city is controlled by the laws of legal liability applicable to an individual sued for fire damage as alleged in the complaint. The question is whether the facts alleged would be sufficient to constitute a cause of action against an individual under the same duties as those imposed upon the city solely because of failure to protect property from destruction by fire caused by another. There is no such liability known to the law unless a duty to the plaintiff to quench the fire or indemnify the loss has been assumed by agreement or imposed by statute. There was no agreement in this case to put out the fire or make good the loss, and so liability is predicated solely upon the above quoted provisions of the city charter defining its powers of government. Quite obviously these provisions were not in terms designed to protect the personal interests of any individual and clearly were designed to secure the benefits of well ordered municipal government enjoyed by all as members of the community. There was indeed a public duty to maintain a fire department, but that was all, and there was no suggestion that for any omission in keeping hydrants, valves or pipes in repair the people of the city could recover fire damages to their property.

An intention to impose on the city the crushing burden of such an obligation should not be imputed to the legislature. Language similar to that found in the Charter of the City of Beacon may be found in many municipal charters. (Cit. Om.) As was said in *Moch v Rensselaer Water Co.*, 247 N.Y. 160, 166, 159 N.E. 896, 62 A.L.R. 1199; "If the plaintiff is to prevail, one who negligently omits to supply a sufficient pressure to extinguish a fire started by another assumes an obligation to pay the ensuing damage, though the whole city is laid low. A promisor will not be deemed to have had in mind the assumption of a risk so overwhelming for such a trivial reward." A fortiori the Legislature should not be deemed to have imposed such a risk when its language connotes nothing more than the creation of departments of municipal government, the grant of essential powers of government and directions as to their exercise.

Such enactments do not import intention to protect the interests of any individual except as they secure to all members of the community the enjoyment of rights and privileges to which they are entitled only as members of the public. Neglect in the performance of such requirements creates no civil liability to individuals. (Cit.Om.)

In the forty years between the *Steitz* decision and the case that immediately follows, have been many fires, not all of which have been extinguished as competently as possible. While the doctrine of Sovereign Immunity was alive and well in Florida in 1985, there was clear language of the court that there was a possibility of liability in certain cases, but the facts had not supported such a finding in the case before it.

Given those particular facts, the court would seem not to have a major problem in finding liability against the city of Daytona Beach.

CITY OF DAYTONA BEACH v PALMER
Supreme Court of Florida (1985)
469 So.2d 121

OVERTON, Justice.

. . . The complaint upon which this action is based alleged that the fire occurred in an office building in which William Palmer (respondent's husband, now deceased) had his office; that Palmer was called to the fire scene and requested by the firemen to unlock his office doors to provide access to his property; that standard firefighting practices required the fire department employees to remove or allow Palmer to remove items of personal property that could be safely removed from his office; that the firemen temporarily terminated their firefighting efforts during a work shift change; that the firefighters opened an upstairs window in Palmer's office in contravention of standard firefighting practices; and that the firefighting unit's platoon commander, by reason of the above conduct, exhibited a clear lack of proper decision making and supervisory skills, which failure was the proximate cause of the destruction of Palmer's office equipment, library and professional records.

The trial court dismissed Palmer's complaint for failure to state a cause of action. On appeal, the district court reversed, finding the complaint stated a cause of action and concluding that this conduct was operational-level negligence for which the city government could be held liable (Cit.Om.).

This Court addressed the issue of government tort liability in the enforcement of laws in *Trianon Park Condominium Association v City of Hialeah*, 468 So.2d 912 (Fla. 1985.) In *Trianon*, we stated that before a governmental entity may be held liable for the negligent acts of its employees, there must first be a determination that there was an underlying common law or statutory duty of care existing with respect to the alleged negligent conduct. At 917. In accordance with our decisions in *Trianon* and *Everton v. Willard*, 468 So.2d 936 (Fla. 1985.), we conclude that there never has been a common law duty of care to individual property owners to provide fire protections services. Further, we find no statutory duty of care upon which to base governmental liability for such conduct.

In *Trianon*, we stated that "there is not governmental tort liability for the action or inaction of governmental officials in carrying out the discretionary governmental functions (of enforcing the laws and protecting the public safety) because there never has been a common law duty of care with respect to these . . . police power functions, and *the statutory waiver of sovereign immunity did not create a new duty of care."* At 921. (emphasis added.)

The decisions of how to properly fight a particular fire, how to rescue victims in a fire, or what and how much equipment to send to a fire, are discretionary judgmental decisions which are inherent in this public safety function of fire protection. A substantial majority of jurisdictions that have addressed the issue of governmental liability for asserted negligent conduct in responding to and fighting fires have reached this same conclusion. (Cit.Om.)

To hold a city liable for the negligent decisions of its firefighters would require a judge or jury to second guess firefighters in making these decisions and would place the judiciary branch in a supervisory role over basic executive branch, public protection functions in violation of the separation of powers doctrine.

We distinguish these types of discretionary firefighting decisions from negligent conduct resulting in personal injury while fire equipment is being driven to the scene of a fire or personal injury to a spectator from the negligent handling of equipment at the scene. Governmental entities are clearly liable for this type of conduct as a result of the enactment of 768.28, Florida Statutes (1983).

In conclusion, we hold that if there is to be a duty to individual property owners upon which the liability of a governmental entity and its taxpayers is to be based for the discretionary acts of firefighters in combatting fires, the duty must be established by an act of the legislature and not by judicial fiat.

For the reasons expressed, we quash the decision of the district court of appeal and remand with directions that the district court reinstate the trial court order granting the motion to dismiss. It is so ordered.

What the court looked for in the above case was whether there was any common law duty on the part of the defendants and found none.

Similarly, an Illinois Appellate Court two years later, had looked for that common law duty, but in the case in Illinois, firefighters had not fought the blaze negligently-they had not fought the blaze at all. The fire had occurred while firefighters were on strike, and the plaintiff argued that the failure to respond to the premises was clearly negligence on the part of the firemen and therefore of the city.

Although there was a statutory immunity, the plaintiff argued that such could not be utilized by the defendants since they were participating in an illegal strike, and such could not be considered to be within the scope of their employment.

JACKSON v CHICAGO FIREFIGHTERS UNION
Illinois Appellate Court, 1ˢᵗ District (1987)
160 Ill.App.3d 975

CAMPBELL, Justice.

. . . In granting the defendants' motion to dismiss, the trial court focused solely on what it found to be the two-fold "threshold issue": (1) whether firefighters have a common law duty to the plaintiffs that is negated by the General Assembly's passage of sections 5-101 and 5-202 of the Tort Immunity Act, except under circumstances where a "special duty" exists: or (2) whether sections 5-101 and 5-102 are simply legislative restatement of the absence of a common law duty between a firefighter and a specific plaintiff. The trial court found that regardless of whether sections 5-101 and 5-102 are statutory restatements of the absence of a duty owed by firefighters, or whether the sections act to negate a common law duty (in the absence of a showing of special duty) by firefighters, dismissal of the cause of action was required on the grounds that "no common law duty exists under the facts alleged in the complaint." In addition, the trial court found that the plaintiffs had failed to sufficiently allege the existence of a special duty between defendants and plaintiffs.

On appeal, plaintiffs contend that the trial court erred in dismissing their complaint because: (1) the defendants were not municipal employees acting within the scope of their employment at the time of the fire at the Ridgeway premises, and, thus are not entitled to the protections of 5-101 and 5-102 of the Tort Immunity Act; and (2), in the alternative, the special duty exception had been properly alleged in the complaint. For the following reasons, we affirm the judgment of the circuit court.

In support of their contention that the court erred in dismissing their complaint, plaintiffs initially argue that defendants' participation in an illegal strike at the time of the fire at the Ridgeway premises triggered two exceptions to the Tort Immunity Act, thereby precluding application of the act's protection to them. First, plaintiffs contend that defendant firefighters were not acting within the scope of their employment while they were on strike. Therefore, because section 2-204 of the Tort Immunity Act limits coverage of the act to public employees who are acting within the scope of their employment, the firefighters were not covered and are liable for their failure to provide fire protection. Second, the plaintiffs argue that pursuant to section 2-202 of the Act, which denies immunity for acts or omissions which constitute wanton and willfull negligence, defendants are liable for the intentional violation of the court order which enjoined the strike and for their refusal to tend to the fire at the Ridgeway premises.

In our view, plaintiffs' scope of employment argument is fundamentally incongruous. Assuming *arguendo* that defendant firefighters were not acting within the scope of their employment at the time they failed to tend to the fire at the Ridgeway premises, then they must have been acting as private citizens. In the latter capacity, defendants were under no duty to provide fire protection. In support of their position, plaintiffs rely on *Bauer v city of Chicago* (1985), 137 Ill.App.3d 228, 484 N.E.2d 422. However, we find that *Bauer* more accurately supports a finding of no duty. In *Bauer*, A suspended police officer was involved in a shooting. The city of Chicago refused to represent the officer on the ground that he had not been acting within the scope of his authority at the time of the shooting. The trial court granted summary judgment in the city's favor. On appeal, the Bauer court held that, ". . . as a matter of law, * * * a suspended police officer cannot be acting within the scope of his employment, even if the officer is engaged in direct police action.* * *A suspended police officer has only the same rights and obligations in preventing and stopping the commission of crime as any private citizen."(Cit.Om.)

Thus, in the present case, whether the defendants were protected by the Tort Immunity Act or whether they acted outside the scope of the public employment as private citizens, we find that they had no legal duty to offer fire protection to plaintiffs.

Special Duty

While the *Jackson* case did not find the defendants liable, it was a critical case nevertheless because it set down the elements of *special duty*, under which public employees could be held liable, the statutory immunity notwithstanding. The court asserted that for the special duty to apply:

a) the municipality must be *uniquely aware* of the danger;
b) there must be *specific acts or omissions*;
c) the acts must be *affirmative or willful*; and
d) the injury must occur when the plaintiff is under the *direct and immediate control* of defendants.

The last element, that of direct and immediate control would become of particular concern to the Corporation Counsel of the city of Chicago, growing out of another fire wherein a civilian at the scene assisted the firefighters by unlocking a door for them; behind the door, unfortunately, was the fire. The once absolute defense, even statutorily codified, was insufficient to protect the public employees under the following facts.

ANTHONY v CITY OF CHICAGO
Appellate Court of Illinois (1988)
523 N.E.2d 22

Following previous dismissals of earlier complaints. on April 9, 1987, Anthony filed a three-count, second amended complaint pursuant to leave of the court. Count I, in relevant part, asserted defendants' negligence in that they permitted Anthony to remain on the premises and "instructed, directed and encouraged" Anthony's aid in opening an elevator door from which smoke was escaping, in a burning building, without providing him with proper training, clothing, assistance or equipment and without warning him of the elevator's dangerous condition. In Count II, Anthony alleged that because defendants "knew or should have known he was likely to be injured" by these same acts, defendants acted wantonly, wilfully and with a reckless disregard for his safety. Anthony attempted in Count III to plead defendants' "special duty" to him and the breach thereof, in that: (1) (d)efendants were uniquely aware of the risk and danger to plaintiff in opening (the elevator) door"; and (2) through their experience, defendants "knew or should have known" either: (a) "elevator shafts are a source of updrafts and associated rapid and explosive combustion"; or (b) "(t)he fire * * * would explode when the elevator door was opened * * *." Anthony further alleged that defendants wilfully and wantonly "allowed, permitted and encouraged" him to remain on the premises, "directed" him to stand in front of and open an elevator door "containing a fire," and failed to "provide him "with proper training, clothing or assistance," although defendants knew or should have known these acts would likely result in injury to Anthony.

The City moved to dismiss, citing sections 5-102 and 5-103 of the Local Governmental and Governmental Employees Tort Immunity Act ("Act") (III.Rev. Stat.1985, ch. 85, pars. 1-101 *et seq.* and asserting that: (1) these sections provide firefighters with blanket immunity from liability for injuries arising from firefighting activities, subject only to the exceptions enumerated in the Act; and (2) the exceptions stated in 5-102 and 5-103 of the Act, relating to the operation of a motor vehicle and fire services provided by "fire protection districts or corporations," are inapplicable to the case at bar. III.Rev.Stat.1985, ch. 85, pars. 5-102, 5-103.

Following a hearing on April 12, 1987, the court refused to recognize a "special duty" exception capable of piercing the statutory immunity sheilding firefighters from liability and dismissed the second amended complaint with prejudice.

Anthony appeals, requesting a vacatur or in the alternative, a reversal of the April 12, 1987 order.

. . . A municipality or its employees may not be held liable for failure to supply general police or fire protection. (Cit.Om.) Where a public employee, however, exercises care or custody over an individual, the individual's status is elevated beyond that of a member of the general public, the "special duty" exception is activated and the employee is liable for injury proximately caused by his negligence (Cit.Om.).

Defendants acknowledge the creation of the special duty exception by our Supreme Court, but argue that it has been applied to police only, and urge that it not be extended to injuries caused by firefighters. (Cit.Om.)

Illinois case law does not limit the exception to a particular class or type of public official; instead the exception has been held relevant to a variety of public entities. (Cit.Om.) Moreover, this court recently recognized that the exception could be applied to firefighters. (See Jackson v. Chicago Firefighters Union, Local 2 (1987), 160 Ill.App.3d 975, 980-82, 112 Ill.Dec. 393, 513 N.E.2d 1002.)

. . . Defendants further maintain that if this court applies the special duty exception to firefighters, Anthony cannot meet the four elements necessary to the cause of action: (1) the municipality must be uniquely aware of the particular danger or risk to which plaintiff is exposed; (2) there must be specific acts or omissions on the part of the municipality; (3) the specific acts or omissions must be affirmative or wilful in nature; (4) the injury must occur while the plaintiff is under the direct and immediate control of municipal employees or agents. (Cit. Om.)

In the case sub judice, the second amended complaint satisfies the first three requirements. The complaint alleges that defendants are experienced in combatting blazes and observing the dangerous effects of updrafts in elevator shafts, and that they permitted an untrained, unequipped civilian to open the door of a burning elevator. (Cit.Om.) Anthony further contends that defendants, through the unknown firefighter, placed him in that hazardous position by affirmatively instructing him to accompany the firefighter in the burning building and open the elevator door. (Cit.Om.)

Defendants are particularly insistent that Anthony failed to allege that he was under the direct and immediate control of the Department and facts sufficient to satisfy the element of control. The fourth requirement of the special duty exception is met where the public employee "(creates) a position of peril" ultimately injurious to plaintiff, as opposed to situations where plaintiff merely seeks protection from the public employee which is not provided (Cit.Om.)

In *Gardner v. Village of Chicago Ridge*, 71 Ill.App.2d at 379, 219 N.E.2d 147, for instance, the court recognized the existence of a special duty where plaintiff acquiesced to police officers' "express request" to identify several criminal suspects and was subsequently beaten by those suspects. No "direct and immediate control" was found however, where plaintiffs alleged injuries arising from a tardy response by police to plaintiffs' 911 emergency telephone call (*Galuszynski v. City of Chicago*, 131 Ill.App.3d at 508, 86 Ill.Dec. 581, 475 N.E.2d 960), or where a police officer refused to accompany plaintiff to a subway platform and plaintiff was later beaten by youths waiting on the platform. (*Marvin v. Chicago Transit Authority*, 113 Ill.App.3d at 177, 86 Ill. Dec. 581, 475 N.E.2d 960.) In *Jackson v. Chicago Firefighters Union, Local 2*, 160 Ill.App.3d at 177, 86 Ill.Dec. 581, 475 N.E.2d 1002, the court ruled that defendant firefighters were nor "responsible" for the fire which destroyed plaintiffs' property and therefore did not maintain "direct and immediate control" over plaintiffs.

The case at bar most closely resembles *Gardner v. Village of Chicago Ridge*, 71 Ill.App.2d 373, 219 N.E.2d 147: the second amended complaint alleged that the unknown firefighter "instructed" and "directed" Anthony to open the elevator door and that Anthony was "instructed, directed and encouraged" to "aid" defendants in combatting the fire. The firefighter arguably assumed responsibility for Anthony's safety when he requisitioned Anthony to assist in fighting the blaze and thereby initiated the events immediately accountable for Anthony's injuries. While the precise phrase "direct and immediate control" is absent from the pleading, Anthony nonetheless alleged facts adequately demonstrating that defendants' affirmative acts created a position of peril (Cit.Om.). The circuit court thus erred in dismissing Anthony's second amended complaint.

For the reasons above stated, the circuit court's order of April 12, 1987 dismissing Anthony's second amended complaint must be reversed and the cause remanded for further proceedings consistent with this opinion.

Reversed and remanded.

STAMOS and BILANDIC, JJ., concur.

In the field of inspections, the doctrine of Sovereign Immunity continued to provide a shield against liability when the inspection proved negligent. The leading case in the area of code inspections, negligent or otherwise, is from Minnesota, which, some years later, would find that even this immunity gave way when the persons to be protected were exceptionally vulnerable.

CRACRAFT v CITY OF ST. LOUIS PARK
Supreme Court of Minnesota (1979)
279 N.W.2d 801

This suit involves the alleged negligent failure of a city inspector to discover a violation of the municipal fire ordinance at Benilde-St. Margaret's High School, St. Louis Park, Minnesota.

On October 27, 1974, a 55-gallon drum of duplicating fluid, an extremely volatile and highly flammable liquid, ignited on the loading dock of the high school. The dock is adjacent to the school's football field and is commonly used by students as a means of ingress and egress.

As a result of the explosion, three youths received first-, second-, and third-degree burns over their entire bodies. Two of the boys died, including Kenneth Kasper. A third boy, plaintiff John Cracraft, received severe burns over 50 percent of his body.

The city fire inspector, Gerald Hines, inspected the entire premises on September 13, 1974. The presence of a drum of duplicating fluid on the dock would be a violation of the fire code. Mr. Hines testified, in deposition, that he did not see the drum at the time of his inspection. He stated that if it was there at the time of the examination, it would have been noticed and removed.

Plaintiffs contend that the city must conduct an inspection with due care, that the city's inspection was negligently performed, and the negligence was a substantial causative factor of the injuries and damages. Defendant municipality, on the other hand, contends that it owed no duty of care for the purposes of a negligence action. Thus, the question in this case becomes: Under what conditions is a duty of care imposed on a municipality which seeks to enforce the law by inspecting for fire code violations?

To hold a municipality liable for negligently inspecting the conduct of third persons for fire code violations, plaintiffs must establish that the municipality has a common law duty to provide a reasonable inspection . . . .

Although recognizing that the Minnesota Legislature had abolished the doctrine of sovereign immunity as it applied to the political subdivision of the state, we held (*Hoffert v Owatonna Inn Towne Motel, Inc.*, 293 Minn. 220, 222; 199 N.W.2d 158, 159 (1972)):

". . . (T)hese statutory provisions (abolishing immunity) merely removed the defense of immunity. They did not create any new liability for a municipality. In order to recover against the city, appellants must show a breach of some duty owed them in their individual capacities and not merely a breach of some obligation owed the general public.

"The purpose of the building code is to protect the public." The court went on to state . . . building inspections are devices used by municipalities to make sure that construction within the corporate limits of the municipality meets the standards established. As such, they are designed to protect the public and are not meant to be an insurance policy by which the municipality guarantees that each building is built in compliance with the building codes and zoning codes. The charge for building permits is to offset expenses incurred by the city in promoting this public interest and is in no way an insurance premium which makes the city liable for each item of defective construction in the premises."

. . . If there were no additional considerations in this case, it could be concluded at this point that the defendant municipality had no duty, public or special, to inspect and correct fire code violations. There are additional considerations, however. The municipality's own ordinances require that it undertake inspections for fire code violations. However, such inspections are required for the purpose of protecting the interests of the municipality as a whole against the fire hazard of the person inspected. The inspections are not undertaken for the purpose of assuring either the person inspected or third persons that the building is free from all hazards, just as the state's issuance of a driver's license is no assurance that the licensed person will be a safe driver. Because the ordinances are designed to protect the municipality's own interest, rather than the interests of a particular class of individuals, only a "public" duty to inspect is created. It is a basic principle of negligence law that public duties created by statute cannot be the basis of a negligence action even against private tortfeasors.

The distinction, therefore, is neither a fiction, nor artificial, nor a relic of the days of sovereign immunity. It is a well established principle of negligence law applicable to tort actions against individuals as well as governments.

. . . At what point, then, does the municipality assume to act for the protection of others as distinguished from acting merely for itself when it inspects the activities of third parties for fire code violations? There is no bright line. But, without intending to be exhaustive, there are at least four factors which should be considered. First, actual knowledge of the dangerous condition is a factor which tends to impose a duty of care on the municipality. Second, reasonable reliance by persons on the municipality's representations and conduct tends to impose a duty of care. Of course, reliance on the inspection in general is not sufficient. Instead, the reasonable reliance must be based on *specific actions or representations which cause the person to forego other alternatives of protecting themselves*. Third, a duty of care may be created by an ordinance or statute that sets forth mandatory acts clearly for a particular class of persons rather than the public as a whole. Finally, the municipality must use due care to avoid increasing the risk of harm.

Applying these factors to this case we find no evidence in the record indicating that a duty was assumed or a special duty was created.

. . . In this situation, there exist viable defendants who allegedly violated the fire codes and may be held responsible at law if their negligence caused injury to the plaintiffs. We are being asked to add another defendant; namely, the municipality involved. If such an expansion and change in the law is to occur, it is better that the legislature act in this field where extensive hearings can be conducted to consider the extent of the financial impact of such a basic change.

. . . Manifestly, then, the creation of a new duty owed by municipalities and other governmental entities to enforce the law with reasonable care is a change which should be made by the legislature. We will not assent to such a change by the judiciary.

KELLY, Justice (dissenting).

. . . Because we have abrogated sovereign immunity, I see no reason why, under general principles of torts, the city, like any other enterprise, should not be held liable for the negligence of its inspectors resulting in foreseeable injury.

. . . The possibility that a municipality may be held liable for the breach of every building code or zoning ordinance within the city, and the consequent enormous drain on the public coffers, is often raised as the prime justification for the "public duty doctrine."

Such arguments, however, were raised a decade ago in opposition to the proposal that the state waive its defense of sovereign immunity. These contentions proved to be false then and are just as likely to be false now.

Moreover, by allowing suits of this type against the state, the state does not assume an absolute duty to enforce its laws and ordinances. Cities will not be held to guarantee compliance with codes and to insure the safety of every building in the city, as the majority seems to indicate. Rather, cities will be held only to a standard of due and reasonable care, liability being limited by such principles as proximate cause and foreseeability.

In addition to the legal justification stated above, there are reasons of public policy which convince me that the decision of the majority is erroneous. By immunizing municipalities from tort liability arising out of the negligent performance of a "public duty," the majority opinion severely undermines any motivation on the part of a municipality to insure that such important duties as fire inspection are properly performed—rendering these duties meaningless. Furthermore, by hanging onto this relic of governmental immunity, the majority is perpetuating the inequity we strove to banish when we abrogated sovereign immunity.

The Minnesota Supreme Court, in 1986, had occasion to apply four part test set forth in *Cracraft*, and did not find that all four were met. In fact, it conceded that only one of the tests had been met, but it was sufficient for the court to find that the county that licensed day care facilities dealt with a special class of individuals that required the special duty of care in providing for their safety. In *Andrade v. Ellefson*, 391 N.W.2d 836, at 842, the court detailed the nature of the particular class to be given special protection:

It is the third *Cracraft* factor, however, that is decisive in this case. "(A) duty of care may be created by an ordinance or statute that sets forth mandatory acts clearly for the protection of a particular class of persons rather than the public as a whole. (Cit.Om.) While the Public Welfare Licensing Act covers the licensing of a variety of facilities, The Act clearly mandates that small children in a licensed day care facility are a particular protected class. The class consists of uniquely vulnerable persons: small children, often infants, left by their working parents in a home other than their own, and left in the care of another person for some period of less than 24 hours of the day. See Minn.Stat. § 245.782, subd. 5 (1984). Provisional licenses for such a facility may, for example, only be issued if any "deviations do not threaten the health, rights, of safety of the persons to be served * * *." Minn.Stat. 245.783 subd. 3 (1984). By Minn.Stat. § 245.802 (1984), state commissioners were instructed to conduct a comprehensive study and prepare a report to the legislature by February 1, 1985, on recommendations for regulations "that will ensure a safe environment for children." The commissioner has promulgated detailed rules governing the needs and well-being of the children in day care facilities. Clearly, the government here is doing more than benefitting the general public and its immediate concern is for the children. Consistent with this concern for the children is the apparent practice of Anoka County to refer parents to those day care facilities which have been licensed on its recommendations.

. . . The operation of day care facilities apparently presents a high risk of liability exposure, and it can be argued that to impose this risk on government may discourage the government from assuming a protective role. On the other hand, the high risk underscores the need for adequate inspection. Here the legislature has addressed this problem. It has conferred governmental immunity on Anoka County under section 3.736, subd. 3 (1984). Liability exists here, however, because Anoka County has elected, as it may, to waive that immunity to the extent set out in its liability insurance.

STATUTORY IMMUNITIES

Legislatures in states that believed that the immunity of their employees had been a very good thing under the common law doctrine, sought to perpetuate that shield from liability by the enactment of statutes that specifically protected their employees, even when they were negligent. Even where their workers had been wanton and willfully negligent, statutes often conferred absolute immunity. As time passed, and the electorate became increasingly dissatisfied with the protection of near reckless personnel whom their tax dollars provided pay, those statutes began to allow recovery for very serious negligence in their operations, and for even less negligence when their apparatus was on the common roadway.

The Illinois statute, as hereinafter set forth, is an example of that changing immunity.

LOCAL GOVERNMENT TORT IMMUNITY ACT

745 ILCS ARTICLE V-FIRE PROTECTION AND RESCUE SERVICES

10/5-101. Establishment of fire department-Fire protection-Rescue or other emergency services.

§ 5-101 Neither a local public entity nor a public employee is liable for failure to establish a fire department or otherwise to provide fire protection, rescue or other emergency service.

As used in this Article, "rescue services" includes, but is not limited to, the operation of an ambulance as defined in the Emergency Medical Services (EMS) Systems Act.

10/5-102. Failure to suppress or contain fire

§ 5-102. Neither a local public entity that has undertaken to provide fire protection service nor any of its employees is liable for an injury resulting from the failure to suppress or contain a fire or from the failure to provide or maintain sufficient personnel, equipment or other fire protection facilities.

10/5-103. Condition of fire protection or fire fighting equipment or facilities-Acts or omissions

§ 5-103. (a) Neither a local public entity, nor a public employee acting in the scope of his employment, is liable for an injury resulting from the condition of fire protection or firefighting equipment or facilities. Nothing in this section shall exonerate a public entity from liability for negligence by reason of the condition of a motor vehicle while it is traveling on public ways.

(b) Neither a local public entity nor a public employee acting in the scope of his employment, is liable for an injury caused by an act or omission of a public employee while engaged in fighting a fire. However, this Section shall not apply if the injury is caused by the willful and wanton conduct of the public employee.

10/5-104. Liability for damages to roads and bridges caused by fire fighting equipment.

§ 5-104. Except as provided in this Article, no trustee, officer or employee of a fire protection district or fire department having a mutual aid agreement with such district, nor any such fire protection district or fire department, shall be liable for damage caused to bridges and roads thereon, owned by the State or a unit of local government, when such damage is caused by fire fighting equipment crossing bridges and roads thereon, for which load limits are lower than the weight of such equipment, when responding to an alarm or returning therefrom.

10/5-106. Emergency Calls.

§ 5-106. Except for willful or wanton conduct, neither a local public entity, nor a public employee acting within the scope of his employment, is liable for an injury caused by the negligent operation of a motor vehicle or firefighting or rescue equipment, when responding to an emergency call, including transportation of a person to a medical facility.

EMERGENCY MEDICAL SERVICES ACT

210 ILCS 50 EMS SYSTEMS ACT

50/17 Immunity from liability
§ 17. Immunity from liability.

(a) Any person, agency or governmental body licensed or authorized pursuant to this Act or its rules, who in good faith performs life support services during a Department approved training course, in the normal course of conducting their duties, or in an emergency call shall not be civilly or criminally liable as a result of their acts or omissions in providing those services unless the acts or omissions, including the bypassing of nearby hospitals or medical facilities for the purpose of transporting a trauma patient to a designated trauma center in accordance with the protocols developed pursuant to Section 27 of this Act, are inconsistent with the person's training or constitute willful or wanton misconduct.

(b) No person, including any private or governmental organization or institution that administers, sponsors, authorizes, supports, finances or supervises the functions of emergency medical services personnel licensed and authorized pursuant to this Act, including persons licensed under this Act and Department rules issued pursuant to this Act, or persons participating in a Department approved training program working for licensure, shall be liable for any civil damages for any act or omission in connection with administration, sponsorship, authorization, support, finance, or supervision of emergency medical services personnel, where the act or omission occurs in connection with their training or with services rendered outside a hospital unless the act or omission was the result of gross negligence or willful misconduct.

(c) Any person who has completed a basic cardiopulmonary resuscitation training course which complies with generally recognized standards, and who in good faith, not for compensation, provides emergency basic cardiopulmonary resuscitation to a person who is an apparent victim of cardiopulmonary insufficiency shall not, as a result of his acts or omissions in providing resuscitation, be liable for civil damages, unless the acts or omissions constitute willful or wanton misconduct.

(d) No local agency, entity of State or local government, or other public or private organization, nor any officer, director, trustee, employee, consultant or agent of such entity, that sponsors, authorizes, supports, finances or supervises the training of persons in a basic cardiopulmonary resuscitation course which complies with generally recognized standards shall be liable for damages in any civil action based on the training of those persons unless an act or omission during the course of instruction constitutes willful or wanton misconduct.

(e) No person who is certified to teach basic cardiopulmonary resuscitation, and who teaches a course which complies with generally recognized standards for basic cardiopulmonary resuscitation, shall be liable for damages in any civil action based on the acts or omissions of a person who received such instruction, unless an act or omission during the course of the instruction constitutes willful or wanton misconduct.

745 ILCS 10/1-210 Willful and Wanton conduct

§ 1-210 "Willful and wanton conduct" as used in this Act means a course of action which shows an actual or deliberate intention to cause harm or which, if not intentional, shows an utter indifference to or conscious disregard for the safety of others or their property.

CIVIL IMMUNITIES/LIABILITIES

LAW ENFORCEMENT EMERGENCY CARE ACT

745 ILCS 20/1. Liability in absence of wilful and wanton misconduct (IRS 70 ¶61)

§ 1. Any law enforcement officer or fireman as defined in Section 2 of the "Law Enforcement Officers and Firemen Compensation Act,"[1] who in good faith provides emergency care without fee to any person shall not, as a result of his acts or omissions, except wilful and wanton misconduct on the part of such person, in providing such care, be liable to a person to whom such care is provided for civil damages.

ACT 75. FIRE FIGHTER LIABILITY ACT

75/1 Liability of fire fighter for injuries to person or property

§ 1. In case an injury to the person or property of another is caused by the negligent operation of any motorized fire fighting equipment by a compensated fire fighter or authorized volunteer fire fighter of a fire protection district or incorporated fire protection organization while he or she is engaged in the performance of his or her duties as fire fighter, and without contributory negligence of the injured person, of the owner of the injured property or of the agent or servant of the injured person or owner, the fire protection district or incorporated fire protection organization in whose behalf the fire fighter is performing his or her duties shall be liable for that injury. While engaged in preventing or extinguishing fires, any fire fighter or authorized volunteer fire fighter may enter upon the lands of any person, firm, private or municipal corporation or the State of Illinois to carry out his or her duties and while so acting shall not be criminally or civilly liable for entering upon such lands. In no case shall such a fire fighter be liable in damages for any injury to the person or property caused by him or her while engaged in the performance of his or her duties as a fire fighter, unless such injury results from his or her wilful and wanton misconduct.

---

[1]   820 ILCS 315/2

CRIMINAL LAW

The 4th Amendment
Search & Seizure   *Indiana v Buxton*
Iowa v Rees
Michigan v Tyler
Michigan v Clifford

CRIMINAL LAW

Just as with tort law, criminal Law is a progeny of the common law, and as such we have inherited many of the basic offenses against society (e.g., theft, burglary, arson). Note that these are considered as wrongs against our *society* even though perpetrated upon an individual. Therein lies a critical distinction between the areas of tort and criminal law.

The law (as administered by our courts) will compensate the individual for a wrong personal to him (Tort), but punishes the criminal because he has wronged society as a whole. This basic distinction should be kept in mind notwithstanding a criminal judge can also order restitution, and some wrongs are *both criminal and tortuous* in nature (e.g., battery).

Another difference is in the proof each requires, and who must prove the issue. In tort, the plaintiff carries the burden of proof throughout the case; that is, he must prove to the judge or jury the issues in his case. The level of proof required of the tort plaintiff is the *preponderance of the evidence* or, that *most* of the evidence satisfies the trier of fact.

In criminal matters, the burden of proof is always upon the government unit that seeks to convict, i.e., the Federal Government, the state, the county, the city, et. al. The level of proof required of the prosecution is that *beyond a reasonable doubt.*

Although we inherited most of our basic crimes from the Common Law, our criminal law has been codified in the United States; i.e., written down in the form of statutes. This is the *substantive* criminal law. Even Louisiana, which as a French, as opposed to English, colony, based its law on the Napoleonic Code, passed statutes that provided that the basis of its criminal law would be English Common Law.

Other statutes that set forth the process itself, from arrest through trial and sentencing, are *procedural* criminal law, and it is here that the Constitutional guarantees of the 4th through the 6th Amendments of the Bill of Rights have critical and considerable force.

It must be remembered that the founding fathers were all too aware of what harm the absence of a process to guarantee a commitment to fairness could do to a people. They were determined to set up restraints against the abuse of power that they had known under the crown. Thus the Constitution applies with particular force in the area of criminal law and criminal procedure.

Specifically prohibited are certain laws, such as *bills of attainder*, which forfeit the property of one convicted of a felony; or any law which makes a crime of conduct which was legal when committed (*ex post facto*).

The Bill of Rights contains a great deal of protection against the abuse of government in the prosecution of the individual, such as the following:

* No evidence may be used which has been secured as the result of an unreasonable search and seizure
* No warrants issued but upon probable cause

* No subsequent prosecution for the same offense
* No compelled testimony against one's self
* No loss of life, liberty or property without due process

* The right to a speedy trial, confrontation of witnesses and assistance of counsel
* No cruel or unusual punishment

The personality of the Supreme Court is etched in its interpretations of the reach of the Constitution, especially in the area of criminal law. To many police officers as well as conservative citizens in the sixties, the decisions of the Supreme Court under Chief Justice Earl Warren represented an excessive concern for the rights of criminal defendants, to the detriment of the effectiveness of law enforcement everywhere. It is doubtful that it could it be honestly asserted that even the Constitution's draftsman, Thomas Jefferson, could have imagined that the protection of the Fifth Amendment would be invoked, successfully, by someone with the colorful name, not to mention lifestyle, of a "Big Tuna".

Generalities can be often stated with regard to the philosophy of any Supreme Court Justice based upon the party of his appointing president; but those labels which attempt to pigeon-hole a justice and thereby effectively predict how his or her vote will be cast, grow more problematic with each election.

Just as politicians are branching off from the main dichotomy of democrat/liberal and/or republican/conservative, so too, party affiliation becomes less meaningful when faced with the issues that continually overlap party boundaries.

When asked if there were any regrets or mistakes during his administration, President Eisenhower replied "Yes; and he's still on the Supreme Court" Obviously, the President expected his appointee to have the same political philosophy on the bench as existed in the White House. Chief Justice Warren surprised both parties, as well as the criminal defendant population for whom he became the greatest advocate. To those that would consider his decisions as at least political treason, it should be remembered that the appointment for life of our Supreme Court Justices was created precisely to remove the reach of politics from their decisions. It is our own, uniquely American system.

Presumption of Innocence

A critical foundation of our criminal law, in fact our basic philosophy of human rights, is the presumption that all defendants are innocent, and remain so unless and until they are proven, beyond a reasonable doubt, to have committed the crime for which they have been charged.

In our system of jurisprudence, a defendant is presumed, as *a matter of law*, to be innocent of any crime until proven guilty by a judge or jury of his peers. The burden of proving him guilty always rests upon the prosecution, to prove the defendant guilty beyond a reasonable doubt (considerably a more difficult standard than that of a civil trial). The reason for the more difficult standard of proof is the potential loss to the defendant; fine, imprisonment or death are the much higher stakes of criminal law.

Instructions to the jury, on how the law requires them to come to their decision, are tendered to the Judge by both of the parties in a criminal case, the prosecution and the defense. The judge may select either of them, or craft one of his own, to instruct the jury how they must apply the law to the facts of the case. Each side, of course, stresses the manner which most favors their result.

A full century ago, a court had two instructions which were requested to be read to the jury before their deliberations. They are reproduced in part below, the court choosing to read the first of the instructions (Note: try to determine which is the instruction requested by the defense) and the appeal was based upon the argument that each did not, in fact, say the same thing.

Instructions to the Jurors

1) You may find the defendants guilty on all the counts of the indictment if you are satisfied that beyond a reasonable doubt the evidence justifies it . . . And if, after weighing all the proofs and looking only to the proofs, you impartially and honestly entertain the belief that

the defendants may be innocent of the offenses charged against them, they are entitled to the benefit of that doubt and you should acquit them.

2) The law presumes that persons charged with crime are innocent until they are proven by competent evidence to be guilty. To the benefit of this presumption the defendants are all entitled, and this presumption stands as their sufficient protection unless it has been removed by evidence proving their guilt beyong a reasonable doubt.

COFFIN v UNITED STATES
156 U.S. 432, 15 S.Ct. 394
Supreme Court of the United States (1895)

This presents the question whether the charge that there cannot be a conviction unless the proof shows guilt beyond a reasonable doubt, so entirely embodies the statement of presumption of innocence as to justify the court in refusing, when requested, to inform the jury concerning the latter . . . .

This confusion makes it necessary to consider the distinction between the presumption of innocence and reasonable doubt as if it were an original question. In order to determine whether the two are equivalent of each other, we must first ascertain, with accuracy, in what each consists. Now the presumption of innocence is a conclusion drawn by the law in favor of the citizen, by virtue whereof, when brought to trial on a criminal charge, he must be acquitted, unless he is proven to be found guilty. In other words, this presumption is an instrument of proof created by the law in favor of one accused, whereby his innocence is established until sufficient evidence is introduced to overcome the proof which the law has created . . . .

The fact that the presumption of innocence is recognized as a presumption of law and is characterized by the civilians as a *presumtio juris* demonstrates that it is evidence in favor of the accused. For in all systems of law legal presumptions are treated as evidence giving rise to resulting proof to the full extent of their legal efficacy.

Concluding then, that the presumption of innocence is evidence in favor of the accused introduced by the law in his behalf, let us consider what is "reasonable doubt." It is of necessity the condition of mind produced by the proof resulting from the evidence in the cause. It is the result of the proof, not the proof itself; whereas the presumption of innocence is one of the instruments of the proof, going to bring about the proof, from which reasonable doubt arises;

thus one is a cause, the other an effect. To say that the one is the equivalent of the other is to say that evidence can be excluded from the jury, and that such exclusion may be cured by instructing them correctly in regard to the method by which they are required to reach their conclusion upon the proof actually before them. In other words, that the exclusion of an important element of proof can be justified by correctly instructing as to the proof admitted. The evolution of the principle of the presumption of innocence and its resultant, the doctrine of reasonable doubt, makes more apparent the correctness of these views, and indicates the necessity of enforcing the one, in order that the other may continue to exist.

. . . (s)ince it is clear that the failure to instruct them in regard to it excluded from their minds a portion of the proof created by law, and which they were bound to consider. "The proofs and the proofs only" confined them to those matters which were admitted to their consideration by the court, and among these elements of proof the court expressly refused to include the presumption of innocence, to which the accused was entitled, and the benefit whereof both the court and the jury were bound to extend him . . .

Judgment reversed and case remanded with directions to grant a new trial.

Corpus Delicti: *The Criminal "Prima Facie" Case*

* *Mens Rea: The Guilty Mind*
* *Actus Reus: The Forbidden Act*

When we examined the area of tort law, we found that the prima facie case was established for negligence when the plaintiff established the duty owed him, breached by the defendant, with injuries to the plaintiff that were proximately caused by the defendant's negligence. All of the elements together were the Prima Facie case, which established the evidence of the tort.

In the area of criminal law, there are but two elements necessary to prove up the "prima facie" case: first, the presence of some *mental state*, such as knowledge or intent, set forth in the statute defining the crime; and second, the *act* or prohibited conduct also defined in the substantive law, i.e., the criminal statute. These two elements, which prove up the evidence of the crime, are called the *corpus delicti.*

A person commits arson, when, by means of fire or explosive, he *knowingly:* damages any real property, (. . .) of another without his consent.

The mental state is that of knowledge *(knowingly)* and the forbidden act the burning *(by means of fire . . . damages . . . property)*

This is the "prima facie" case of arson; the knowledge is enough, however, when of the probable effect that his actions will have. We are all presumed to have knowledge of, and therefore intend, the likely and probable results of our actions.

Other states have the words "with intent to . . .", or "with malice," which form the required *mens rea* for criminal liability. How much of the maliciousness must be proven was addressed by many jurisdictions, with results not unlike the decision of the Massachusetts Supreme Court in 1961.

The defendant, as proven by the evidence, was "drinking in the Moody Gardens on Moody Street, Lowell." About 8:00 pm he left, walked to the rear and up the steps of the back porch on the second floor, and then set fire to some papers there and left. The building was damaged, and when he was arrested and questioned as to "why he set the fire, . . . (he) said that he had *no reason for doing it . . .*"

The Massachusetts statute punished anyone who "willfully and *maliciously* . . ." burned or tried to burn property.

COMMONWEALTH V LOUIS L. LAMOTHE, Jr.
Supreme Judicial Court of Massachusetts (1961)
179 N.E.2d 245

SPALDING, Justice.

Both exceptions present the same question, namely, whether malice can be inferred from the willful attempt to burn the property.

The offense charged . . . reads, "Whoever willfully and maliciously attempts to set fire to, or attempts to burn . . . any of the buildings, structure, or property . . . shall be punished," etc. The defendant concedes that the Commonwealth has proved all that is necessary to sustain a conviction except the element of malice. Proof of willfullness, he contends, is not enough; there must, he asserts, he proof also that the act was done out of motive of cruelty, hostility or revenge.

At common law the offense of arson consisted of the willful and malicious burning of the house of another. (4 Blackstone, Commentaries 21st Ed., p.220). But the meaning given to the word "malicious" when used in defining the crime of arson is quite different from its literal meaning. Sir Matthew Hale in his Pleas of the Crown (Vol. 1 at page 569) gives the following illustration, "But if A has a malicious intent to burn the house of B and in setting fire to it burns the house of B and C or the house of B escapes by some accident, and the fire takes in the house of C and burneth it, tho A did not intend to burn the house of C yet in law it shall be said the malicious and willful burning of the house of C, and he may be indicted for the malicious and willful burning of the house of C." (Citations omitted). The malice which a necessary element in the crime of arson need not be express, but may be implied; it need not take the form of malevolence of will, but it is sufficient if one deliberately and without justification or excuse sets out to burn the dwelling house of another."

Support for this view may be found in *Commonwealth v. Mehales*, 284 Mass. 412, at page 415, . . . where it was said, "The malice now essential under that statute is not necessarily against the owner of the building, but that malice which 'characterizes all acts done with an evil disposition, a wrong and unlawful motive or purpose; the willful doing of an injurious act without lawful excuse.'

This distinction has been well stated in *Commonwealth v. Goodwin*, 122 Mass. 19. There it was said at page 35, "The doing of an unlawful act without excuse is ordinarily sufficient to support the allegation that it was done maliciously and with criminal intent"

Judgment affirmed.

Corpus Delicti

It seemed, in the Lamothe case, the Massachusetts Court was creating a lesser corpus delicti for the crime of arson, or perhaps all crimes. If the court was saying that the state of mind could be deduced, inferred from the forbidden act without any other rational explanation for it, did they really reduce the elements of the crime to a single one?

When we analyze the statute that defines the crime of Arson, identify those specific words that set forth the act which is made unlawful and those which identify the state of mind necessary as part of the corpus delicti.

The corpus delicti in criminal law is what the prima facie case was in tort: the basic elements to prove up the matter, the fact of commission of a crime. It is the elements of the crime which must be proven up before any conviction is possible. Generally, that is the existence of a mental state, coupled with a specific act which has been made illegal by the statute.

For arson, the basic corpus delicti is:

1) Property damaged by fire/explosive, and
2) intentional burning.

The burning need not be complete, and jurisdictions vary in the extent of damage or charring required, but it *must* be intentional. The following is the current statute defining the crime of arson, with its particular state(s) of mind, and forbidden acts.

Arson 720 ILCS 5/20-1

Sec. 20-1 Arson.

A person commits arson when, by means of fire or explosive, he knowingly:

(a) Damages any real property, or any personal property having a value of $150 or more, of another without his consent; or

(b) With intent to defraud an insurer, damages any property or any personal property having a value of $150 or more.

Property "of another" means a building or other property, whether real or personal, in which a person other than the offender has an interest which the offender has no authority to defeat or impair, even though the offender may also have an interest in the building or property.

(c) Sentence.

Arson is a Class 2 felony.
(Source: P.A. 77-2638.)

Note that in Section 20-1 (a) several specific words are used to describe and define the particular act in question, yet only one is necessary for the state of mind. In Section 20-1 (b) we see that another kind of state of mind must be present for the commission of this type of arson.

Sec. 20-1.1. Aggravated Arson

(a) A person commits aggravated arson when in the course of committing arson he or she knowingly damages, partially or totally, any building or structure, including any adjacent building or structure, including all or any part of a school building, house trailer, water craft, motor vehicle, or railroad car, and (1) he knows or reasonably should know that one or more persons are present therein or (2) any person suffers great bodily harm, or permanent disability or disfigurement as a result of the fire or explosion or (3) a fireman, policeman, or correctional officer who is present at the scene acting in the line of duty is injured as a result of the fire or explosion. For purposes of this section, property "of another" means a building or other property, whether real or personal, in which a person other than the offender has an interest that the offender has no authority to defeat or impair, even though the offender may also have an interest in the building or property; and "school building" means any public or private preschool, elementary or secondary school, community college, college or university.

(b) Sentence. Aggravated arson is a Class X felony.

(Source: P.A. 93-335, eff. 7-24-03; 94-127, eff. 7-7-05; 94-393, eff. 8-1-05.)

Sec. 20-1.2. Residential Arson

(a) A person commits the offense of residential arson when, in the course of committing an arson, he or she knowingly damages, partially or totally, any building or structure that is the dwelling place of another.

(b) Sentence. Residential arson is a Class 1 felony.

(Source: P.A. 90-787, eff. 8-14-98.)

Sec. 20-1.3 Place of worship arson.

(a) A person commits the offense of place of worship arson when, in the course of committing an arson, he or she knowingly damages, partially or totally, any place of worship.

(b) Sentence. Place of worship arson is a Class 1 felony.

(Source: P.A. 93-169, eff. 7-10-03

Sec. 20-2 Possession of explosives or explosive or incendiary devices.

(a) A person commits the offense of possession of explosives or explosive or incendiary devices in violation of this Section when he or she possesses, manufactures or transports any explosive compound, timing or detonating device for use with any explosive compound or incendiary device and either intends to use such explosive or incendiary device to commit any offense or knows that another intends to use such explosive or device to commit a felony.

(b) Sentence.

Possession of explosives or explosive or incendiary device in violation of this section is a Class 1 felony for which a person, if sentenced to a term of imprisonment, shall be sentenced to not less than 4 years and not more than 30 years.

(c) (Blank).

(Source: P.A. 93-594, eff. 1-1-04; 94-556, eff. 9-11-05)

The Mental State

The issue of the mental state of the defendant in a criminal trial varies as to the time in question and the time of trial.

Often a court will determine at the outset of a trial whether or not an individual is *competent to stand trial*, which relates to his understanding of the proceedings and whether he can understand sufficiently to prepare, with his counsel, a proper defense.

The defense of insanity, like other affirmative defenses, must be pleaded by the defendant or his counsel, and generally states that the defendant lacked substantial capacity to either appreciate the criminality of his conduct or could not conform his conduct to the requirements of the law.

The above can be caused by a mental defect (physical) or a mental disease (functional mental disorder), but the existence of either is relevant only to the time of the crime.

Motive

Motive, or the reason for committing the act, is always relevant in any criminal action, no less the case in arson prosecutions. It should not be confused with intent, however, inasmuch they are critically distinct matters which address separate issues.

Intent is a critical part of the corpus delicti of arson, without which there is no crime; motive on the other hand, can be non existent, (as seen in the earlier *Lamothe* case) and is not necessary for a conviction for the crime of arson, or any other crime. It is however, relevant to the issue of whether someone may have committed a crime, inasmuch as its existence more logically leads, when coupled with other evidence showing the commission of the crime, to a conclusion that a defendant more likely committed a crime than not.

Without a showing of intent, however, no weight of the evidence of motive can ever suffice to substitute as part of the corpus delicti.

Legal Presumptions: Age and State of Mind

Several states have codified legal presumptions which may or may not be rebutted at trial, depending upon the age of the defendant at the time of the commission of the crime. Generally, there is a presumption that anyone under the age of seven cannot form the required legal intent for the commission of any crime, and this may not be rebutted at trial. It operates as a complete defense to criminal liability.

Between seven and fourteen, there is still a presumption that there is not any intent, but this may be rebutted at trial by competent evidence of the defendant's mental ability; from fourteen to twenty-one, the presumption is that the defendant in fact had the requisite intent, and only only satisfactory showing that he could not have formed such intent, will the presumption be overcome. The above are *general* principles with regard to age and within each jurisdiction, the actual law should be examined as controlling; e.g., in Illinois, no one can be convicted of a crime for an act which they committed prior to their thirteenth birthday.

Affirmative Defenses: Lack of Intent

1. Insanity

While most common as a defense to murder, insanity is a defense to any crime in that it destroys the evidence of intent. There are several variations on this theme, and differing results that obtain if it is successful. No version will be successful in either Montana or Idaho, however, based upon the statutory elimination of the defense of insanity. Four basic versions of the defense are as follow:

1) The Durham Test: a person's acts were
   the product of a mental disease or defect
2) The M'Naghten Test: a person
   did not know that what he did was wrong;
   did not understand the nature or quality of his acts

3) The Irresistible Impulse Test: a person
   could not control his conduct even if he knew that it was wrong
4) The Model Penal Code Test: the person
   lacked substantial capacity to appreciate the criminality of his conduct
   or conform his conduct to the law

The current Illinois statute on the matter defines four states of mind, one of which must be asserted in the criminal complaint, as the following:

1) **Knowledge**
2) **Intent**
3) **Recklessness**
4) **Negligence**

Entrapment

The defense of entrapment is an affirmative defense also, meaning it must be pleaded by the defendant; the court will not provide it for him. The reason it goes toward intent is that its basis is that the defendant never had the intent in the first place but was lured into committing the crime by the actions of police. The policy behind the defense is that police should be enforcing the law and preventing crime, not "creating" it.

It is not a defense, however, where the police have only provided the opportunity for the party charged to have committed the crime, where the disposition toward the offense already existed. Thus the businessman cruising Sunset Boulevard who makes a "date" with the sauntering female who is also a vice detective has no defense of entrapment; nor the drug dealer who makes his buy from the narcotics officer.

A person in public office, is approached by an old friend, perhaps a former lover, who invites him to her hotel room. There, to renew the relationship, or for old times sake, she suggests that they do some drugs. At first he refuses, but later inhales some drugs from a small pipe which she supplied. Moments later, the police force entry and place him under arrest. The police had only provided the wrongdoer with an opportunity to commit the crime and there was no entrapment, the court had ruled, with what seemed as a stretch of the logic in lieu of the rationale for the defense.

Intoxication

Unless the intoxication was involuntary, the fact that one was under the influence of drugs or alcohol will not affect his responsibility for the commission of a crime. There are great variations in the statutes of individual states, from qualified defense to the charges, to none at all.

Compulsion

A person is not guilty of an offense he is forced to commit under the threat of serious harm. This defense is not allowed for capital offenses, such as murder, rape, et al., and may also be allowed to be interposed when the harm is threatened to a loved one.

Self Defense

Self-defense is most often utilized in cases of aggression, i.e., assault, battery, rape, attempted murder and if proven, would allow an acquittal for the would be victim of the original attack. The extent to which the repulsing of the initial attack may cause great bodily harm or death is limited to certain circumstances by nature of the original felony, defense of person versus defense of property, etc., but each will negate criminal liability if appropriate to the circumstances. It is not so much a defense going to lack of intent as it is a justification for what otherwise would be a crime.

Inchoate Offenses

Incomplete Act and the Completed Crime

Where the intended act is not completed, there is often another completed act or acts which constitute a separate crime, called inchoate (incomplete) offenses.

When a party asks or requests assistance of another in the commission of a crime, he has committed the crime of *solicitation*.

When the other person or persons agree to assist or commit the criminal act, there is a *conspiracy*, and each of them has committed that offense as a co-conspirator.

When anyone tries, but fails through no fault of his own to complete the act which is the offense, he has committed the crime of *attempt.* Attempt occurs when someone goes beyond just contemplating a criminal offense, and takes steps in furtherance of the crime intended. The degree of steps taken in furtherance may vary in different jurisdictions, of course, and the evidence is often in the form of testimony from one who participated to some extent in the criminal act. His testimony usually buys him immunity from prosecution for that offense.

*   *   *

W.A. Maner owned the Durham Medical Institute in Atlanta, and when he was apprehended and charged (with attempt to commit arson) he had strewn excelsior (light shavings of wood that served as packing for fragile goods prior to the invention of styrofoam; it most resembled wooden spaghetti) over boxes and on barrels in his office, then soaked them with alcohol and gasoline. He also put "croker" sacks (burlap bags) under his roll top desk and doused them with alcohol and gasoline.

He did not try to deny the acts at trial, but argued that he had committed no crime, at that point, but that he was merely preparing to do so, and should be found not guilty.

MANER v STATE
Court of Appeals of Georgia (1931)
159 S.E. 902

LUKE, J.

We recognize, of course, that one may intend to commit a crime and do certain acts towards its consummation, and repent of his intention and refrain from his original purpose before the commission of the act; and that "mere prepatory acts for the commission of a crime, and not proximately leading to its consummation, do not constitute an attempt to commit the crime." *Groves v. State*, 116 Ga. 516, 42 S.E. 755, 59 L.R.A. 598. The question for determination is: Does the indictment allege such prepatory acts as "proximately lead to the consummation of the crime?' We think it does. How much further could the defendant have gone and still be guilty only of attempt? If he had actually set fire to the building, he would be guilty of the crime of arson, rather than an attempt to commit this crime, because the laws of 1924 (Ga. Laws 1924, p.193, § 2) provide that one is guilty of the offense who willfully or maliciously or with intent to defraud "sets fire to or burns or causes to be burned, or who aids, counsels or procures the burning" of the buildings named in this section. Any one of these acts would constitute the crime of arson. Since setting fire to the building would constitute the crime of arson, and the law makes it an offense to attempt to commit this crime, at what stage of the defendant's acts would he be guilty of the latter offense? Where is the dividing line between preparation and attempt? Mr. Clark in his work on Criminal Law (2d Ed.) p. 126, says "An attempt to commit a crime is an act done with intent to commit that crime, and tending to, but falling short of, its commission," and that two of the essential elements of the offense are: "(a) The act must be such as would be proximately connected with the completed crime, and (b) There must be an apparent possibility to commit the crime in the manner proposed." And on page 127 he says: "To constitute an attempt there must be an act done in pursuance of the intent, and more or less directly tending to the commission of the crime. In general, the act must be inexplicable as a lawful act, and must be more than mere preparation. Yet *it cannot be accurately said that no preparations can amount to an attempt.* It is a question of degree and depends upon the circumstances of each case." Bishop says that, "An attempt is an intent to do a particular criminal thing, with an act towards it falling short of the thing intended." See 1 Bish. New Crim. L. § 728. A reasonable construction of the acts alleged in the indictment force one to the conclusion that such acts were committed for no other reason than to set fire to the building, and thereby commit arson. Whether the defendant repented before the consummation of the crime intended would be a question of fact for the jury after the trial had reached that stage of the proceedings.

Strewing excelsior along and upon barrels and boxes, pouring alcohol and gasoline over and upon the same, putting croker sacks under a roller-top desk and saturating them with alcohol and gasoline, are overt acts, "inexplicable as lawful acts," "tending to the commission of the crime" of arson. The indictment sufficiently alleged an attempt to commit such crime, and the court did not err in overruling the general demurrer thereto.

Judgment affirmed.

The following case might have been the inspiration for one of the poems of Robert Service: In the back room of a saloon in Athena, Oregon, on July 30, 1904, Taylor was commiserating with McGrath regarding the testimony of one John Bannister, which did not serve Taylor too well in his divorce proceedings. Taylor asked McGrath if he would help him get even by burning neighbor Bannister's barn and wheat crop inside. McGrath in turn asked Palmer to help, who in turn told his boss, Bannister's friend.

Back in the back room again, Taylor gave them some training in how to set a slow burning fire with overalls, and agreed to pay them $100.00 for the work. When the three met at Taylor's house at midnight, he gave them a pair of overalls, reminded them how to start the fire, paid McGrath the $100, and provided a horse for McGrath. "Good luck go with you," he stated as they rode off toward Bannister's barn.

Taylor's agents noticed fresh tracks en route to Bannister's and when McGrath caught sight of some buggies behind the barn, he became frightened and rode off. He was, with Palmer, a witness for the prosecution in the trial of Taylor for attempt arson.

STATE v TAYLOR
Supreme Court of Oregon (1906)
84 P. 82

BEAN, C.J.

The question as to what constitutes an attempt to commit a crime is often intricate and difficult to determine, and no general rule has or can be laid down which can be applied as a test in all cases. Each case must be determined on its own facts, in light of certain principles which appear to be well settled. An attempt is defined as an "intent to do a particular criminal thing, with an act toward it falling short of the thing intended," 1 Bishop, New Crim. Law § 728. Or, according to Wharton, "An attempt is an intended apparent unfinished crime." 1 Wharton, Criminal Law (9th Ed.) § 173. Another author says: "An attempt to commit a crime is an act done in part execution of a criminal design, amounting to more than mere preparation, but falling short of actual consummation, and possessing, except for failure to consummate, all the elements of the substantive crime." 3 Am. & Eng. Law (3rd Ed.) 250. An indictable attempt, therefore, consists of two important elements: First, an intent to commit the crime; and, second, a direct, ineffectual act done toward its commission. To constitute an attempt, there must be something more than a mere intent to commit the offense, and preparation for its commission is not sufficient. Some overt act must be done toward its commission, but which falls short of the completed crime. It need not be the last proximate act before the commission of the offense, but it must be some act directed toward the commission of the offense after the preparations are made. It is often difficult to determine the difference between preparation for the commission of a crime and an act toward its commission. There is a class of acts which may be done in pursuance of an intention to commit a crime, but not, in legal sense, a part of it, and do not constitute an indictable offense; such as the purchase of a gun with the design of committing murder, or the procuring of poison with the same intent. These and like acts are considered in the nature of mere preliminary preparation, and not as acts toward the consummation of the crime. It is upon this principle that most of the cases cited by the defendant rest although some of them seemed to have carried the doctrine to the utmost limit. (Cit.Om.)

In the case at bar, we have something more than mere intention or preparation, so far as the defendant is concerned. His part in the transaction was fully consummated when he employed McGrath and Palmer to commit the offense, gave them materials with which to do it, showed them how to start a slow burning fire, paid them compensation for their services, furnished a horse for one of them to ride, and started them on their way. He had thus done all that he was expected to do, and his felonious design and action was then just as complete as the crime had been consummated, and the punishment of such an offender is just as essential to the safety of society. The failure to commit the crime was not due to any act of his, but to the insufficiency of the agencies employed for carrying out his criminal design.

In *People v. Bush*, 4 Hill, 133, . . . Mr. Justice Cowen (said): . . . "A mere solicitation to commit a felony is an offense, whether it be actually committed or not. This was held in the *King v. Higgins*, 2 East, 5. In the case before us there was more. The solicitation was followed by furnishing the instrument of mischief . . . .

The same principle was again applied in *Mcdermott v. People*, 5 Parker Cr. R. 102 . . . . The court court held the defendant properly convicted of an attempt to commit arson, saying: "The two important and essential facts to be established to convict a person of an offense are, first, an intent to commit the offense; and second, some overt act consequent upon that intent towards its commission. So long as the act rests in bare intention, it is not punishable. *'Cogitationis poenam nemo patitur.'* It is only when the thought manifests itself by an outward act in or toward the commission of an offense that the law intervenes to punish. As we cannot look into the mind and see the intent, it must, of necessity, be inferred from the nature of the act done, and, if that be unlawful, a wicked intent will be presumed. These are fundamental legal principles. Now applied to the facts of this case, what do we find? We find that the defendant intended to commit the crime of arson. Indeed, he had committed the offense 'already in his heart.' What were the overt acts toward the commission? He had prepared camphene and other combustibles, and had them in his room, and then he went a step further and solicited McDonnell to use those combustibles to burn the building, promising him, if he would do so, to 'give him the deeds of the place, and assign to him his right in the same.' We have, then, the fixed design of the defendant to burn this barn, and overt acts toward the commission of the offense, and a failure in the perpetration of it. The offense, then, is fully made out . . ."

Missouri has a similar statute. In *State v. Hayes*, 78 Mo. 307, the defendant solicited one McMahan to set fire to a building, furnished him a can of oil for the purpose, and gave him instructions for the burning. The court held that he was properly convicted of the offense of an attempt, although McMahan was acting under the advice of the police, and did not himself intend to commit the arson. The court said: "The evil intent which imparts to the act its criminality must exist in the mind of the procurer. And how the fact that the party solicited does not acquiesce or share in the wicked intent, exonerates the solicitor, baffles reason."

. . . In *Commonwealth v. Peaslee*, 177 Mass. 267, 59 N.E. 55, the evidence was that the defendant had arranged combustibles in a building in such a way that they were ready to be lighted, and, if lighted, would have set fire to the building and contents. The plan, however, required a candle which was standing on a shelf about six feet away from the combustibles to be placed on a piece of wood standing in a pan of turpentine and lighted. The defendant offered to pay a young man in his employment if he would go to the building, seemingly some miles from the place of the dialogue, and carry out the plan. This was refused. Later the defendant and the young man drove toward the building, but, when within about a quarter of a mile of the place, defendant said he had changed his mind and drove away. This was the only act he ever did toward accomplishing what he had in contemplation, and yet the court held that it was sufficient to convict him of an attempt to burn the building and its contents with intent to injure insurers of the same.

We conclude, therefore, that the conviction of the defendant was right, and the judgment will be affirmed.

For the crime of arson, the mental state is that of knowledge, or intent, a purposeful act as contrasted with a negligent one; the act is the deliberate burning, the illegal destruction of property by the agent of fire. Absent either of these two basic elements and there is no corpus delicti, no crime of arson has been committed. While the mental state required can be proven, or inferred from the act itself, the same does not hold true for the fire; in fact there exists a presumption in direct opposition to the second element of the corpus delicti of arson, the statements of some arson investigators notwithstanding.

HAWAII v DUDOIT
Supreme Court of Hawaii (1973)
514 P.2d 373

RICHARDSON, Chief Justice.

The facts of this case are simple, if not sparse. Defendant Dudoit was seen leaving a rooming house lavatory. At the same time Dudoit was observed leaving, a small fire was discovered in that lavatory. Some testimony was presented as to Dudoit's actions and reactions regarding the fire. There was also testimony as to the presence of newspapers, cardboard, and pieces of rug inside the washroom in question. There was expert testimony that the fire was not electrical in origin. No evidence was introduced as to the origin of this fire other than the physical presence of newspapers, cardboard and pieces of rug . . . .

In order to convict the defendant Dudoit of the crime of arson, an essential element that the state of Hawaii had the burden of proving beyond a reasonable doubt was that the fire was kindled by other than natural or accidental means. The only proof submitted by the state to meet that burden was evidence of the presence of debris in the washroom. The presence of these newspapers, pieces of rug, and a cardboard box are all that the state relies on to raise the inference of a criminal agency in kindling the fire.

The state's main witness testifies that he was employed for the purpose of cleaning such debris out of the washroom. It further appears from the testimony that it was not unusual for the items in question to be in the washroom. State witness Kahalekomo testified that he sometimes saw newspapers in the washroom. We find the presence of this debris equivocal proof at best . . . .

The presence of material which has incendiary properties only incidental to their primary purpose is not substantial evidence. We could distinguish this case from *Republic of Hawaii v Tokuji*, 9 Haw. 548 (1894), where facts showed the fire to have started in three distinct places and where oily wicking and matches were found nearby. In the case at hand, only the presence of debris is shown, a presence that is susceptible to more than one interpretation.

The state did not establish nor attempt to show that the materials' presence were somehow related to the fire's origin. The state has resources not available to defendants especially indigent defendants. City fire inspectors or other experts could have been used to tie the debris to the cause of the fire. The burden is on the state to overcome the presumption that the fire has natural or accidental origins. (Cit.Om.) We feel that the equivocal presence presented did not overcome this presumption nor was it substantial evidence of a criminal agency . . . .

We reverse for failure of the *corpus delicti* . . . .

Marumoto, Justice, with whom Justice Abe, joins.

I dissent. This court reverses the defendant's conviction in this case on the ground that the state had the burden of proving beyond a reasonable doubt that the fire was kindled by other than natural or accidental means, and that "(t)he only proof submitted by the state to meet the burden, was evidence of the presence of debris in the washroom."

The record shows more than that. The fire took place in a small four feet by seven feet room in a tenement building containing toilet facilities.

The police officer, who investigated the fire, testified that the areas in the room where the electrical wiring ran were not burned at all. From that testimony, the trial court concluded that the fire was not caused by any short-circuiting in the electrical wiring system.

The testimony of the officer showed the following: five pieces of three inch wide boards were burned from floor to ceiling; the toilet seat was also burned; the top of the porcelain water tank was blackened; items which could have been used to start the fire were spread on the floor in front of the toilet. The trial court concluded from that testimony that the fire was of incendiary origin.

The caretaker of the building testified that he saw the fire in the room and the defendant walking out of the room, "just like nothing business, just keep on walking."

A tenant of the building testified to the same effect, his testimony being as follows:

"Q. Now, while you were putting out the fire, *pioing* the fire, did you see Duprie around?"
"A. Yeah; this man stop.
"Q. Was he helping you folks putting out the fire?
"A. No.

In finding the defendant guilty, the trial court stated: "Defendant, when seen, certainly didn't express any concern for the fire; expressing concern for the fire would be normal. Its grossly abnormal that he did not express any concern. I think it is also grossly inordinate that he would step into the bathroom when the bathroom is that small, when a fire that size is going on at that time that it is not necessary for him to step into the bathroom to see that fire."

Would your opinion change if Dudoit had been locked in the small public washroom? What if he had been an inmate in prison, locked in a single cell alone, and a fire started from combustibles in the corner of the cell? What more would you need to know before determining cause and origin? What more would you have to know before convicting? What doubts would you consider reasonable, and what would be beyond reasonable doubt?

Testimony may be in the form of direct evidence ("I saw John strike the victim with the club.") or, more likely, in the form of circumstantial evidence, from which an inference must drawn, such as the testimony in the Dudoit case ("Just like nothing, . . ."). A particular type of testimony comes from someone who should know as much about the intent and the commission of the crime as the perpetrator: another perpetrator: the co-conspirator. Often his testimony has been secured by police or with the prosecuting attorney's office who have agreed to intercede on his behalf at trial in exchange for his testimony against the principal defendant, sometimes granting immunity from prosecution in exchange for testimony.

The co-conspirator, it should be remembered, is someone who usually is a criminal himself (unless the agent of the police), and the defense has every right to attack his credibility. Whether someone who would have, or already has committed serious crimes in the past should have their word taken as truth, simply by swearing that they will tell the truth in open court, is always an issue for the judge or jury.

Beyond attacking their credibility on the general basis of their character, an aggressive defense counsel may raise the issue of the accomplice's motive to tell falsehoods against the defendant.

To bolster their witness's testimony, corroboration is necessary, in the form of some evidence to support the statements of the co-conspirator.

BORZA v MARYLAND
Court of Special Appeals of Maryland (1975)
335 A.2d 142

MOYLAN, Judge.

Late in the afternoon of Saturday, October 2, 1971, a fire occurred at the Castro Convertible furniture store at 315 North Howard Street in Baltimore. It was during business hours. The site of the fire was on the fifth floor, an area used for the storage of furniture. The business was one of three furniture stores in Maryland and New Jersey operated by the appellant, as franchisee of the Castro Convertible Company. The Hartford Mutual Insurance Company paid $13,917.52 for damages to the store and $24,655.57 for damages to the contents. An accountant testified that as of June, 1971, three months earlier, the store was operating at a net loss of $104,000.

Captain John Richter of the Baltimore City Fire Department's Fire Investigation Bureau arrived at the fire scene at 5:05 pm. He estimated that the fire had been burning about one hour when he arrived. The first alarm had been turned in at 4:36 pm by a parking lot attendant next door who saw smoke and flames coming from the building. Captain Richter could not fully ascertain the cause of the fire. He found a large pile of trash burning on the fifth floor. The fire had also spread to the sixth floor. He effectively eliminated electrical or heating fixtures as a cause of the fire. He could not eliminate spontaneous combustion, noting that the source of possible combustion would have been consumed in the fire. He surmised that the fire probably started from careless smoking. He did interview the employee who had worked on the fifth floor that day, however. That employee was not a smoker, and he had not been in the store after 12:30 that day.

The testimony of the assumed accomplice now comes into play; Joseph Credge.

Credge testified that the Baltimore store was losing money and that in April or May of 1971, he and the appellant began discussions of how to dispose of it. They finally determined to burn the Baltimore Store. It was agreed that one or the other of them would go to the fifth floor of the Baltimore store and set fire to the packing materials and rubbish which were usually piled there awaiting disposal. On two occasions, on two successive Saturdays in September, 1971, Credge traveled from Trenton to Baltimore to set the fire. On, both occasions, he abandoned the attempt because of fear. On the night of Friday, October 1, 1971, the appellant told Credge he was going to Baltimore the next day and would set the fire if the opportunity presented itself. As a signal to the appellant upon his return to Trenton that the mission had succeeded, Credge was to leave the lights on in the Trenton store if word came in that the Baltimore store had caught fire. Late on the afternoon of October 2, Credge, in Trenton, received a telephone call from the manager in the Baltimore store informing him that the store had caught fire.

The corroboration of Credge's testimony came largely from three employees of the Baltimore store. John Martin, the manager of appellant's Towson store, received a call from the appellant on the morning of October 2. The appellant informed Martin that he was taking a train in from Trenton and asked to be picked up at the Pennsylvania Station. Martin picked him up at the station between

3:30 and 4:00 pm. and drove him immediately to the Howard Street store. The appellant spent a few minutes on the first floor talking to various employees. A customer came in, and the appellant took him upstairs. The employees assumed that they were going to a second floor showroom. They were not certain whether the appellant returned to the first floor simultaneously with the customer. All that was certain was that the appellant was out of their sight on some upper floor. The appellant returned to the first floor about fifteen minutes after he had left it and within several minutes told Martin that he had to catch a train. They immediately departed. Martin dropped the appellant at the Pennsylvania Station "at most one hour after he had picked him up."

Martin was just three blocks away from the station when he heard on his car radio about the store fire on Howard Street. He returned there immediately. The appellant took the stand and acknowledged the account of his visit to Baltimore as given by the three employees.

Out of chance phrases in *McDowell v State*, 231 Md. 298, 189 A.2d 913, and *Bollinger v State*, 208 Md. 298, 117 A.2d 913, the dissent spins the theory that the *corpus delicti* of arson may never be established by evidence which goes to show criminal agency. Because an uncritical reading of the dicta in *Bollinger* might give rise to such a misperception in others, it may be well to try to lay the ghost to rest.

In *McDowell*, the critical question was whether the testimony of an accomplice had been adequately corroborated. The court held that it had, and the conviction for arson was affirmed.

McDowell is also instructive on the further point of what is independent evidence tending to corroborate the testimony of an accomplice. In *McDowell*, an apartment was burned. The defendant was a subtenant enjoying residential privileges through January 3, 1962, the day of the fire. His presence in the apartment house, like the presence of the present appellant in the Howard Street store, was, therefore, not remarkable. Notwithstanding the relative innocuousness of such presence, standing alone, that presence was nevertheless held to be independent evidence corroborating the accomplice's testimony.

The *McDowell* court also considered as independent, corroborative evidence, the inference of a motive arising out of the fact that the defendant was being ejected from the apartment. Further evidence of motive came from the mouth of the accomplice, but the inference was held to be corroborative. In the present case also, direct testimony as to motive came from the accomplice Credge. The fact of the insurance being carried on the appellant's business and the independently established fact that the business had been operating at a net loss of over $100,000.00 during the months immediately preceding the fire certainly give rise to an inference of motive as forcefully as did the ejectment by a landlord in *McDowell*. In referring to these two independent items of evidence, *McDowell* said, *passim*, at 231 Md. 212-214, 189 A.2d at 615:

> "Here the evidence of McDowell's presence, of his having to leave the apartment, and of his being the last person to have been in the immediate vicinity of the scene of the crime with both the opportunity and a possible motive to commit the offense serves as corroboration of the identification of the defendant with the commission of the crime, which is the other branch of the Polansky (*Polansky v State* 205 Md. 362, 109 A.2d 52) rule . . .
>
> In an arson case the presence of the defendant in the vicinity of the fire, whether before or after its occurrence, is always relevant. *Bollinger v State supra*, at 208 Md. 307, 117 A.2d at 917 . . . As to both presence and motive the defendant's testimony corroborates that of the accomplice. He was in the immediate vicinity of the fire, before it was set, and he was being put out of the apartment along with Aldrich.

It is easy to see where the dissent was logically ensnared, because the passage in Wharton, cited with apparent approval by *Bollinger*, is a model of poor exposition. It joins in a single sentence—"The *corpus delicti* cannot be established by proof of the burning alone, or by the naked confession of the accused."—two very disparate propositions, without so much as a break of paragraph or even a period to make them twain."

That freakish accident of murky exposition cannot give birth to the notion that the *corpus delicti* of an arson cannot be proved by *the combination of* proof of burning *and* the confession of the accused.

As to the first proposition, Wharton reiterates the universally accepted truth that the confession of a crime cannot, standing alone, warrant a conviction, absent some independent evidence of the *corpus delicti*. The thrust of the principle is to prevent mentally unstable persons from confessing to, and being convicted of, crimes that never occurred. * * *

Bollinger makes it very clear, in discussing specifically the proof of the *corpus delicti* itself, that a confession may well be one of the factors entering into that equation. It said at 208 Md. 305-306, 117 a.2d at 917:

> "It is also not necessary that the evidence independent of the confession be full and positive . . . In addition, the evidence necessary to corroborate a confession need not establish the *corpus delicti* beyond

a reasonable doubt. *It is sufficient if, when considered in connection with the confession, it satisfies the jury beyond a reasonable doubt that the crime was committed and that the defendant committed it.* As Judge Learned Hand said in *Daeche v United States*, 2 Cir., 250 F. 566, 571, circumstances corroborating a confession need not independently establish the truth of the *corpus delicti* at all, either beyond a reasonable doubt, or by a preponderance of proof, *but any such circumstances will serve which in the judge's opinion go to fortify the truth of the confession. (Cit. omitted.) (Emphasis added)*

"Of course, proof of the *corpus delicti* in an arson case is usually a difficult matter, as the burning is almost invariably done in a most secretive manner. The prosecution usually has to depend on circumstantial evidence.

As to the second very distinct proposition, *Wharton* is simply pointing out that one of the elements of the crime of arson, which needs be proved by the State, is the special *mens rea* that the burning be "wilful and malicious." Again, however, the ill-advised language of *Wharton* has led latter-day readers astray, particularly where *Wharton* said:

"Where nothing but the burning appears, the law presumes it to have been accidental, and not by criminal design; and the state must overcome this presumption of law, and prove a criminal design beyond a reasonable doubt."

This, of course, is not a presumption of law. It is simply a statement that the State has the burden of proving all elements of a crime. A presumption has the legal effect of shifting to an opponent the burden of going forward and producing evidence. 9 Wigmore on Evidence (3rd Ed. 1940) § 2490, "Presumptions." No burden, of course, shifted to the State in this instance, since the State had the burden from the very outset. This is one more instance of the word presumption having too many meanings. The presumption referred to here, like the so-called presumption of innocence, is neither a true presumption of law nor an inference of fact, but a statement as to burden of proof. The State has the burden of proving the special *mens rea* in an arson case beyond a reasonable doubt, just as it has the burden of proving every other element of this or any other offense. Indeed, later editions of Wharton have refrained from this loose use of the word "presumption." 2 Wharton's Criminal Law and Procedure (Anderson Ed., 1957) now describes, in dealing with arson, the mental state at §390:

"In the absence of contrary evidence, it is assumed that every burning is accidental or is due to natural causes, and not criminal design. The burden is, accordingly, on the prosecution to establish that it was wilful and malicious. Because of this, the *corpus delicti* is not established by the proof of burning alone, such fact does not prove the intent with which the act was done."

We note, moreover, that the words of the appellant at issue in this case were operative words of the then ongoing conspiracy spoken by the appellant to Credge and were not a confession within the contemplation of *Bollinger*.

Bollinger lends further support to our holding that there was in this case ample independent evidence to corroborate the testimony of an assumed accomplice. Their presence, like the presence of the appellant here at the North Howard Street store, was, therefore, unremarkable. Nonetheless, such presence near the scene of the crime was held to be independent evidence of guilt(.)

Curiously opposite also in the *Bollinger* case was that the court there found relevant to the establishment of the corpus delicti the facts that the barn owners had been present in their barn a little more than an hour before the fire occurred, that neither of the owners smoked, and that the barn had recently been wired by an electrician and the wiring was apparently all right.

Setting down the nubs of the instruction requested and the instructions given side by side, it is clear that the difference is only stylistic.

Instruction Requested	Instruction Given
"It is necessary that the burning be willful and malicious. In the absence of contrary evidence it is assumed that every burning is accidental or due to natural causes and not criminal design. The burden is, accordingly, on the prosecution to establish that it was willful and malicious."	"In that regard you are advised that to constitute the offense of arson, it is necessary that the burning be wilful and malicious. The burden is upon the State to establish beyond a reasonable doubt that it was willful and malicious."

Every essential point of law was properly covered . . .
Judgments affirmed; costs to be paid by appellant.

LOWE, Judge (dissenting).

I must respectfully depart from the majority because it is obvious to me that the State failed to meet its burden.

Borza was convicted *solely* on the testimony of his accomplice, Credge, who, after a homosexual affair with Borza had been rejected by him in preference for a more natural relationship with one of the opposite sex. The testimony was gratuitously volunteered after two years of silence following the fire. Suffice to say, Credge was not a reluctant witness. More than that, his testimony at most established only that he and appellant had discussed burning the store preceding April or May, that he, Credge, had twice traveled to Baltimore in September to burn the store, and that on the night before the fire, appellant had mentioned that he might set fire to the store. This factual posture presented at least four possibilities:

1) That Credge told the truth and that the appellant willfully and maliciously set fire to the store;
2) That Credge told the truth but that the fire was accidental and Credge wrongfully deduced appellant's guilt;
3) That Credge lied about the previous conversations;
4) That Credge himself set the fire, knowing that the appellant would be in the store that day.

Assuming Credge told the truth, his testimony did no more than establish that appellant was contemplating setting the fire, *not* that he set it. Had the State then proven that the fire was deliberately set-indicating a criminal act-the evidence may have been sufficient to convict. The State did just the opposite.

The only permissible evidence submitted by the State to meet its burden of overcoming the presumption of accident was that of Captain Richter of the Fire Investigation Bureau. From the majority's depiction of his testimony we are told:

"Captain Richter could not fully ascertain the cause of the fire . . .

He could not eliminate spontaneous combustion . . .

He surmised that the fire probably resulted from careless smoking . . ."
although the employee on the fifth floor had been a non-smoker.

The majority has transformed evidence of criminal agency, i.e., if there was a crime, appellant probably committed it, into evidence of agency and *corpus delicti*, i.e., the fire was deliberately set and appellant set it. That is a leap of faith wholly unwarranted by the evidence and diametrically opposed to the Court of Appeals clear and simple expression of the State's burden . . . .

The majority dismisses the requirement of independently proving the *actus rea* of arson simply because it is a crime requiring "a special *mens rea*," i.e., proof of willful and malicious intent. Because *mens rea* is also an element of criminal agency does not excuse the necessity of independently proving the act charged was a crime. "Where nothing but the burning appears, the law presumes it to have been accidental, and not by criminal design; and the State must overcome this presumption of law, and prove a criminal design beyond a reasonable doubt." *Bollinger*, 208 Md. at 304, 117 A.2d at 916. However you read that sentence, whether in or out of context, its clarity dispels the notion that it is a "freakish accident of murky exposition." It is not conceivable that the Court of Appeals meant that an accusation that a defendant discussed committing a crime, is sufficient to prove that a crime was committed. In laying their "ghost to rest" the majority may find themselves haunted by the apparition of a dormant *corpus delicti*.

Corroboration is the other fundamental legal protection that this case erodes.

The only corroborative evidence of Credge's testimony was the presence of the accused in his own store on the day of the fire.[1] Significantly, this evidence in no way detracts from either of the third or fourth exculpatory hypotheses suggested above . . . .

Appellant's presence in his own store, though perhaps relevant, surely cannot be regarded as insuring Credge's verity by supporting "some of the material points" of his testimony. Presence of an accused may be adequate corroboration when it is "under unusual or suspicious circumstances." Wharton, Criminal Evidence (Torcia Ed., 1973) §649 at 368. But the presence of a furniture store owner at his own store can hardly be regarded as unusual or suspicious. In that situation, mere presence is not sufficient corroboration . . . .

The potentially vengeful motivations of appellant's lone accuser and the unexplained delay of two and one half years before he made the accusation create a most tenuous setting in which to undermine the safeguards provided by the requisites of proof of *corpus delicti* and corroboration. Strain we have and strain we should to meet a technical mischance in a case where guilt and culpability of the accused is otherwise readily apparent. But what meaning can we give to the platitudes upon which our system of justice is said to rely if we need strain so hard here, even to ascertain if a crime was committed. To permit a rejected homosexual

---

[1]   Although prior to the fire Credge contacted an FBI agent and told him about his and appellant's fire discussions, it would be the ultimate in tautological thinking to treat such self-serving groundwork-whether or not termed "operative verbal acts"—as corroboration.

paramour to supply that plus every other element necessary for conviction, is to allow the accuser to make a mockery of our time honored safeguards. In trying to stabilize the tenuous structure upon which this case is built, the majority has exacted another chip from the foundation structure of the system.

Evidence

Relevance

Facts and testimony which will go directly to convincing the trier of fact (judge or jury) that something was more likely true or untrue, are relevant to the issue and are admitted into evidence. As an example, in determining whether or not a person saw a defendant at the scene of a crime, evidence of his vision is relevant to both the witnesses' creditability as well as to the capacity of the defendant to commit the crime. Evidence of the witnesses' hearing ability is not relevant. The key issue in relevant evidence is logic.

Materiality

For evidence to be material it must be probative, relate to some issue that is before the court. Evidence that the defendant in an arson trial had the property insured against fire is material to the issue whether he had the intent to defraud an insurer; coverage for flooding is not material to the issue (or relevant). Note that it does not prove, by itself, that the defendant committed arson, or even that he had such intent; it is merely admissible evidence to prove that it is more likely than not that he did have such an intent. Key in determining materiality is whether it is important to the issue.

Competence

The evidence which is offered must be from a source that is reliable, and is qualified to offer such evidence. The opinion of an expert would be competent to offer as to the origin of a fire, but not the average citizen, or even firefighter.

Direct

Real
Evidence which does not require any inference on the part of the trier of fact; a bullet identified as the one taken from the victim; a policy of insurance

as proof that person had insurance coverage; a sum of money as an evidence exhibit in a trial for bribery

Testimony

Given the same issues as above, real evidence in the form of testimony would be the testimony of the medical examiner who removed the bullet; the testimony of the agent who wrote the insurance policy; and the testimony of the undercover police officer who paid the congressman, representative, alderman or trustee.

Circumstantial

In our same factual situations, where the medical examiner testifies that he removed the bullet from the back of the victim's skull, it is circumstantial evidence ruling out suicide, i.e., the jury must infer that is unlikely that someone would commit suicide in such a way; our insurance agent testifies that the defendant increased his fire coverage 90 fold and reduced all other coverages the month before the fire; this is circumstantial evidence of intent to defraud an insurer; and finally, the tactical officer testifies that in response to his question of the defendant, the reply was "You get me the cash, at least 50 big ones, and I'll take care of the assault weapons provision; get me 2 million and I'll get the whole crime bill scuttled; ask anyone who's done business here, I've been in this business since Watergate." (Admittedly, it is difficult to distinguish the about exchange from those of a lobbyist and his targeted elected official.)

Testimony and cross examination

When we read our history concerning the infamous Star Chambers, and how evidence was "secured" from the defendant and from those who testified against him, we have little problem understanding the concern of the drafters of the Constitution and the Bill of Rights for fair procedures in open court which allowed for the questioning of the witness by both the prosecution and the defense.

This of course cannot exist where the party making a statement is not even in the courtroom for the defense counsel to examine. Thus the courts fashioned rules of procedure by their decisions which would not admit any testimony from someone whom the defendant could not cross examine. Such statements were called hearsay, and ruled inadmissible, save for some limited exceptions to the otherwise powerful protection against false testimony.

Hearsay

An out of court statement, offered to prove the truth of what is being asserted, whose value rests upon the creditability of the out of court asserter

Exceptions to Hearsay

Spontaneous Declarations

A person often exclaims things immediately following either powerfully significant events or traumatic ones, which do not allow time for reflection prior to speaking out. Thus, they are more likely than not to have a high degree of trustworthiness

Dying Declarations

The basis for the exception for dying declarations is that someone who is, or feels they are, in imminent danger of death, is unlikely to have a motive for not telling the truth, and as such, his last statements are afforded great consideration notwithstanding the fact that he *will not* be available for cross examination.

Prior Statements

Statements made prior to current testimony are often allowed to be used, not for the purpose of proving the truth or falsity of the statements, but for purposes of impeaching the creditability of the defendant or witness.

The statements may be consistent or inconsistent, since they are not offered for their truth.

Prior Testimony

Again, if the previous testimony was in court, then there should be a presumption that it was truthful, since it was made under oath. If the statements made in the current case contradict previous testimony, the likely question from the cross examiner is: "Tell us, Mr. Sampson, were you lying then, or are you lying now?"

Statements to Treating Physicians (Paramedics)

Generally, it can be taken as true that we do not lie to the people who will make us well, treat our injuries or save our lives. Thus, statements made to those persons have a high degree of reliability and are accordingly accepted into evidence.

Statements concerning State of Mind

Statements made prior to the commission of a crime, while they may not be used to prove the principal matter may be used to demonstrate the defendant's state of mind, relevant to another issue, such as an insanity defense.

Admissions against interest

Since the privilege against self-incrimination under the Fifth Amendment operates to shield someone from saying anything that could be used as a basis to prosecute them, an admission which also implicates them as perpetrators is likely to have a good deal of reliability, i.e., why would anyone also subject themselves to liability.

Co Conspirator Statement

Of course, there may be many reasons, especially when the party is dealing with the prosecutor, to win favorable terms for himself by cooperation with the state. While their creditability is rigorously attacked by defense counsel, the admissibility of their testimony is regularly granted.

As evidenced in the *Borza* case, there must be some form of corroboration of testimony of the accomplice or co-conspirator to prove up the case in chief, but its admissibility is permitted under the exception of a statement against interest.

The above and foregoing is but a brief survey of the kinds of evidence that are used as proof in criminal cases, and is not meant to be a definitive exposition of hearsay, let alone the laws of evidence. For Fire Service members, there is a single crime in which we are inextricably involved; initially, we are involved with mitigation of the effects of the crime, thereafter in its discovery, and finally in its prosecution and thereby, its ultimate prevention. The restrictions upon us, and the law enforcement officers and prosecuting attorneys with whom we form an interrelated unit, must be understood so that we provide the most clear, compelling and professional evidence available in securing conviction.

Search & Seizure: The Reach of the Fourth Amendment
Amendment Four.

> *The right of the people to be secure in their persons, houses, papers and effects against unreasonable searches and seizures, shall not be violated,*

upon liberty was and has been continually fought. The early decision of Lord Camden in *Entick v Carrington*, (1765), 19 Howell's State Trials 1029, held these general writs to be invalid and laid the basis of the Fourth Amendment. Thus the doctrine "Every man's home is his castle" was founded. (Footnote omitted)

The problem that we must resolve is that of harmonizing the constitutional right against unreasonable search and seizure with the rights of the people collectively to life, liberty, *safety*, and the pursuit of happiness as guaranteed by our state and federal constitutions . . . .

What legislation may be passed for the safety of its people without violating other sections of the Constitution? Admittedly the safety of the people is the first law of the land and will prevail as against private rights provided by the Constitution. (Citations omitted). But, to be justified, such encroachment upon private rights must be reasonable and necessary.

Relevant parts of such legislative enactments deemed to have important bearing on this case are as follows:

§20-802, Burns' 1950 Repl.:
"It shall be the duty of the state fire marshal to enforce all laws of the state and ordinances of the several cities and towns in Indiana, providing for any of the following:

"4. The investigation, prosecution and suppression of the crime of arson and other crimes connected with the destruction or attempted destruction of property by fire or explosion, and the crime of swindling or defrauding an underwriter or attempting to do so; and for the investigation of the cause, origin and circumstances of fires.

"It shall be the further duty of the state fire marshal to make, . . . inspections of property and place orders thereon, when needed, for the prevention of fires and fire losses, and to enforce and to carry out such orders, . . ."

§20-807:
"The state fire marshal, his deputies or assistants, on the complaint of any person or whenever he or they shall deem it necessary, shall inspect all buildings, premises, property, conditions, and things comprehended in this act within their jurisdiction."

§20-808:
"The state fire marshal or his deputies may, in addition to the investigation made by any of his assistants, at any time investigate as to the origin or circumstances of any fire occurring in this state . . .

"The state fire marshal or his deputies or any of his assistants may at all reasonable hours enter any building, property or premises within his jurisdiction for the purpose of making an inspection or investigation which, under the provisions of this act, or any law which may have been or may be from time to time enacted requiring the fire marshal to enforce or carry out, he or they may deem necessary to be made."

It is urged by the state that investigations as to the cause of fires, authorized by the law, are necessary to the public safety as a means of fire prevention. Furthermore, the state argues that the circumstances surrounding such a situation make it necessary that such investigations be initiated without a search warrant because, the cause of the fire being unknown, there is no probable cause upon which a search warrant could issue.

Finally the state contends that, it being necessary to initiate such investigations without a search warrant, evidence so obtained as to the cause of such fire, whether it was of accidental or incendiary origin, should be admissable in evidence by the state in any action wherein the cause of such fire is an issue.

The state contends to hold otherwise would, for all practical purposes, be to deny the state the right to prosecute persons for arson in every instance where, at the outset, the cause of a fire is unknown. Upon this issue the state's contention is not well taken. Under the facts before us, it cannot well be maintained that the search made was a mere civil inspection and, even if it began as such as the state contends it may have, no good reason is shown why a search warrant was not obtained at a point in time when the evidence believed to be incriminating was discovered. From the point in time when the investigation was conducted for the purpose of obtaining incriminating evidence against the owner of property, a search warrant was necessary. In support of its position to the contrary the state has cited numerous cases in which the right of inspection has been upheld without the necessity of a search warrant. However it must be noted that in each instance referred to the inspection or investigation was civil and not criminal in nature. It was permitted as relating to the regulation of the use or occupancy of the property itself. In no instance was the information obtained used in a criminal prosecution against the proprietor of the property.

Having held that a search warrant is required by the fire marshal and his deputies in criminal investigations, regarding the cause of fires, not made at the time of the fire we are now required to consider whether or not the Fire Marshal Law is unconstitutional, because of the duty and authority it vests in the fire marshal and his deputies without reference to a search warrant. If the law is construed to provide that criminal investigations may be made without a search warrant, the law is unconstitutional, for the reasons above stated. If, however, the law can be construed to have adopted and incorporated by implication the constitutional requirement that the fire marshal and his deputies obtain a search warrant before making an investigation intended to lead to a criminal prosecution, it is constitutional. In deciding this question we are committed to holding the statute constitutional, if we can . . .

Upon examination of the Fire Marshal Law we note that it makes no reference to the use or non use of search warrants in connection with the inspections and investigations authorized by the fire marshal and his deputies. Therefore, we cannot say that it clearly purports to grant authority to make criminal investigations without resort to this constitutional limitation upon the police power of the state. On the other hand, the law does expressly describe the police power of the fire marshal and his deputies ". . . in all cases . . . of arson . . ." as that "possessed by a constable, sheriff or police officer of the state." §20-802 *supra*. The above named officers have no authority of search and seizure preliminary to a criminal prosecution, without a search warrant.

We therefore hold that under the Fire Marshal Law the fire marshal and his deputies and his agents must obtain a search warrant prior to searching a person's dwelling, effects or possessions for the purpose of obtaining evidence, to be used in a criminal prosecution and that this basic constitutional requirement can be and is by implication incorporated as a necessary part of the responsibility and activity incorporated by the law.

We conclude that the state's Exhibit No. 5 was properly excluded from the evidence.

Compare both the facts of the above case and the reasoning of the Indiana court with that of the Iowa court some years later:

The Cedar Rapids Fire Department responded to a fire in a printing plant, and extinguished the fire at approximately 0550 hours. The fire chief, with a team of investigators, began their investigation of the fire while the firemen were overhauling and picking up. They went in and out of the building several times, during the pre-dawn hours and thereafter, without any warrant and without objection by the owner.

The evidence recovered at the scene in the investigations was used to charge the owner with arson, and at trial, his attorney made a motion to suppress the evidence as having been recovered in violation of the Fourth Amendment, and the trial court granted the motion. The state appealed the trial court's ruling directly to the state's Supreme Court on the issue of the point of Constitutional law.

The Supreme Court of Iowa reversed the lower court, but by the narrowest of margins (5-4).

IOWA v REES
Supreme Court of Iowa (1966)
139 N.W.2d 406

SNELL, Justice . . .

. . .

On August 15, 1964, a fire was reported at 324 7th St., in Cedar Rapids. The fire department and extinguished the flames at 5:50 a.m. The building involved was being used as a printing plant operated by Citizen's Publications, Inc., lessee. One Joseph W. Grant, Jr., the defendant in the criminal action, had an interest in the business and occupied an apartment on the premises.

Immediately after the fire had been extinguished the fire chief and his employees, a city electrical inspector, a foreman of the light and power company, a deputy state fire marshal, an agent of the National Board of Fire Underwriters, and others entered the premises for the purpose of investigating the cause and origin of the fire. The investigation was prolonged and the building reentered several times as part of a continuing investigation. The defendant said no search warrant was ever requested or secured. However, there is no claim of harassment, abuse, subterfuge, force or even objection.

Based in part at least upon the evidence obtained by this extended investigation, the Linn County grand jury returned an indictment charging accused with the crime of arson. He was arraigned and entered a "not guilty" plea. Prior to trial he filed the subject motion to suppress testimony of grand jury witnesses, * * *. By his motion accused requested the court to suppress all evidence gained by these persons as a result of their investigation in connection with the fire.

* * * The statutory authority for investigation into the origin and cause of fires is found in chapter 100, Code of Iowa, 1962.

Section 100.1, subparagraph 2, requires an investigation by the state fire marshal.

Section 100.2 provides: "The chief of the department of every city or town in which a fire department is established . . . shall investigate into the cause, origin and circumstances of every fire occurring in such city . . . and determine whether such fire was the result of natural causes, negligence or design. The state fire marshal may assist . . . superintend and direct . . ."

Section 100.3 requires a report to the state fire marshal.

Section 100.9 provides that when the state fire marshal is of the opinion that there is evidence sufficient to charge any person with arson or related offenses he shall cause arrest and prosecution and shall furnish to the county attorney all evidence.

Section 100.10 authorizes the fire marshal and his subordinates to enter any building and examine the same and contents.

Section 100.12 authorizes entry and examination by the chief of the fire department.

Under these statutes the entry and examination by the officers was legal and mandatory.

What was done here is exactly what is required by the statutes, *i.e.*, investigation, determination of opinion as to cause of the fire, prosecution and furnishing of evidence. The trial court held that any evidence obtained after the date and time of the extinguishment of the fire would be inadmissible as having been the fruits of an unlawful search and seizure.

Here there was no unlawful search and seizure. What was done was pursuant to statute. We use the word unlawful as meaning without statutory support or in violation of statute. The question is was it unreasonable and violative of constitutional limitations.

Statutes and ordinances authorizing civil inspections have long been acknowledged and sanctioned as incident to the police power of a state or municipality but they must be within constitutional limits. (Cit.Om.)

In *Frank v. State of Maryland*, 359 U.S. 360, 79 S.Ct. 804, 3 L.Ed.2d 877, it was held that a health officer under authority of a civil ordinance could go on property at reasonable times without the aid of a search warrant for the limited purpose of an inspection to ascertain whether conditions are present which do not meet minimum standards and might be inimical to the health, welfare and safety of the public.

The case recognizes two basic constitutional protections.

"(1) the right to be secure from intrusion into personal privacy, the right to shut the door on officials of the state unless their entry is under proper authority of law. The second, and intimately related protection is self-protection: the right to resist unauthorized entry which has as its design the securing of information to fortify the coercive power of the state against the individual, information which may be used to effect a further deprivation of life or liberty or property. Thus, evidence of criminal action may not, save in very limited and closely confined situations, be seized without a judicially issued search warrant."

Mr. Justice Frankfurter traced the history of and necessity for certain inspections and held there was no violation of due process. * * *

The reasoning of the court was sound and appropriate to the case before us.

In the case at bar except for the fact that the evidence was obtained pursuant to a statutory mandate instead of a search warrant there is not a word in the record to support the order of suppression.

It is argued that when the investigation uncovered evidence of crime its investigatory status ended; that the statutory authority came to an end; that it became an accusatory search and could be supported only by a search warrant. We do not agree. The statutes clearly contemplate the discovery of evidence of crime, the arrest and prosecution of the person to be charged, and the delivery of all evidence, names of witnesses and all information to the county attorney. The statutory authority of the investigating officials did not terminate when evidence of arson was found. * * *

In the case at bar . . . (t)he original entry was lawful and mandatory under the statute. No one contends that the original entry was unreasonable. As we said . . . it did "not change character from its success." (Cit.Om.) The entry did not become unlawful or the search become unreasonable just because evidence of arson was found. There is nothing in the record before us, except the finding of evidence of arson, to support a holding that there was a change from a lawful to an unlawful procedure.

The fact that an investigation becomes accusatory does not make it unconstitutional. It does go beyond proper limits when it extends into fields unrelated to the authorized investigation or is unduly prolonged over the objection of the accused. Not even a search warrant is good indefinitely. See section 751.12, Code of Iowa. The question is not before us but it may be that the defendant could have, after a reasonable time for completion, terminated the investigation by telling the investigators to stay out. In that event further search and seizure would have required a search warrant. However, the record is silent as to any search beyond the limits of the statutory mandate or over any objection, timely or otherwise, by the defendant.

We find nothing in the Constitution of the United States, the pronouncements of the United States Supreme Court, the Constitution of the State of Iowa or our pronouncements requiring the suppression of the evidence obtained during the search involved. * * *

The trial court apparently proceeded from the premise that a reasonable search and seizure can only proceed from the foundation of a search warrant issued on an affidavit showing probable cause. We do not think that is what the Constitution says nor what the cases hold.

Mapp v. Ohio, 367 U.S. 643, 81 S.Ct. 1684, 6 L.Ed.2d 1081 holds that evidence obtained by unconstitutional search is inadmissible. The rights guaranteed by Amendment 4 are enforceable against the states by the Due Process Clause of Amendment 14. With these basic rights of the people no one has any legitimate quarrel. * * *

It is the indiscriminate search and seizure without benefit of a warrant issued on affidavit of probable cause that is proscribed. Nowhere do we find any proscription against the use of evidence obtained during a reasonable and legally authorized investigation. It is unreasonable and illogical to say that when officers are carrying on a legal or as in this case a mandatory investigation they must stop and get a search warrant before they can seize and later use the evidence for which they were making their original investigation.

The present case is a far cry factually from *Mapp*.

In *Mapp*, a reinforced group of seven or more officers, in search of a person wanted for questioning on an unrelated matter and for possible evidence of an unrelated offense, forcibly entered a house over the objection of defendant, pretended to have a warrant, manhandled the defendant and refused to permit defendant's lawyer to enter or see defendant. Proceeding "in this highhanded manner" the officers searched thoroughly and incident thereto found some obscene materials for possession of which defendant was ultimately convicted. * * *

What is proscribed by the Amendment is not the seizure of incriminating evidence but the unreasonable invasion of the right of privacy. If the search is unreasonable and without authority then in that event seizure of the evidence is without authority and the evidence inadmissible.

In the case at bar the officers had a right to investigate. There is nothing unreasonable about searching for the cause of a fire. When evidence is so found it is not necessary for officers to desist from further action and wait for a search warrant before they may pick up what they have found, or testify as to what they have seen, or complete their investigation.

The test is the reasonableness of the search under proper authority and not the source of the authority under which the search is made. A reasonable search mandatory under a legislative enactment is clothed with as much dignity and is entitled to as much consideration as a search under a warrant issued by a Justice of the Peace. It would be illogical to say that the evidence would have been admissible if seized under a search warrant but inadmissible if seized under the statute. This assumes, of course, that the entry was reasonable and legal and no one contends otherwise. Within the constitutional limitations as to reasonableness the legislature may and has authorized such an investigation as was made here. * * *

The foundation for a search after a fire is the statute. The legislature has said that when there has been a fire there shall be an investigation. There is nothing in the constitution that says the legislature may not, within the limits of reasonableness and by positive mandate, direct a search upon the happening of an event of such public interest as a fire. The fire is the reason and the statute is the authority for the procedure.

It is unrealistic and unsound to say that when a constitutionally reasonable investigation or search has been directed by the legislature upon the happening of a certain event, *i.e.*, a fire, there must also be a search warrant that can only be issued upon affidavit of probable cause.

It is not logical to say that a mandatory entry and examination of the cause of a fire is unreasonable. The fact that the statutory investigation may uncover evidence of a crime does not mean that further search becomes constitutionally unreasonable or that evidence obtained thereby is inadmissible.

It is unlikely that before beginning the statutory investigation there would be information as to "probable cause" sufficient to support a search warrant. The constitution does not say that there can be no investigation without "probable cause" as to a specific crime when "probable cause" can only be determined by investigation or that when probable cause develops the right to search ends. That would draw too fine a line between investigation and search.

In the case at bar the officers were acting under explicit statutory authority. We find nothing unreasonable or violative of constitutional rights in the statutory procedure. There is no claim of arbitrary force, subterfuge, coercion or objection.

The accused did not meet the burden of demonstrating that the evidence had been illegally procured.

There is no showing that the search was violative of any constitutional rights or that the evidence is inadmissible on the grounds urged.

The writ of *certiorari* is sustained, the order of the trial court suppressing the evidence is reversed and the case remanded to the trial court for entry of an order in harmony herewith.

Writ sustained and case remanded.

GARFIELD, C.J., and MOORE, STUART and MASON, JJ., concur.
RAWLINGS, LARSON, THORNTON, and BECKER, JJ., dissent.

Justice Rawlings set forth a lengthy dissent in this case in which he clearly felt that the investigation was, even if not at the outset criminal in nature, it quickly became just that during the reentries to the premises with his subordinates. He stated that the investigator who had the authority of the statute could only rely on his five senses under that authority to provide the probable cause to secure a warrant to seize further evidence of the commission of arson.

Citing another Supreme Court decision (*Johnson v. United States*, 333 U.S. 10,13, 68 S.Ct. 367,369, 92 L.Ed. 436), he argued:

"The point of the Fourth Amendment, which is often not grasped by zealous officers, is not that it denies law enforcement the support of the usual inferences which reasonable men draw from evidence. Its protection consists in requiring that those inferences be drawn by a neutral and detached magistrate instead of being judged by the officer engaged in the often competitive enterprise of ferreting out crime."

The difficult question to be answered then, is when does the fire investigator change from one whose duty it is to determine the origin and cause of a fire, into the agent of law enforcement, collecting evidence to be used in a criminal prosecution, against whom all the protections of the Fourth Amendment stand?

While the line may be far from a hard and fast one, clearly where the investigator has determined the cause of the fire as incendiary, any further seizure of evidence must be done under the authority of a search warrant or with the effective consent of someone with the authority to grant such consent.

Over a decade after the *Rees* decision, the United States Supreme Court decided a case involving a warrantless search which produced evidence of arson for which the defendants were convicted in a Michigan trial court of conspiracy to burn real property. Their conviction had been reversed on appeal to the Michigan Supreme Court, and the state of Michigan appealed that decision to the Supreme Court, which granted certiorari.

That line, drawn at different junctures by different jurisdictions, was now drawn for fire investigators by the final interpreters of the reach of the Fourth Amendment. It would be binding upon all others, save for future Supreme Courts.

MICHIGAN v TYLER
Supreme Court of the United States (1978)
436 U.S. 499

MR. JUSTICE STEWART

* * * Shortly before midnight on January 21, 1970, a fire broke out at Tyler's Auction, a furniture store in Oakland, Mich. The building was leased to respondent Loren Tyler, who conducted the business in association with Robert Tompkins.

According to trial testimony of various witnesses, the fire department responded to the fire and was "just watering down smoldering embers" when Fire Chief See arrived on the scene about 2 a.m. It was Chief See's responsibility "to determine the cause and make out all reports." Chief See was met by Lt. Lawson, who informed him that two plastic containers of flammable liquid had been found in the building. Using portable lights, they entered the gutted store, which was filled with smoke and steam, to examine the containers. Concluding that the fire "could possibly have been an arson," Chief See called Police Detective Webb, who arrived around 3:30 a.m. Detective Webb took several pictures of the containers and of the interior of the store, but finally abandoned his efforts because of smoke and steam. Chief See briefly "(l)ooked throughout the rest of the building to see if there was any further evidence, to determine what the cause of the fire was." By 4 a.m., the fire had been extinguished and the fire fighters departed. See and Webb took the two containers to the fire station, where they were turned over to Webb for safekeeping. There was neither consent nor a warrant for any of these entries into the building, nor for the removal of the containers. The respondents challenged the introduction of these containers at trial, but abandoned their objection in the State Supreme Court. (Cit.Om.) Four hours after he had left Tyler's Auction, Chief See returned with Assistant Chief Somerville, whose job was to determine the "origin of all fires that occur within the Township." The fire had been extinguished and the building was empty. After a cursory examination they left, and Somerville returned with Detective Webb around 9 a.m. In Webb's words, they discovered suspicious "burn marks in the carpet, which (Webb) could not see earlier that morning, because of the heat, steam and the darkness." They also found "pieces of tape, with burn marks, on the stairway." After leaving the building to obtain tools, they returned and removed pieces of the carpet and sections of the stairs to preserve these bits of evidence suggestive of a fuse trail. Somerville also searched through the rubble, "looking for any other signs or evidence that showed how this fire was caused." Again, there was neither consent nor a warrant for these entries and seizures. Both at trial and on appeal, the respondents objected to the introduction of evidence thereby obtained.

On February 16, Sergeant Hoffman of the Michigan State Police Arson Section returned to Tyler's Auction to take photographs. During this visit or during another about the same time, he checked the circuit breakers, had someone inspect the furnace, and had a television repairman examine the remains of several television sets found in the ashes. He also found a piece of fuse. Over the course of his several visits, Hoffman secured physical evidence and formed opinions that played a substantial role at trial in establishing arson as the cause of the fire and in refuting the respondents' testimony about what furniture had been lost. His entries into the building were without warrant or Tyler's consent, and were for the sole purpose "of making an investigation and seizing evidence." At the trial, respondents' attorney objected to the admission of physical evidence obtained during these visits, and also moved to strike all of Hoffman's testimony "because it was got in an illegal manner."

The Michigan Supreme Court held that with only a few exceptions, any entry onto fire-damaged private property by fire or police officials is subject to the warrant requirements of the Fourth and Fourteenth Amendments. "Once the blaze (has been) extinguished and the fire fighters have left the premises, a warrant is required to reenter and search the premises, unless there is consent or the premises have been abandoned." (Cit.Om.) Applying this principle, the court ruled that the series of warrantless entries that began after the blaze had been extinguished at 4 a.m. on January 22 violated the Fourth and Fourteenth Amendments. It found that the "record does not factually support a conclusion that Tyler had abandoned the fire-damaged premises" and accepted the lower court's finding that "'(c)onsent for the numerous searches was never obtained from the defendant Tyler,'" (Cit.Om.) Accordingly, the court reversed the respondents' convictions and ordered a new trial.

* * * Thus, there is no diminution in a person's reasonable expectation of privacy nor in the protection of the Fourth Amendment simply because the official conducting the search wears the uniform of a fire fighter rather than a policeman, or because his purpose is to ascertain the cause of a fire rather than to look for evidence of a crime, or because the fire may have been started deliberately. Searches for administrative purposes, like searches for evidence of crime, are encompassed by the Fourth Amendment. And under that Amendment, "one governing principle, justified by history and current experience, has consistently been followed: except in certain carefully defined classes of cases, a search of private property without proper consent is 'unreasonable' unless it has been authorized by a valid search warrant." (Cit.Om.) The showing of probable cause necessary to secure a warrant may vary with the object and intrusiveness of the search, but the necessity for the warrant persists.

The petitioner argues that no purpose would be served by requiring warrants to investigate the cause of a fire. This argument is grounded on the premise that the only fact that need be shown to justify an investigatory search is that a fire of undetermined origin has occurred on those premises. The petitioner contends that this consideration distinguishes this case from Camara, which concerned the necessity for warrants to conduct routine building inspections. Whereas the occupant of premises subjected to an unexpected building inspection may have no way of knowing the purpose or the lawfulness of the entry, it is argued that the occupant of burned premises can hardly question the factual basis for fire officials wanting access to his property. And whereas a magistrate performs the significant function of assuring that an agency's decision to conduct a routine inspection of a particular dwelling conforms with reasonable legislative or administrative standards, he can do little more than rubber stamp an application to search fire-damaged premises for the cause of the blaze. In short, where the justification for the search is as simple and as obvious to everyone as the fact of a recent fire, a magistrate's review would be a time-consuming formality of negligible protection to the occupant.

The petitioner's argument fails primarily because it is built on a faulty premise. To secure a warrant to investigate the cause of a fire, an official must show more than the bare fact that a fire has occurred. The magistrate's duty is to assure that the proposed search will be reasonable, a determination that requires inquiry into the need for the intrusion on the one hand, and the threat of disruption to the occupant on the other. For routine building inspections, a reasonable balance between these competing concerns is usually achieved by legislative or administrative guidelines specifying the purpose, frequency, scope and manner of conducting the inspections. In the context of investigatory fire searches, which are not programmatic but are responsive to individual events, a more particularized inquiry may be necessary. The number of prior entries, the scope of the search, the time of day when it is proposed to be made, the lapse of time since the fire, the continued use of the building, and the owner's efforts to secure it against intruders might all be relevant factors Even though a fire victim's privacy must normally must yield to the vital social objective of ascertaining the cause of the fire, the magistrate can perform the important function of preventing harassment by keeping that invasion to a minimum. (Cit.Om.) * * *

In short, the warrant requirement provides significant protection for fire victims in this context, just as it does for property owners faced with routine building inspections. As a general matter, then, official entries to investigate the cause of a fire must adhere to the warrant procedures of the Fourth Amendment. In the words of the Michigan Supreme Court: "Where the cause (of the fire) is undetermined, and the purpose of the investigation is to determine the cause and to prevent such fires from occurring or recurring, a . . . search may be conducted pursuant to a warrant issued in accordance with reasonable legislative or administrative standards or, absent their promulgation, judicially prescribed standards; if evidence of wrongdoing is discovered, it may, of course, be used to establish probable cause for the issuance of a criminal investigative search warrant or in prosecution." But "(i)f the authorities are seeking evidence to be used in a criminal prosecution, the usual standard (of probable cause) will apply." (Cit.Om.) Since all the entries in this case were "without proper consent" and were not "authorized by a valid search warrant," each one is illegal unless it falls within one of the "certain carefully defined classes of cases" for which warrants are not mandatory. (Cit.Om.)

* * * A burning building clearly presents an exigency of sufficient proportions to render a warrantless entry "reasonable." Indeed, it would defy reason to suppose that firemen must secure a warrant or consent before entering a burning structure to put out the blaze. And once in a building for this purpose, firefighters may seize evidence of arson that is in plain view. (Cit.Om.) Thus, the Fourth and Fourteenth Amendments were not violated by the entry of the firemen to extinguish the fire at Tyler's Auction, nor by Chief See's removal of the two plastic containers of flammable liquid found on the floor of one of the showrooms.

Although the Michigan Supreme Court seems to have accepted this principle, its opinion may be read as holding that the exigency justifying a warrantless entry to fight a fire ends, and the need to get a warrant begins, with the dousing of the last flame. (Cit.Om.) We think this view of the fire fighting function is unrealistically narrow, however. Fire officials are charged not only with extinguishing fires, but with finding their causes. Prompt determination of the fire's origin may be necessary to prevent its recurrence, as through the detection of continuing dangers such as faulty wiring or a defective furnace. Immediate investigation may also be necessary to preserve evidence from intentional or accidental destruction. And, of course, the sooner the officials complete their duties, the less will be their subsequent interference with the privacy and the recovery efforts of the victims. For these reasons, officials need no warrant to remain in a building for a reasonable time to investigate the cause of a blaze after it has been extinguished. And if the warrantless entry to put out the fire and determine its cause is constitutional, the warrantless seizure of evidence while inspecting the premises for these purposes is also constitutional.

The respondents argue, however, that the Michigan Supreme Court was correct in holding that the departure by the fire officials from Tyler's Auction at 4 a.m. ended any license they might have had to conduct a warrantless search. Hence, they say that even if the firemen might have been entitled to remain in the building without a warrant to investigate the cause of the fire, their departure and re-entry four hours later that morning required a warrant.

On the facts of this case, we do not believe that a warrant was necessary for the early morning entries on January 22. As the fire was being extinguished, Chief See and his assistants began their investigation, but visibility was severely hindered by darkness, steam and smoke. Thus they departed at 4 a.m. and returned shortly after daylight to continue their investigation. Little purpose would have been served by their remaining in the building, except to remove any doubt about the legality of the warrantless search and seizure later that same morning. Under these circumstances, we find that the morning entries were no more than an actual continuation of the first, and the lack of a warrant thus did not invalidate the resulting seizure of evidence.

The entries occurring after January 22, however, were clearly detached from the initial exigency and warrantless entry. Since all of these searches were conducted without valid warrants and without consent, they were invalid under the Fourth and Fourteenth Amendments, and any evidence obtained as a result of those entries must, therefore, be excluded at the respondents' retrial.

In summation, we hold that an entry to fight a fire requires no warrant, and that once in the building, the officials may remain there for a reasonable time to investigate the cause of the blaze. Thereafter, additional entries to investigate the cause of the fire must be made pursuant to the warrant procedures governing administrative searches. (Cit.Om.) Evidence of arson discovered in the course of such investigations is admissible at trial, but if the investigating officials find probable cause to believe that arson has occurred and require further access to gather evidence for a possible prosecution, they may obtain a warrant only upon a traditional showing of probable cause applicable to searches for evidence of crime. (Cit.Om.)

These principles require that we affirm the judgment of the Michigan Supreme Court ordering a new trial.

Affirmed.

The Supreme Court had finally, it was thought, drawn the line on what could be seized and the parameters of a legal, and reasonable search of fire damaged premises for the state of Michigan; and, in doing so for all fire investigators in the United States. The decision was not unanimous, however, and there were some questions to which the Court alluded, but did not fully address.

Some of the issues that recur in these (arson) cases are:

* *the right of privacy*
* *consent*
* *reasonableness*
* *administrative vs.criminal search warrant*
* *cause and origin (origin/cause)*
* *criminal evidence*
* *statutory authority*
* *probable cause*

In just six years, the Supreme Court would again grant certiorari to the Michigan Supreme Court, in a criminal case; the crime once more was arson, and again the critical issue was that of the reach of the Fourth Amendment with regard to searches of premises which had been damaged by fire.

As you read the Supreme Court decision, try to observe the parallels between the two cases in terms of the factual settings. Does the Court follow its own precedent, or does it distinguish the cases to lay its foundation for a different ruling? What is clearly the same in the two cases; what is different? Does it always require a different decision if the facts are different?

The purpose of our analysis is to become familiar with the issues that the Court addresses, and the interpretation of the Court as it applies the Constitution to the facts of those cases it has chosen to review. The purpose of the Court is to help us conform our actions within the requirements of the Constitution, and, understanding its provisions and protections, to follow its mandates in the area of criminal law, in order to secure a conviction based upon professional and legal evidence and prosecution: a goal that all good fire investigators share.

MICHIGAN v. CLIFFORD
464 US 287 (1984)

POWER, Justice.

. . .

The trial court conducted an evidentiary hearing and denied the motion on the ground that exigent circumstances justified the search. The court certified its evidentiary ruling for interlocutory appeal and the Michigan Court of Appeals reversed.

That court held that there were no exigent circumstances for the search. Instead, it found that the warrantless entry and search of the Clifford residence were conducted pursuant to a policy of the Arson Division of the Detroit Fire Department that sanctioned such searches as long as the owner was not present, the premises were open to trespassers, and the search occurred within a reasonable time of the fire. The Court of Appeals held that this policy was inconsistent with Michigan v. Tyler, 436 US 499, 56 L Ed 2d 486, 98 S Ct 1942 (1978), and that the warrantless, nonconsensual search of the Cliffords' residence violated the Fourth and Fourteenth Amendments.

We granted certiorari to clarify doubt that appears to exist as to the application of our decision in Tyler.

In the early morning hours of October 18, 1980, a fire erupted at the Clifford home. The Cliffords were out of town on a camping trip at the time. The fire was reported to the Detroit Fire Department, and the fire units arrived on the scene about 5:40 a.m. The fire was extinguished and all fire officials and police left the premises at 7:04 a.m.

At 8 o'clock on the morning of the fire, Lieutenant Beyer, a fire investigator with the arson section of the Detroit Fire Department, received instructions to investigate the Clifford fire. He was informed that the Fire Department suspected arson. Because he had other assignments, Lieutenant Beyer did not proceed immediately to the Clifford residence. He and his partner finally arrived at about 1 p.m. on October 18.

When they arrived, they found a work crew on the scene. The crew was boarding up the house and pumping some six inches of water out of the basement. A neighbor told the investigators that he had called Mr. Clifford and had been instructed to request the Cliffords' insurance agent to send a boarding crew out to secure the house. The neighbor also advised that the Cliffords did not plan to return that day. While the investigators waited for the water to be pumped out, they found a Coleman fuel can in the driveway that was seized and marked as evidence.

By 1:30 p.m., the water had been pumped out of the basement and Lieutenant Beyer and his partner, without obtaining consent or an administrative warrant, entered the Clifford residence and began their investigation into the cause of the fire. Their search began in the basement and they quickly confirmed that the fire had originated there beneath the basement stairway. They detected a strong odor of fuel throughout the basement, and found two more Coleman fuel cans beneath the stairway. As they dug through the debris, the investigators also found a crock pot with attached wires leading to an electrical timer that was plugged into an outlet a few feet away. The timer was set to turn on at approximately 3:45 a.m. and to turn back off at approximately 9 a.m. It had stopped somewhere between 4 and 4:30 a.m. All of this evidence was seized and marked.

After determining that the fire had originated in the basement, Lieutenant Beyer and his partner searched the remainder of the house. The warrantless search that followed was extensive and thorough. The investigators called in a photographer to take pictures throughout the house. They searched through drawers and closets and found them full of old clothes. They inspected the rooms and noted that there were nails on the walls but no pictures. They found wiring and cassettes for a video tape machine but no machine.

Respondents moved to exclude all exhibits and testimony based on the basement and upstairs searches on the ground that they were searches to gather evidence of arson, that they were conducted without a warrant, consent, or exigent circumstances, and that they therefore were per se unreasonable under the Fourth and Fourteenth Amendments. Petitioner, on the other hand, argues that the entire search was reasonable and should be exempt from the warrant requirement.

In its petition for certiorari, the state does not challenge the state court's finding that there were no exigent circumstances justifying the search of the Clifford home. Instead, it asks us to exempt from the warrant requirement all administrative investigations into the cause and origin of a fire. We decline to do so.

In Tyler, we restated the Court's position that administrative searches generally require warrants. (Cit. Om.). We reaffirm that view again today. Except in certain carefully defined classes of cases, the nonconsensual entry and search of property are governed by the warrant requirement of the Fourth and Fourteenth Amendments. The constitutionality of warrantless and nonconsensual entries onto fire-damaged premises, therefore, normally turns on several factors: whether there are legitimate privacy interests that are protected by the Fourth Amendment; whether exigent circumstances justify the government intrusion regardless of any reasonable expectations of privacy; and, whether the object of the search is to determine the cause of the fire or to gather evidence of criminal activity.

. . . Privacy expectations will vary with the type of property, the amount of fire damage, the prior and continued use of the premises, and in some cases the owner's efforts to secure it against intruders. Some fires may be so devastating that no reasonable privacy interests remain in the ashes and ruins, regardless of the owner's subjective expectations. The test is essentially an objective one: whether "the expectation [is] one that society is prepared to recognize as 'reasonable.'" (Cit. Om.) If reasonable privacy interests remain in the fire-damaged property, the warrant requirement applies, and any official entry must be made pursuant to a warrant in the absence of consent or exigent circumstances.

A burning building of course creates an exigency that justifies a warrantless entry by fire officials to fight the blaze. Moreover, in Tyler we held that once in the building, officials need no warrant to remain for "a reasonable time to investigate the cause of a blaze after it has been extinguished." (Cit. Om.) Where, however, reasonable expectations of privacy remain in the fire-damaged property, additional investigations begun after the fire has been extinguished and fire and police officials have left the scene, generally must be made pursuant to a warrant or the identification of some new exigency.

The aftermath of a fire often presents exigencies that will not tolerate the delay necessary to obtain a warrant or secure the owner's consent to inspect fire-damaged premises. Because determining the cause and origin of a fire serves a compelling public interest, the warrant requirement does not apply in such cases.

If a warrant is necessary, the object of the search determines the type of warrant required. If the primary object is to determine the cause and origin of a recent fire, an administrative warrant will suffice. To obtain such a warrant, fire officials need only show that a fire of undetermined origin has occurred on the premises, that the scope of the proposed search is reasonable and will not intrude unnecessarily on the fire victim's privacy, and that the search will be executed at a reasonable and convenient time.

If the primary object of the search is to gather evidence of criminal activity, a criminal search warrant may be obtained only on a showing of probable cause to believe that relevant evidence will be found in the place to be searched. If evidence of criminal activity is found during the course of a valid administrative search, it may be seized under the "plain view" doctrine. (Cit. Om.) This evidence may then be used to obtain a criminal search warrant. Fire officials may not, however, rely on this evidence to expand the scope of their administrative search without first making a showing of probable cause to an independent judicial officer.

The object of the search is important even if exigent circumstances exist. Circumstances that justify a warrantless search for the cause of a fire may not justify a search to gather evidence of criminal activity once that cause has been determined. If, for example, the administrative search is justified by the immediate need to ensure against rekindling, the scope of the search may be no broader than reasonably necessary to achieve its end.

. . . In Tyler we upheld a warrantless postfire search of a furniture store, despite the absence of exigent circumstances, on the ground that it was a continuation of a valid search begun immediately after the fire. The investigation was begun as the last flames were being doused, but could not be completed because of smoke and darkness. The search was resumed promptly after the smoke cleared and daylight dawned. Because the postfire search was interrupted for reasons that were evident, we held that the early morning search was "no more than an actual continuation of the first, and the lack of a warrant did not invalidate the resulting seizure of evidence." (Cit. Om.)

As the State conceded at oral argument, this case is distinguishable for several reasons. First, the challenged search was not a continuation of an earlier search. Between the time the firefighters had extinguished the blaze and left the scene and the arson investigators first arrived about 1 p.m. to begin their investigation, the Cliffords had taken steps to secure the privacy interests that remained in their residence against further intrusion. These efforts separate the entry made to extinguish the blaze from that made later by different officers to investigate its origin. Second, the privacy interests in the residence-particularly after the Cliffords had acted-were significantly greater than those in the fire-damaged furniture store, making the delay between the fire and the midday search unreasonable absent a warrant, consent, or exigent circumstances. We frequently have noted that privacy interests are especially strong in a private residence. These facts-the interim effort to secure the burned premises and the heightened privacy interests in the home-distinguish this case from Tyler. At least where a homeowner has made a reasonable effort to secure his fire-damaged home after the blaze has been extinguished and the fire and police units have left the scene, we hold that a subsequent postfire search must be conducted pursuant a warrant, consent, or the identification of some new exigency. So long as the primary purpose is to ascertain the cause of the fire, an administrative warrant will suffice.

Because the cause of the fire was then known, the search of the upper portions of the house, described above, could only have been a search to gather evidence of the crime of arson. Absent exigent circumstances, such a search requires a criminal warrant.

Even if the midday basement search had been a valid administrative search, it would not have justified the upstairs search. The scope of such a search is limited to that reasonably necessary to determine the cause and origin of a fire and to ensure against rekindling. As soon as the investigators determined that the fire had originated in the basement and had been caused by the crock pot and timer found beneath the basement stairs, the scope of their search was limited to the basement area. Although the investigators could have used whatever evidence they discovered in the basement to establish probable cause to search the remainder of the house, they could not lawfully undertake that search without a proper judicial determination that a successful showing of probable cause had been made. Because there were no exigent circumstances justifying the upstairs search, and it was undertaken without a prior showing of probable cause before an independent judicial officer, we hold that this search of a home was unreasonable under the Fourth and Fourteenth Amendments, regardless of the validity of the basement search.

The warrantless intrusion into the upstairs regions of the Clifford house presents a telling illustration of the importance of prior judicial review of proposed administrative searches. If an administrative warrant had been obtained in this case, it presumably would have limited the scope of the proposed investigation and would have prevented the warrantless intrusion into the upper rooms of the Clifford home An administrative search into the cause of a recent fire does not give fire officials license to roam freely through the fire victim's private residence.

The only pieces of physical evidence that have been challenged on this interlocutory appeal are the three empty fuel cans, the electric crock pot, and the timer and attached cord. Respondents have also challenged the testimony of the investigators concerning the warrantless search of both the basement and the upstairs portions of the Clifford home. The discovery of two of the fuel cans, the crock pot, the timer and cord-as well as the investigators' related testimony-were the product of the unconstitutional postfire search of the Cliffords' residence. Thus, we affirm that portion of the Michigan Court of Appeals that excluded that evidence. One of the fuel cans was discovered in plain view during the initial investigation by the firefighters. It would have been admissible whether it had been seized in the basement by firefighters or in the driveway by the arson investigators. Exclusion of this evidence should be reversed. It is so ordered.

EMPLOYMENT LAW

Common Law: Employment at Will

Workers Compensation

Statutory Applications/Judicial Construction

Workers Compensation
> *City of Huntington v Fisher*

FLSA   *Bell v Porter*
> *Bridgeman v Ford, Bacon & Davis*
> *Alex v Chicago*

OSHA   *Marshall v Barlow's Inc*

The "Right" to Employment:

A) Federal Statutory Protection

The Civil Rights Acts

* 1868
* 1964

The Suspect Criteria

Race, color, religion, sex or national origin

Blair v Freehold (1971)

Vulcan Society v New York Civil
> *Service Commission (1973)*

Boston NAACP v Beecher (1974)

Constitutional Interpretation of Civil Rights

Disparate Treatment

Disparate Impact

> *Griggs v Duke Power Co (1971)*

Balancing the Rights

> *Univ. of Cal Regents v Baake (1978)*
> *United Steelworkers v Weber (1979)*
> *Loc. 93 IAFF v Cleveland (1986)*

Civil Rights Act of 1991: the pendulum arc

2) Sex Discrimination
      Berkman v City of New York
   Sexual Harrassment: The reach of Title VII
      Meritor Savings & Loan v Vinson (1986)
      Harris v Forklift Systems, Inc. (1993)
3) Age
   Age Discrimination in Employment Act (ADEA)
      EEOC v Wyoming
4) Physical/Mental Handicap
   Americans with Disabilities Act (ADA)

EMPLOYMENT LAW

Common Law Doctrines

Agency Principles: the relationship defined

Agency is the area of law which defines the relationship of the Principal and his agent (at Common Law, the Master and his Servant) especially the responsibility of the principal/master for the acts and conduct of the agent/servant. It is a theory of whereby the master, at common law, was held to be responsible for the acts of his servant, within certain prescribed limitations.

The underlying concept and policy was twofold:

1) the master exercised control over the employee by reason of his authority in determining the work or assignment of tasks which the servant did for the master; the principal authorizes his agent to enter into agreements which are to bind the third party and the principal to a definite set of rights obligations, usually in the form of a contract; the employer hires the employee to perform a particular job for the employer;

2) the master is more able to pay for the damages caused by the negligent acts of his servant, and much more able to provide for compensation for the injured party than the servant, as evidenced by securing of insurance.

Thus the party employed (servant, agent or employee), together with his respective master, principal or employer, all were under the general principles which legally bound the employing party to be responsible for the acts of his employee.

This sometime was in the form of a contract to which the party was bound by his agents intentional acts, or legal liability for negligent acts of his employee, even though he had not authorized such.

Vicarious tort liability: the doctrine of respondeat superior

The principle involved in this imposition of vicarious liability in the area of tort law is called *respondeat superior*:

"Let the master answer" (for the negligence of his servant). While the terms "master" and "servant" were part of the common law in a society with rigid class distinctions, the growth of employment relationships in a democratic society substituted the more acceptable "principal" and "agent" for the area of business law where sales agents were authorized and expected to bind their principals into contracts for the purchase and sale of goods in commerce. In addition to the contractual type liability for the agents actions, the principal was clearly liable in tort for the negligent acts of his agent, subject to some limitations as we shall examine herein. While the firefighter might be surprised to be considered a "government agent", the principle of *respondeat superior* clearly applies, especially with the erosion of sovereign immunity, to the relationship of "Employer" and "Employee". Thus where an employee has committed a negligent act, his employer will have to answer in damages, under certain conditions, as follow:

1) *Scope of Employment.* The employee must be acting within the scope of his employment, that is, doing the work or performing the acts for which he has been employed. A firefighter who is engaged in driving an apparatus to a fire, extinguishing a fire, ventilating, or performing rescue is clearly within the scope of his employment, but apprehending a criminal is not one of the duties for which he has been employed.

A delivery truck driver who has an accident while he is working would normally be considered to be within the scope of his employment, but if he is not on the routed course of his deliveries, will the employer still be liable for his negligence? That depends upon the reason for his excursion; if the reason he is off the route is because there is a vehicle disabled in the road and he seeks the most convenient way around the obstruction, it is considered in the law a *detour*. The employer will still be liable since his driver was still acting in furtherance of his duties to the employer. A different case, and result arises when the purpose for which he strays from his course is not the interests of the employer but his own, e.g., he takes the truck well off the route to visit friends at the local fire station, and accidentally backs into the chief's buggy when leaving. This departure is not a detour, but a *frolic*, and negligence for which the employer would not be liable. (A note might be appropriate here that while the principle of law is sound, a practical evaluation in terms of real dollars could cause acceptance of the liability in lieu of the cost of legal defense).

Borrowed Servant

The doctrine of vicarious liability and *respondeat superior* continues to apply where one "borrows" the services of an employee for a short period of time, and negligence of the employee occurs. The borrowing employer will be liable, provided that what the employee is doing is within the scope of his duties for the borrowing employer. Some legal scholars have suggested that a paramedic, "borrowed" from the fire service entity by the emergency facilities of the hospital, falls into such classification. This would mean that while performing service for the hospital project medical director, negligence of the paramedic will become the liability of that "employing" hospital.

Independent Contractors

An exception to the doctrine of respondeat superior is that of one who does work for another, and is paid to do the work, but is not considered an employee. This is the independent contractor and the critical issue of whether one is determined to be such is that of *control*. Where the party determines himself how the work will be performed, uses his own tools and equipment, and the work is limited in scope to a particular job or project, then he will likely be considered an independent contractor, who will provide both liability and workers compensation insurance, often as part of an agreement, which also specifies the exact terms of the work. The more that the party paying for the work exercises control over the job, however, (providing equipment, directing employees, or the like) the more the independence of the contractor will dissipate, and the more likely that he will be considered an employee, with the more probable result that his negligence will be answered by his "Employer".

Workers Compensation

The agency principles and the doctrine of vicarious liability was to define the responsibilities of the Employer to third parties (often employers themselves); it was a more difficult task to secure those principles on behalf of the employee.

Just as the social policy of placing liability for an employee's negligence on an Employer was based on the concept that he was in the best position to provide compensation to the injured party, the industrial revolution in the United States provided the impetus for a logical corollary to that doctrine. While the 13th Amendment legally broke the shackles for blacks enslaved in an agricultural system, the growth of an industrial system in the north left masses of workers economically enslaved to work in unsafe factories that ran incessantly on their muscle and too often, blood. Whether in the fields of Alabama, the sweatshops of New York or slaughterhouses of Chicago, labor was simply a commodity of unlimited supply. Professor William L. Prosser, in his treatise on tort law, analyzes the historical underpinnings of the development of workers compensation:

> The rule that the employer was not liable for injuries caused solely by the negligence of a fellow servant first appeared in England in 1837, and almost immediately afterward in the United States, . . .
>
> The reasons usually assigned for (the rule) however, were that the plaintiff upon entering the employment *assumed the risk* (emphasis supplied) of negligence on the part of his fellow servants, and the master did not undertake to protect him against it; . . . and that it would promote the safety of the public and of all servants to make each one watchful of the conduct of others for his own protection.
>
> The explanation of the rule probably lay in the highly individualistic viewpoint of the common law courts, and their desire to encourage industrial undertakings by making the burden on them as light as possible.
>
> Under the common law system, by far the greater proportion of industrial accidents remained uncompensated, and the burden fell upon the workman, who was least able to support it. Furthermore, the litigation which usually was necessary to any recovery meant delay, pressure on the injured man to settle his claim in order to live, and heavy attorney' fees and other expenses which frequently left him only a small part of the money finally paid. Coupled with this were working conditions of an extreme inhumanity in many industries, which the employer was under no particular incentive to improve.

Statutory Construction

A critical part of the job of the court is that of interpreting the law which has been created by another branch of government: the legislature. The court can utilize several methods of determining what the legislature intended including examining the debates concerning the passage of the statute, or compare the statute with other related laws. The court may simply read the statute itself, giving it the effect that a common sense reading of the language should produce.

When Isaac Fisher was killed while fighting a fire, other members of the city of Huntington Fire Department were comforted by the fact that the compensation was granted by the Industrial Commission. They were then angered by the fact that the city appealed the issue of whether the widow should have been granted compensation.

In the Appellate Court, the judgment was rendered for the city, in reliance upon an earlier case, *City of Fort Wayne v Hazelett, 1939, 107 Ind.App. 184, 23 N.E.2d 610*. The widow then requested the Supreme Court of Indiana to consider whether the Appellate Court was correct in its ruling.

CITY OF HUNTINGTON v. FISHER
Supreme Court of Indiana (1942)
40 N.E.2d 699

FANSLER, Judge

* * * In the Hazlett case it was pointed out that a city acts in a governmental capacity in maintaining a fire department, and is controlled by statute in hiring and firing firemen, and that there is a statute providing for a pension system for members of the fire department, and the court concluded, in view of these facts, firemen are not in the service of a city under a contract of hire within the meaning of the Workmen's Compensation Law.

Nor can we agree that the fact that the city acts in a governmental capacity, and that the manner of hiring and discharging firemen is regulated by statute, and that a pension system is provided for firemen, furnishes a basis for concluding that it was not intended that they should come within the terms of the Compensation Law. The state is included within the definition of employer, and it acts in a governmental capacity, and the manner of its employment and discharge of employees is regulated by statute, and it may be noted that, under federal statutes, private employers are regulated in the employment and discharge of men where labor union membership is involved. The statute providing for pensions for municipal utility workers expressly excludes them from the provisions of the Workmen's Compensation Act. Section 48-6607, Burns' Ind. Stat. 1933, Section 12321, Baldwin's Ind. St. 1934. But we find no similar provisions in the Firemen's Pension Law, Burns' Ann. St. 48-6501 *et seq.*, and we must assume, in the light of the express exclusion of municipal utility employees, that if an exception was intended because of the Firemen's Pension Law, it would have been expressed.

The judgment is reversed, and the cause remanded to the Appellate Court for further proceedings not inconsistent with this opinion.

Probably no better argument for the passage of workers' compensation was the simple slogan chanted by the workers themselves: "The cost of the product should bear the blood of the workman."

The first of the workers' compensation statutes were passed in England in 1837, and in the United States for Government employees only (1908), the first state statute in New York in 1910, and by 1921 most of the states had followed suit. By 1963, all 50 of the states had such statutes.

The statutes provided for a continuation of wages during the time of incapacity, together with an evaluation of the loss that was permanent, payment of medical bills and today, the cost of rehabilitation. The wages were not equal to the worker's normal wages, but were placed at a percentage.

Of most critical importance, however, was the fact that all of the statutes abolished the common law tort defenses: contributory negligence, assumption of risk, and the fellow servant rule. Thus the only issue was whether the injury had occurred at the workplace, which could be proven via witnesses, and there had to be adequate notice to the employer, again, no difficulty for the injured worker.

In 1938, The Fair Labor Standards Act provided federal regulations for working conditions such as child labor, minimum wage, hours of employment as part of the Roosevelt administration's efforts to raise the nation from the mire of the Depression.

Two cases, decided the in the same year (1946), dealt with the application of the FLSA on firefighters who were employed by independent contractors for the government at ordnance plants, one in Illinois, one in Arkansas. Each court came to the same result, although by different reasoning, for an issue that is taken for granted in our time: compensation while sleeping.

The firm of Sanderson and Porter was an independent contractor whose employees were hired to operate the ordnance plant at Elwood, Illinois under a contract with the U.S. Government. They had complete supervision of all the employees and maintained their own fire department in which the plaintiffs were employed as firefighters. Since they were required to be at work for twenty-four hours, on a two-platoon system, they sought overtime compensation based upon the Fair Labor Standards Act.

BELL *et al v.* PORTER *et al.*
Court of Appeals, 7th Circuit (1946)
159 F.2d 117

KERNER, Circuit Judge.

We now consider whether the employees' eight-hour sleeping time was compensable under the Act.

Appellees' duties were to fight fires, scrub the premises, drill, make inspection and trial runs, pick up and deliver reports, fill extinguishers, attend school after supper, and clean equipment. These duties ordinarily took about five hours per day of their time, the remainder of the time between 7:30 am and 11:30 pm being spent in playing cards, reading, listening to radio programs, eating and other personal activities. They were permitted to retire at 10:00 pm, except that one fireman in each station was required to remain awake until 11:30 pm. During the period in question, appellees spent 338,265 hours at the plant of which 229,545 were hours worked between 7:30 am and 11:30 pm, for which they were paid at overtime rates for hours worked in excess of 40 hours per week. The remaining 108,720 hours were sleeping period hours between 11:30 pm and 7:30 am, for which no compensation was paid.

The (appellate) court found that the two-platoon system was proposed to the men in December, 1943, at which time they voted unanimously in favor of the plan; that the plan was put into effect on February 27, 1944, and continued in effect until December 1, 1945; . . .

The court also found that during the period in question there were six occasions on which the sleeping periods of the men were interrupted by fire alarms, three occasions when certain of the men were required to remain during a portion of their sleeping period at the scene of a fire that had occurred prior to 11:30 pm, and on one occasion on which two of the men were detailed for a portion of their sleeping period to stand by at the scene of hazardous operations. The total number of hours spent by all appellees on such night duty amounted to 136 out of a total of 108,720 sleeping period hours. Four of the appellees were never called out for such duty and the remainder spent from 30 minutes to 8 hours on such duty.

The court concluded that the time spent by appellees at the plant during the period between 11:30 pm and 7:30 am was predominantly for appellants' benefit as an incident of their employment and as the only practical means for getting instant service in case of fire, and that the eight hour period between 11:30 pm and 7:30 am constituted working time.

Appellees argue that the sleeping quarters were uncomfortable and unsanitary.

The court in the instant case did not find that the sleeping quarters were inadequate or of such a character that the men were unable to obtain normal rest. But be that as it may, the ultimate finding was clearly a mixed question of fact and law, *United States v. Anderson*, 7 Cir., 108 F.2d 475, and if based upon a misapplication of the law, it is not binding on the reviewing court. (*Citation omitted*) Here, under the facts and circumstances, as in the *Bowers v. Remington Rand* case, it is clear that appellees, in consideration of their employment as firemen, were willing to sleep on the premises and keep themselves available for duty if called upon during their rest period; their contract was to wait to be engaged; hence the time spent in sleeping is not compensable.

The judgment is reversed and the cause is remanded to the District Court with instructions to dismiss the complaint.

On a superficial level, the following case seems fairly identical to the previous one, but there is a qualitative difference in how the court arrived at its decision, which was also similar.

BRIDGEMAN et al v. FORD, BACON & DAVIS, Inc.
District Court, E.D. Arkansas, W.D. (1946)
64 F.Supp. 1006

We further conclude that time spent by an employee in a rest or sleeping period- the employee being subject to call for emergencies, and being compensated specially therefore-may, but need not necessarily, be considered as employment hours under the provisions of the Fair Labor Standards Act. Whether or not such sleeping time constitutes working hours depends upon the facts in each particular case. In this connection, it is important to determine the degree with which the employee is free to obtain normal rest and the degree of interference with his normal mode of living and freedom of action is that the employee is required to sleep away from home, the time devoted to rest and sleep should not be considered as employment hours. But if the rest period be interrupted to such an extent as to deprive the employee of a normal period of consecutive hours for sleeping, then such period should be considered as hours of employment under the provisions of said Act.

After the first two months they were allowed, under their agreement with the company, a similar eight hour period of rest extending from 11:00

pm to 7:00 am, but, in practice, were permitted to retire at 9:30 pm. Their contention is that the rest periods were so interfered with by outside noises and emergency calls that they were unable to enjoy the same or obtain a normal night's sleep. The plaintiffs have failed to sustain the burden of proof in this regard.

In the course of the first two months, the plaintiffs were required, during the rest period, to answer fire calls only, and the proof shows that only sixteen fire runs were made during the rest period between November 29, 1943 and May 27, 1945, a period of eighteen months, and of average duration of slightly less than one hour.

Some three and one half months after the change was made, the ambulances were moved from the hospitals to the fire stations, and emergency calls were more frequent. A compilation of defendant's records, filed as an exhibit herein, and which we accept, discloses however, that, taking into consideration both fire and ambulance runs made during the eight hour rest period, over the entire period from November 29, 1943 to May 27, 1945, thirty eight plaintiffs averaged forty-one minutes per hundred hours rest or sleeping time on both fire and ambulance calls, or, conversely, ninety-nine hours and nineteen minutes of each one-hundred hour's rest or sleeping time were uninterrupted by reason of emergency calls of any nature.

Some of the firemen testified that they were disturbed by the fire inspectors who had an office on the first floor of the fire station, but the fire chief, Mr. Lawrence A. Pluche, testified that he had received only one complaint in this regard during the entire period under consideration, which was on account of the fire inspectors storing their clothes in lockers on the second floor; and that he immediately moved the lockers downstairs; also, that the inspectors spent practically all of their nighttime in inspecting various parts of the ordnance area, which comprised about 7,400 acres. Some of the men complained that the beds were not comfortable. These were small iron beds, fitted with mattresses and springs, such as are frequently used in dormitories occupied by numbers of men. Chief Pluche stated that he and his wife sleep on identical beds every night. Others complained of snoring. Doubtless it took time for the men to adjust themselves to sleeping in a dormitory along with a number of others, but, on the whole, the court finds that their rest period was not materially interrupted, and that they obtained a normal night's rest.

In our opinion, the only substantial interference with the men's normal mode of living and freedom of action during the rest period was that they were required to sleep away from their homes.

Judgment in accordance with opinion.

F.L.S.A. Then and Now

The issues in the Fair Labor Standards Act before the courts in the above cases were whether and how the Act's provisions were to apply to employees, and thus employers, who were under its jurisdiction; in 1938 those were the workers in private companies.

But in 1974, Congress amended the FLSA to include public employees of federal, state and local governments, and with it, imposed the Act's mandate regarding wages and hours. The historical setting for the Court's decision had been some three decades of increased federal regulation of state enterprise, based on the power of Congress to regulate under the Commerce Clause. Several agencies and representative groups had challenged the reach of the Congress into what had been traditionally, and constitutionally, they argued, the province of state government.

The Court, in *National League of Cities v Usery*, 426 US 833, 96 S.Ct 2465 (1976) agreed with the states, with Justice Blackmun making a majority of five with some reservation.

Justice Renquist delivered the reasoning of that majority:

Judged solely in terms of increased costs in dollars, these allegations show a significant impact on the functioning of the governmental bodies involved. The Metropolitan Government of Nashville and Davidson County, Tenn., for example asserted that the Act will increase its costs of providing essential police and fire protection, without any increase in service or in current salary levels, by $ 938,000 per year . . .

Increased costs are not, of course, the only adverse effects which compliance with the Act will visit upon state and local governments, and in turn upon the citizens who depend upon those governments. In its complaint in intervention, for example, California asserted that it could not comply with the overtime costs (approximately $ 750,000 per year) which the Act required to be paid to California Highway Patrol cadets during their academy training program. California reported that it had thus been forced to reduce its academy training program from 2,080 to only 960 hours, a compromise undoubtedly of substantial importance to those whose safety and welfare may depend upon the preparedness of the California Highway Patrol . . .

Quite apart from the substantial costs imposed upon the states and their political subdivisions, the Act displaces state policies regarding the manner in which they structure delivery of those governmental services which their citizens require. The Act, speaking directly to the States qua States, requires that they shall pay all but an extremely limited minority of their employees the minimum wage rates currently chosen by Congress. It may well be that as a matter of economic policy it would be desirable that States, just as private employers, comply with these minimum wage requirements. But it cannot be gainsaid that the federal requirement directly supplants the considered policy choices of the States' elected officials and administrators as to how they wish to structure pay scales in state employment. The State may wish to employ persons with little or no training, or those who wish to work on a casual basis, or those who for some other reason do not possess minimum employment requirements, and pay them less than the minimally prescribed federal wage. It may wish to offer part-time or summer employment to teenagers at a figure less than the minimum wage, and if unable to do so, may decline to offer such employment at all. But the Act would forbid such choices by the States . . .

Thus, even if appellants have overestimated the effects which the Act will have upon their current levels and patterns of governmental activity, the dispositive factor is that Congress has attempted to exercise its Commerce Clause authority to prescribe minimum wages and maximum hours to be paid by the States in their capacities as sovereign governments. In doing so, Congress has sought to wield its power in a fashion that would impair the States' "ability to function effectively in a federal system." (Fry). This exercise of congressional authority does not comport with the federal system of government embodied in the Constitution. We hold so far in that the challenged amendments operate to directly displace the States' freedom to structure integral operations in areas of traditional governmental functions, they are not within the authority granted Congress by Art. I, § 8, cl. 3.

National League of Cities should not stand for the proposition that Congress may not constitutionally prescribe to the states, but rather for the fact that the reach of the authority of the federal government, in any of its branches, has always been an issue which sharply divided political philosophies, the national parties and even the Supreme Court.

When the issue of the authority of Congress (especially under the Commerce Clause) had finally been upheld against the doctrine of states' rights under the tenth amendment, it was by a divided Court.

Congress had also amended the Age Discrimination in Employment Act in 1974 (extending the age range to make impermissible any actions impacting employees between 40 and 70), but it was the Supreme Court that extended its application to public employees. The mandatory retirement of a supervisor in Wyoming's Fish and Game Department, at age 55, was held violative of the ADEA by The Court. In so finding that the protection of the ADEA should apply to public employees, every budget of every state, local government or municipality was thereby destroyed, since almost all required some mandatory retirement of at least its public safety workers.

In 1983, in another 5-4 decision of The Court, the Congressional authority was again upheld as constitutionally permissible regulation of the state.

Two years later, The Court addressed the issue of regulation of a mass-transit system under the FLSA, which would be exempt under the Renquist reasoning in *National League of Cities*. Justice Blackmun, the deciding vote in that earlier case, then stating that he "may have misinterpreted the Court's reasoning," and now spoke for the majority of six in allowing the application of the FLSA to the states.

Justices Powell, O'Connor and of course, Chief Justice Renquist dissented.

If the predictability of the Supreme Court seems to be a most difficult thing to grasp, it should be remembered that a sharply divided decision evidences the very real split of political philosophy in determining what the forefathers had intended, in the very seminal questions of what the Constitution means.

What remains constant, however, is the simple truth that the Constitution continues to be what the Supreme Court finds it to be, always adaptable to changing circumstances.

There are several ways in which the judiciary can interpret the law, and it should be kept in mind that the justices themselves are the products of their society, their environments and political philosophies, which are brought to bear in making their decisions and influencing others to concur with their reasoning.

The court may look to the legislative history of a law in determining what the legislature intended, where there is more than one reasonable interpretation of a statute. It may also examine the history involved with the issues in the case, i.e., what led these parties to seek the intervention of the court; or what rights are being abridged or curtailed, and whether such restrictions run afoul of constitutional mandates.

Finally, the court may simply read the statute itself; compare it with other statutes that the legislature has passed, and decide whether something was intentional, or an accidental omission.

Paramedics in the state of Washington had worked without the benefit of any additional day off to reduce the weekly aggregate hours of their 24 hour platoon system, notwithstanding the fact that the firefighters in that jurisdiction had such a day to reduce their working hours.

The Fair Labor Standards Act had allowed exemptions for certain public safety people based upon the fact that a week was not an appropriate block of time upon which to calculate their hours, i.e., a 28 day cycle had been used for police and firemen. Such a cycle then reflected their special weekends and days off that brought their aggregate, and average hours down within statutory reason.

The court found no such hours in the (Washington) paramedics schedule and concluded that they could not be exempted simply because of their close association with fire service. The decision carried eastward, where paramedics who *did* enjoy additional days off, similar to the firefighters' schedule, believed that the court's decision applied to them as well.

Several of the paramedics also believed that, should the city of Chicago be faced with the liability of back pay overtime, they would more readily provide them with cross-training as firefighters to secure their exemption from further FLSA liability.

The paramedics won their case(s) in the U.S. District Court for the Northern District of Illinois, and the city of Chicago appealed the court's interpretation of the federal statute. Notwithstanding the central fact that Chicago paramedics worked exactly the same work schedule as their firefighter bretheren, the court held that the city did not prove that they should be exempt similarly to firefighters since they failed to show that 80% of their runs were fire-related, or that they were so integral to firefighting since they were not permitted into fire buildings nor were they trained even in extrication.

The Court of Appeals' decision affirmed that of the lower court and no appeal from this decision to the Illinois Supreme Court occurred; the city of Chicago stemmed the financial hemorrhage by adding the tourniquet of another platoon to the existing three. The EMS ranks, have since worked twenty fours hours, followed by seventy two hours off, gladly giving up the compensatory "Daley Day," and the firefighters rejected that schedule in contract negotiations.

Federal Protection of Individual Rights

The Civil Rights Act of 1964: Title VII

It shall be an unlawful employment practice for an employer—(1) to fail or refuse to hire or to discharge any individual or otherwise to discriminate against any individual with respect to his compensation, terms, conditions, or privileges of employment, because of such individual's race, color, religion, sex, or national origin . . .

When President Johnson signed the 1964 Civil Rights Act into law on July 2, 1964, it was the culmination of not only the march on Washington in the summer of 1963, but also the congressional mandate to eliminate the effects of discrimination in society by addressing it in the workplace.

The Supreme Court, in *Brown v. the Board of Education*, had established clearly that the doctrine of *separate but equal* was no longer in conformity with the principles of the Constitution and had directed that the dismantling of segregation in public schools proceed with all deliberate speed. To the degree that the Supreme Court forced the nation to apply "Equal Justice Under Law" to the school house, Title VII was its legislative counterpart in the workplace.

Underlying both are the basic tenets of the Constitution, and the history of our country has been written largely, and continues to be written, by our adherence to, or violation of those principles, as finally determined by the Supreme Court.

The Constitution evolves with each decision of The Court, and its ability to be adapted and shaped by those decisions is a testament to the belief and draftmanship of our founding fathers.

No political system has existed with such dedication to the maximum possible freedom attainable on behalf of a nation of such diversity of cultures, beliefs and hopes.

Where the labor of the worker was simply treated as a commodity, without regard to the conditions within the workplace, or the well-being of the worker and his family, it is hardly a mystery to understand why *The Communist Manifesto* began with a call to the workers of the world to assert their political and human rights. Since immigrants poured into the New World with few skills and less knowledge, there was always a ready supply of labor, often in competition for their very livelihood. This led to the full acceptance of such theories of Social Darwinism by the factory owners, as well as the almost universal concept of employment at will.

Since profit was the single motivating factor, the abuses of the industrial system continued to grow exponentially, and while the crash of 1929 probably sobered up many of the high riding robber barons, it had an even worse effect upon the workers. Instead of a poor paying, dangerous job working long hours, now they had no job at all.

The Civil War had been fought, at least after the Emancipation Proclamation, to insure the rights and blessings of liberty on all Americans, regardless of color or creed. The Roosevelt Administration believed the

Government could now help the common worker by passing legislation which would help him gain economic freedom.

It was necessary, in a real political sense, for the survival of Democracy, supported by the Capitalist engines of Commerce. All too inviting were the promises of a new order which would begin with the destruction of monarchies and capitalist war machinery; the American worker had nothing too lose by trying out a new system of government; the current one had failed, as witness the Great Depression.

Roosevelt tried to lift the economy, at least to one knee, by various attempts at legislative relief, all of which, the Supreme Court had said, failed Constitutional muster. But when he was inspired to propose the Supreme Court itself be remodeled to an expanded fifteen member version, it seemed as if he hard learned a great deal, constitutionally speaking, for his attempts at legislative reform of the economic problems were thereafter within the mandates of the Constitution.

(This analysis might be challenged as suggesting that The Court was intimidated by the "Court Packing Plan;" but the timing of events seems more than coincidental.)

The Wagner Act (The National Labor Relations Act), passed in 1935, was the most comprehensive legislation ever enacted to secure the rights of workers to form unions and bargain collectively for themselves. It was not the beginning of a long, hard struggle for economic independence, it was rather the culmination of the growing political power of the labor movement, the response to years of violent and disruptive strikes, and the means of insuring to the American worker that there was more to be gained through democratic processes than anarchy.

The good fight, depending upon which side of the struggle one sat, continued with the tide moving to management after the war with the passage of the Taft-Hartley Act (1947) and the enactment of the Landrum-Griffin Act (1959).

But apart from the dichotomy of the labor-management struggle, there continued another struggle just underneath the larger battles between employees and employers. The election of John F. Kennedy in 1960, followed by the marches on Washington through the summer of 1963, led to the passage of the 1964 Civil Rights Act. In Title VII of that act was the most powerful law ever passed to guarantee the rights of minorities to equal employment opportunities since the Emancipation Proclamation. The 1868 Civil Rights Act, passed three years following the end of the Civil War, did not accomplish anywhere near the goals attained by the impact of Title VII.

The Disparate Treatment Cases

When an employee, who is of a protected class, is treated in an adverse manner, than other employees not in that protected class, there exists a case of disparate (different) treatment.

McDonnell Douglas Corp., v Green was the first of Supreme Court cases setting forth the Disparate Treatment doctrine. The case involved a black mechanic who had been laid off by his employer, and participated in a "stall-in" to protest racial discrimination by his employer. When workers were called back to work, he was not rehired though he continually answered their ads for workers.

What was critical in the case was the standards set forth by the Court in establishing a *prima facie* case of discrimination. The plaintiff had to show (in the context of a hiring complaint):

1) plaintiff was a member of the protected class (Minority);
2) plaintiff was qualified, and applied for a job for which the employer was seeking applicants;
3) plaintiff was rejected in spite of qualifications; and
4) the position the plaintiff sought remained open, and the employer continued to seek applicants.

Once the plaintiff established his prima facie case, the burden shifted to the employer to "articulate some legitimate, nondiscriminatory reason for the employee's rejection." (Cit.Om.) Although some appellate courts had interpreted this to mean that the employer had to *prove* that there was no discriminatory motive, the Supreme Court reversed and remanded those cases to hold consistently that the burden remained always with the plaintiff. The burden on the defendant was only one of production, but the burden on the plaintiff was one of persuasion.

Finally, the plaintiff had the opportunity, and in fact the burden of persuading the court, that the reason given was simply pretextual. The critical issue was one of intent, which could be proven by direct or circumstantial evidence, but it had to be proven to the satisfaction of the court nonetheless.

In determining intent, the court could look to the following:

a) history of employer's practices;
b) evidence of other employees' experiences;

c) employer's opportunity to appraise employees unfairly;
d) statistical evidence of a pattern or practice
   (statistics were not determinative, however)

Finally, in *Texas Department of Community Affairs v. Burdine*, 450 U.S. 248 (1981), the Court once more pulled together the wandering appellate courts regarding the burdens of the plaintiff and respondent (at 256):

> In summary, once a claimant establishes a prima facie case, a presumption arises that the employer unlawfully discriminated against the employee. The burden that shifts to the defendant is the burden to rebut that presumption. The way in which the defendant can do this is to present admissible evidence of the reasons for the action taken against the plaintiff. If the defendant succeeds in carrying this burden of production, the presumption raised by the prima facie case is dissolved. The inquiry then turns to whether the plaintiff can show that the stated reason for the employment decision was not the true reason. In this sense, the plaintiff's "burden (then) merges with the ultimate burden of persuading the court that she has been the victim of intentional discrimination."

The reason for the employer's action against the plaintiff must be that the plaintiff was a member of the protected class, and "but for" his class status (race, religion, sex, age . . .), the action would not have been taken. This is the "causation" test which the Supreme Court set down for the edification of the rest of the judiciary, as well as employers in general.

The Disparate Impact Cases

As indicated, intent was a critical factor in proving up the Disparate Treatment claim. It was not as easy for defendant employers to counter the charges in cases where intent was not a material issue before the court.

In 1955, Duke Power Company was a steam generating facility located on the Dan River, in Draper, North Carolina. The plant was divided into five departments: (1) Labor, (2) Coal Handling, (3) Operations, (4) Maintenance and (5) Laboratory and Test. Blacks were employed only in the Labor Department; jobs in that department, even the highest paying ones, paid less than the lowest paying ones in any of the other departments.

The company, in 1955, began a policy of requiring a high school education for initial assignment to any department other than labor. In 1965, the company abandoned its policy of restricting blacks to the Labor Department, but at the same time required a high school diploma for transference to any department from Labor. The white employees, hired prior to the high school diploma policy, continued to perform satisfactorily in the other departments, and secured promotions. The employer did not dispute any of the above facts.

On July 2, 1965, the Company added the requirement of passing two professionally prepared aptitude tests in addition to the high school diploma; in September, the company dropped the high school requirement for incumbent employees, but they had to pass two tests successfully: the Wonderlic Personnel Test (a general intelligence test) and the Bennett Mechanical Comprehension Test. The scores required for passing were the national median for high school graduates.

The District Court found that although there had been racial discrimination prior to the passage of the (Civil Rights) Act, Title VII was prospective in its application. On appeal, the Court was concerned with the intent of the company, and since it found no intent to discriminate by using a high school diploma and the test requirements, there was no violation of the Act.

The plaintiff appealed to the Court of last resort.

GRIGGS v DUKE POWER CO.
United States Supreme Court (1971)
401 US 424

BURGER, Chief Justice.

* * *

The objective of Congress in the enactment of Title VII is plain from the language of the statute. It was to achieve equality of employment opportunities and remove barriers that have operated in the past to favor an identifiable group of white employees over other employees. Under the Act, practices, procedures or tests neutral on their face, and even neutral in terms of intent, cannot be maintained if they operate to "freeze" the status quo of prior discriminatory employment practices.

The Court of Appeals' opinion, and the partial dissent, agreed that, on the record in the present case, "whites register far better on the company's alternative requirements" than Negroes. 420 F2d 1225, 1239 n. 6. This consequence would appear to be directly traceable to race. Basic intelligence must have the means of articulation to manifest itself fairly in a testing process. Because they are Negroes, petitioners have long received inferior education in segregated schools and this Court expressly recognized these differences in Gaston County v United States, 395 US 285, 23 LEd2d 309, 89 SCt 1270, (1969). There, because of the inferior education received by Negroes in North Carolina, this Court barred the institution of a literacy test for voter registration on the ground that the test would abridge the right to vote indirectly on account of race. Congress did not intend by Title VII, however, to guarantee a job to every person, regardless of qualifications. In short, the Act does not command that any person be hired simply because he was formerly the subject of discrimination, or because he is a member of a minority group. Discriminatory preference for any group, minority or majority, is precisely and only what Congress has proscribed. What is required by Congress is the removal of artificial, arbitrary, and unnecessary barriers to employment when the barriers operate invidiously to discriminate on the basis of racial or other impermissible classification.

 * * * The Act proscribes not only overt discrimination but also practices that are fair in form, but discriminatory in operation. The touchstone is business necessity. If an employment practice which operates to exclude Negroes cannot be shown to be related to job performance, the practice is prohibited.

 On the record before us, neither the high school completion requirement nor the general intelligence test is shown to bear a demonstrable relationship to successful performance of the jobs for which it was used. Both were adopted, as the Court of Appeals noted, without meaningful study of their relationship to job-performance ability. Rather, a vice-president of the company testified, the requirements were instituted on the Company's judgment that they generally would improve the overall quality of the work force.

 The evidence, however, shows that employees who have not completed high school or taken the tests have continued to perform satisfactorily and make progress in departments for which the high school and test criteria are now used. * * *

 The Court of Appeals held that the Company had adopted the diploma and test requirements without any "intention to discriminate against Negro employees." 420 F2d at 1232. We do not suggest that either the District Court or the Court of Appeals erred in examining the employer's intent; but good intent or the absence of discriminatory intent does not redeem employment procedures or testing mechanisms that operate as "built-in headwinds" for minority groups and are unrelated to measuring job capability * * *

The Company contends that its general intelligence tests are specifically permitted by §703(h) of the Act. That section authorizes the use of "any professionally developed ability test" that is not "designed, intended *or used* to discriminate because of race . . . ." (Emphasis added)

The Equal Employment Opportunity Commission, having enforcement responsibility, has issued guidelines interpreting §703(h) to permit only the use of job-related tests. The administrative interpretation of the Act by the enforcing agency is entitled to great deference. (Cit.Om.) * * *

From the sum of the legislative history relevant in this case, the conclusion is inescapable that the EEOC's construction of §703 (h) to require that employment tests be job related comports with congressional intent.

Nothing in the Act precludes the use of testing or measuring procedures; obviously they are useful. What Congress has forbidden is giving these devices and mechanisms controlling force unless they are demonstrably a reasonable measure of job performance. Congress has not commanded that the less qualified be preferred over the better qualified simply because of minority origins. Far from disparaging job qualifications as such, Congress has made such qualifications the controlling factor, so that race, religion, nationality and sex become irrelevant. What Congress has commanded is that any tests used must measure the person for the job and not the person in the abstract.

The judgment of the Court of Appeals is, as to that portion of the judgment appealed from, reversed.

The Proof of Disparate Impact: Statistics

The Court had set forth the alternative theory of disparate impact in the *Griggs* decision, and what developed in the courts' struggle to balance rights of individuals, was the continued examination of the relatedness of the procedure or qualifying test to the job being sought.

Statistics were evidence used by the plaintiff alleging racial discrimination; job-relatedness was the defense used by the responding employer to attempt to justify its selection procedures. In New York, at the beginning of the 70's, their Civil Service Commission employed screening standards which included a minimum height requirement, absence of any criminal convictions, and the passing of a written examination.

The District Court had held that there was evidence of a racially disproportionate impact, and the finding was upheld by the Appellate Court. Neither the plaintiffs nor the respondents, nor a group that had intervened as a friend of the court were pleased with the decisions of the lower courts, which had included hiring on a quota system of 3:1 until the testing procedures were reconciled.

Select the *best* answer from the following:

99. The New York State Legislature recently passed a welfare requirement that has been challenged in the courts. This requirement provides that

   (a) people who seek welfare must be residents of the State for a year.
   (b) everyone on welfare must take a job.
   (c) drug addicts must give up their habit before they can receive any money.
   (d) people who receive money must agree to vote in state elections.

VULCAN SOCIETY OF the NEW YORK CITY FIRE DEPARTMENT
v
CIVIL SERVICE COMMISSION OF the CITY OF NEW YORK

Nicholas M. Cianciotto et al, Intervenors
U.S. Court of Appeals, 2d Cir. (1973)
490 F2d 387

* * * The municipal defendants do not here challenge the findings of racially disproportionate impact, but the intervenors do. The basic facts are these: Roughly 11.5 percent of the 14,168 applicants who entered the examination halls were black or Hispanic. Yet minority members comprised only 5.6 percent of those who had passed the written, physical and medical examinations at the time of the hearing. Nonminority candidates thus survived the screening process at a rate of more than twice that of minority candidates. Perhaps even more important, 18.4 percent of the whites who took the examination ranked in the top 4,000 and survived the physical while the comparable figure for minority candidates was 6.6 percent, a disparity of 2.8 to 1.

* * * The intervenors also criticize the plaintiff's comparison of the number of minority candidates who took the written examination with the number who finally qualified for appointment as a means of proving the racially disproportionate impact of the written test. The comparison was invalid, they claim, because minority members might have been disproportionately eliminated by either the physical or medical examinations, rather than by the written test. In theory this is true, and since there is no claim that the physical and medical examinations were biased, such a result would vitiate the plaintiffs' constitutional claim. But plaintiffs' statistical expert produced an analysis showing that on the hypothesis that the written examination did not discriminate against minority applicants, the nonminority candidates must have passed the physical and medical examinations at a rate almost three times that of the minority candidates, a result he properly regarded as extremely unlikely.

The intervenors point to several other factors which they claim may undercut the validity of plaintiffs' statistics, but none of them casts serious doubt on the court's finding. They contend first that a substantial number of minority candidates may have done well on the written examination but had been prevented from becoming "finally qualified" by the diploma or height requirement or criminal conviction bar. Yet since the factors requiring automatic disqualification were publicized prior to the administration of the examination, it seems unlikely that a substantial number of candidates took the written test in the face of certain rejection. Second, the intervenors point to the large number of candidates who passed the written test but did not appear for their physical or medical examinations; however, there is no reason to suppose that minority candidates were significantly overrepresented among the "no-shows." Finally, the intervenors claim that the "character review" procedure may have been responsible for eliminating a large number of minority candidates. This claim is frivolous, as it appears that only four candidates had been eliminated by the character review screening process at the time of the hearing.

It may well be that the cited figures and other peripheral data relied on by the district judge did not prove a racially proportionate impact with complete mathematical certainty. But there is no requirement that they should. "Certainty generally is an illusion, and repose is not the destiny of man." (Holmes, *The Path of the Law*, 10 Harv. L. Rev. 457, 461 (1897). We must not forget the limited office of the finding that black and Hispanic candidates did significantly worse in the examination than others. That does not at all decide the case; it simply places on the defendants a burden of justification which they should not be unwilling to assume.

* * * We shall first consider the written examination. No one challenges Judge Weinfield's conclusion that questions 81-100 entitled "City Government and Current Events" were not job-related. Taking this as a given, appellants advance two major contentions: One is that the judge found nothing else wrong with the written examination, with the consequence that if he erred in insisting on a competitive physical, the only relief required would be to regrade the examination

on the basis of the first 80 questions. The alternative is that if he found more to be wrong, he was in error. We reject both.

Although the judge placed particular emphasis on the unrelatedness of the civic affairs questions, this was not the limit of his criticism of the written examination. He sustained plaintiffs' contention that the defendants failed to perform an adequate job analysis in preparing the examination (footnote omitted) and said that "The record compels the conclusion that the procedures employed by defendants to construct Exam 0159 did not measure up to professionally accepted standards concerning content validity." He added that "Even if the defendants were not required to conform precisely to all the requirements of a professional job analysis, it is clear that the methods actually employed were below those found unsatisfactory in *Chance* . . ." Turning to defendants' contention that a faulty method of developing the examination should not be fatal if the result is satisfactory, he said that "Even if this contention is accepted, under these circumstances only the most convincing testimony as to job-relatedness could succeed in discharging their (defendants') burden," but that "The testimony of defendants' expert . . . not only failed to meet this burden, but even acknowledged the presence of a major flaw in the examination which is in itself fatal." The "major flaw" that the court pointed to was the inclusion of twenty civics questions, but we do not think that the mention of this serious defect indicated that, in the judge's view, the resitting of the examination was without substantial flaws . . .

The defendants and the intervenors ask us to set aside Judge Weinfield's finding that Exam 0159 was insufficiently job-related because of the lack of a competitive, as distinguished from a merely qualifying, physical examination. We decline to do so.

We can speedily reject the first ground of attack, namely, the absence of evidence that the minority candidates would do better than whites on a competitive physical examination. This misinterprets Judge Weinfield's opinion. He did not hold that the use of a merely qualifying physical in itself necessarily or even probably worked against the minorities; what he held was that the absence of a competitive physical in the selection process of a largely physical vocation was additional evidence of the lack of job-relatedness of the selection procedure considered as a whole. * * *

We stress the limited nature of our holding. We do not read Judge Weinfield as having said that if a written examination were sufficiently job-related, a competitive physical would *always* be constitutionally required, although he obviously would view such a physical with favor. There are considerations of cost and convenience that militate against giving a competitive physical to an extremely large group, including some who will rank so low on a proper written examination that even an Olympic score on a competitive physical would not put them within hiring range. Plaintiffs say these difficulties can be readily overcome, but they do not tell us how. In any event, there is no need to decide the question at this time. All that we regard the Judge as having held, and all that we now approve, is that, in combination with the defects in preparation and content of Exam 0159 which we have described, the use of a merely qualifying physical examination rendered the Fire Department's selection procedures insufficiently job-related to withstand constitutional attack.

All parties objected to the interim relief directed by the trial judge. * * * . . . (W)e approach the use of a quota system "somewhat gingerly" and approve this course only because no other method was available for affording appropriate relief without impairing essential city services. As to the ratio chosen, the intervenors argue that the appropriate ratio should be seven majority candidates to one minority candidate, and the plaintiffs contend that the ratio should be 1:1.

The argument for the 7:1 ratio is that the ratio of whites to minority members who took the examination was 8:1 and that only a slight adjustment in that figure is needed to take account of improper disparities in appointments already made. Arguing against this and in support of a 1:1 ratio, plaintiffs argue that the nature of Exam 0159 and its predecessors had discouraged minority members from taking the examination; that although there was no specific evidence as to the discriminatory effect of previous examinations, on which Exam 0159 was patterned in considerable measure, this could be gleaned, sufficiently for the purpose of framing relief, from the fact that only 5 percent of the New York City Fire Department consisted of minority members as against a 32 percent city-wide minority population in the eligible age group; and that at most the district court's 3:1 ratio up to June 30, 1974 would bring the percentage of minority firemen up to only 6.7 percent.

The judgment is affirmed . . .

Affirmative Action: Quotas, Goals and Preferences

Following the passage of the Civil Rights Act of 1964, the Judiciary was fully occupied with structuring the appropriate relief when it found evidence of past discrimination. Often hiring or promotional quotas were established by the court with the 'forced agreement' of the parties, with these consent decrees operating to move the parties ahead toward resolution of the conflict. Timetables were often utilized with goals to be attained by projected targeted 'deadlines.'

The courts, and The Court itself, found themselves divided over the determination of what was permissible and impermissible discrimination, and what the intent of the Title VII was, and how far any order of the court could go in achieving discrimination-free workplaces.

Courts of Appeals in some circuits aligned themselves with the more conservative decisions, dicta and reasoning of the Supreme Court; others with the more liberal interpretations.

When the Supreme Court held that an affirmative action program which set aside a number of positions for minority students in the entering class of medical school students was violative of the Constitution, many felt that the death knell for affirmative action had sounded

The court had held that where there was no other reason for the denial of the plaintiff's admission than the color of his skin, and such was not permitted even under the cloak of affirmative action. He had scored higher than any of the minority students in the qualifying entrance examination, but had been denied entrance to the University of California's Medical School.

Justice Powell expressed the concern of just how far The Court could extend its judicial protection of any group:

> The concepts of "majority" and "minority" necessarily reflect temporary arrangements and political judgments . . . . (T)he white majority itself is composed of various minority groups, most of which can lay claim to a history of prior discrimination at the hands of the state and private individuals . . . . There is no principled basis for deciding which groups would merit "heightened judicial solicitude" and which would not . . . Those whose societal injury is thought to exceed some arbitrary level of tolerability would be entitled to preferential classifications at the expense of . . . other groups. Those classifications would be free from judicial scrutiny. As these preferences began to have their desired effect, and the consequences of past discrimination were undone, new judicial rankings would be necessary. The kind of variable sociological and political analysis necessary to produce such rankings simply does not lie within the judicial competence-even if they otherwise were politically feasible and socially desirable. *University of California Regents v. Bakke*, 438 US 265, 296-297 (1978).

The reason that *Bakke* was not as significant as one might expect was probably twofold. First, the case was moot, since Baake had enrolled in medical school in Mexico, and had finished his basic curriculum by the time the court had decided that he had improperly been denied entrance to the school of his choice; second, the Court clearly let it be known that there might have been other reasons which the Board of Regents could have set forth in developing an affirmative action program that would have passed constitutional muster.

Any lingering doubts about the effectiveness and the legality of race-conscious plans in increasing minority representation were resolved by the Court in a case that seemed to most identical with the *Bakke* decision.

Brian Weber had applied for a training program with Kaiser Aluminum and Chemical Company, which had been developed with the United Steelworkers of America to provide a competent craft workforce from which the employer could hire as vacancies arose.

Brian was rejected because the training program, which had been established as part of a collective bargaining agreement with the Steelworkers, mandated that at least 50 percent of the applicants would be black, and he had not been in the half of trainees that were white.

Weber then sued the union, arguing that the arrangement was violative of Title VII by allowing racial discrimination in employment, and the District Court as well as the Court of Appeals agreed. Both Kaiser and the Union appealed to the United States Supreme Court.

UNITED STEELWORKERS of AMERICA v. WEBER
United States Supreme Court (1979)
443 US 193

BRENNAN, Justice.

Weber argues that Congress intended Title VII to prohibit all race conscious affirmative action plans. His argument rests on a literal interpretation of sections 703(a) and (d) of the Act. Those sections make it unlawful to "discriminate . . . because of . . . race" in hiring and in the selection of apprentices for training programs. Since, the argument runs, Title VII forbids discrimination against whites as well as blacks, and since the plan operates to discriminate against white employees solely because they are white, the plan violates Title VII.

Weber's argument is not without force. But it overlooks the fact that the Kaiser-USWA is voluntarily adopted by private parties to eliminate the traditional patterns of racial segregation. In this context, Weber's reliance on a literal construction of section 703(a) and (d) is misplaced. It is a familiar rule that a thing may be within the letter of the statute and yet not within the statute, because not within its spirit, nor within the intention of its makers. The prohibition against racial discrimination in Title VII must therefore be read against the background of the legislative history of Title VII and the historical context from which the Act arose. Examination of those sources makes clear that an interpretation of the sections that forbade all race-conscious affirmative action would bring about an end completely at variance with the purpose of the statute and must be rejected.

Congress' primary concern in enacting the prohibition against racial discrimination in Title VII was the plight of the Negro in our economy. Before 1964, blacks were largely relegated to unskilled and semi-skilled jobs. Because of automation, the number of such jobs was rapidly decreasing. As a consequence, the relative position of the Negro was steadily worsening. Congress feared that the goals of the Civil Rights Act-the integration of blacks into American society-could not be achieved unless this trend were reversed. Accordingly, it was clear to Congress that the crux of the problem was to open employment opportunities for Negroes in occupations traditionally closed to them. It was to this problem that Title VII's prohibition against racial discrimination in employment was primarily addressed.

We need not define in detail the line between permissible and impermissible affirmative action plans. It suffices to hold that the Kaiser-USWA plan falls on the permissible side of the line. The purposes of the plan mirror those of the statute. Both were designed to break down old patterns of racial segregation and hierarchy. The plan does not unnecessarily trammel the interests of the white employees (or) require the discharge of white workers and their replacement with new black hires. Nor does the plan create an absolute bar to the advancement of white employees; half of those trained in the program will be white. Moreover, the plan is a temporary measure; it is not intended to maintain racial balance, but simply to eliminate a manifest racial imbalance. Preferential selection of craft trainees will end as soon as the percentage of black skilled workers approximates the percentage of blacks in the local labor force.

Reversed.

Within a year of the *Weber* decision, Chicago Firefighters had struck against the city to obtain a written contract. After twenty-three bitter days, Local 2, IAFF, had its first written contract, and in it, and in every contract thereafter was Appendix G, and its specific provisions:

2. Hiring and Recruitment
   a. Goals

   The parties agree that hiring and recruitment programs of the Fire Department shall have as a goal to achieve in the shortest possible time a total force in which approximately thirty per cent shall be Black and fifteen per cent Hispanic. To this end, the hiring and recruitment programs should aim to assure that at least 45 % of all recruits added to the force hereafter shall consist of Blacks and Hispanics. Within 90 days of the effective date of this agreement, the city will publish the initial steps it plans to take to remove all racial inequalities in the Chicago Fire Department.

3. Transfers and Promotions
   a. Goal

   The parties agree that the transfer and promotional policies of the Fire Department shall have, as a goal, the inclusion of Black and Hispanic personnel in all categories and in all ranks in order to reach as quickly as is reasonably possible a level as close to 45 % as is reasonable (sic) achievable.

The written goals of Appendix D, as part of the Labor Contract that ended the firefighters' strike of 1980, did not end the dispute over conflicting rights between white, black and Hispanic members. Hiring goals were fairly consistent in their apportionment by race, but each promotional test, and list that followed, were met with legal challenges. The earliest were resolved by a consent decree (an agreement between the parties that was sanctioned by order of the federal court) that set a ratio of 4:1 for promotions to Engineer and Lieutenant.

Chicago was by no means unique in either the problems of affirmative action implementation, or the proposed resolutions or the litigation that challenged those resolutions.

Nor did the Supreme Court itself remain static.

Carl Stotts had brought a Title VII action against the Memphis Fire Department, alleging racial discrimination. In 1980, the parties entered into a consent decree that provided for hiring quotas of black applicants at 50 % and promotions for Blacks at 20 % for a specified time. The 1981 budget called for layoffs of firefighters, and the *bona fide* seniority system in their contract required "last hired, first fired" in its implementation. (A *bona fide* seniority system was one which was not designed to effect racial discrimination).

Stotts returned to court to secure an injunction against the use of the seniority system, which would negate the gains made under the consent decree. The district court granted the injunction that had the effect of laying off white firefighters with more seniority, and the appellate court affirmed the district court. The union appealed to the U.S. Supreme Court.

FIREFIGHTERS LOCAL UNION NO. 1784 v STOTTS
United States Supreme Court (1984)
467 U.S. 561

WHITE, Justice.

Section 703(h) of Title VII provides that it is not an unlawful employment practice to apply different terms, conditions or privileges of employment pursuant to a bona fide seniority system, provided that such differences are not the result of an intention to discriminate because of race. It is clear that the city had a seniority system, that its proposed layoff plan conformed to that system, and that in making the settlement the city had not agreed to award competitive seniority to any minority member whom the city later proposed to lay off. The District Court held that the city could not follow its seniority system in making its proposed layoffs because its proposal was discriminatory in effect. Section 703(h) permits the routine application of a seniority system absent proof of an intention to discriminate. Here, the layoff proposal was not adopted with the purpose or intent to discriminate on the basis of race

(The injunction to implement the consent decree) overstates the authority of the trial court to disregard a seniority system in fashioning a remedy after an employer has followed a pattern or practice having a discriminatory effect on black applicants or employees. If individual members of a plaintiff class demonstrate that they have been actual victims of the discriminatory practice, they may be given their rightful place on the seniority roster. However, mere membership in the disadvantaged class is insufficient to warrant a seniority award; each individual must prove that the discriminatory practice had an impact on him. Here, there was no finding that any of the blacks protected from layoff had been a victim of discrimination and no award of any competitive seniority to any of them.

Reversed.

The Court also quoted the staunchest proponent of the Civil Rights Act, Senator Hubert Humphrey, from the Senate debate on the Act:

> ". . . There is nothing in (the Act) that will give any power to any court to require firing of employees in order to meet a racial quota or to achieve a certain racial balance."

The Vanguards was an association of black and Hispanic firefighters who had filed Title VII suits against the city for discrimination in promotions, and after lengthy litigation, in which Local 93, the firefighters' union had intervened. The final consent decree required that the city promote in the following numbers and ranks: 66 lieutenants, 32 captains, 16 battalion chiefs and 4 assistant chiefs, with the 66 lieutenants divided equally between minority and non-minority firemen. Only 10 minorities had qualified for the upper-level positions, and the decree included the immediate promotion of all 10, and goals based upon percentage promotions during the two-year life of the decree. The District Court approved the decree over the objections of the intervors (Union), with the observation "It is neither unreasonable nor unfair to require non-minority firefighters who, although they committed no wrong, benefited from the effects of the discrimination to bear some of the burden of the remedy." (Cit.Om.) The appellate court affirmed on the basis that it was not an unreasonable plan and did not cause promotion of unqualified minorities or the discharge of any non-minority firefighters, or any absolute bar to non-minority advancement. Local 93 then appealed to the Supreme Court, which granted certiorari regarding the issue of the power of the court with regard to § 706(g) of Title VII:

> "*(n)o order of the court shall require* the admission or reinstatement of an individual as a member of a union, or *the hiring, reinstatement, or promotion of an individual as an employee,* or the payment to him of any back pay, *if such individual* was refused admission, suspended, or expelled, or *was refused employment or advancement* or was suspended or discharged *for any reason other than discrimination on account of race,* color, religion, sex, or national origin or in violation of section 2000e-3(a) of this title." 42 U.S.C. § 2000e-5(g) (emphasis added).

LOCAL # 93, I.A.F.F. v CITY OF CLEVELAND
United States Supreme Court (1986)
478 U.S. 501

BRENNAN, Justice

The question presented in this case is whether § 706(g) of Title VII of the Civil Rights Act of 1964, 78 Stat. 261, as amended, 42 U.S.C. § 2000e-5(g), precludes the entry of a consent decree which provides relief that may benefit individuals who were not the actual victims of the defendant's discriminatory practices.

* * * (v)oluntary action available to employers and unions seeking to eradicate race discrimination may include reasonable race-conscious relief that benefits individuals who were not actual victims of discrimination. This was the holding of *Steelworkers v Weber*, 443 U.S. 193 (1979). * * * Of course, *Weber* involved a purely private contractual agreement rather than a consent decree. But, at least at first blush, there does not seem to be any reason to distinguish between voluntary action taken in a consent decree and voluntary action taken entirely outside the context of litigation.

* * * Local 93 and the United States . . . contend that § 706(g) establishes an independent limitation on what *courts*-as opposed to employers or unions-can do, prohibiting any "order of the court" from providing relief that may benefit non-victims. They argue that a consent decree should be treated as an "order" within the meaning of § 706(g) because it possesses the legal force an character of a judgment decreed after a trial. They rely for this conclusion on several characteristics of consent decrees: first, that a consent decree looks like and is entered as a judgment; second, that the court retains the power to modify a consent decree in certain circumstances over the objection of a signatory (Cit. Om.); third, that noncompliance with a consent decree is enforceable by citation for contempt of court (Cit.Om.) * * *

Because this Court's cases do not treat consent decrees as judicial decrees in all respects and for all purposes, we think that the language of § 706(g) does not so clearly include consent decrees as to preclude resort to the voluminous legislative history of Title VII . . . . In addition to the fact that consent decrees have contractual as well as judicial features, the use of the verb "require" in § 706(g) suggests that it was the coercive aspect of a judicial decree that Congress had in mind. * * * Indeed, it is the parties' agreement that serves as the source of the court's authority to enter any judgment at all. * * * But the difference between contractual remedies and the contempt power is not significant in any relevant sense with respect to § 706(g). For the choice of an enforcement scheme-whether to rely on contractual remedies or to have an agreement entered as a consent decree-is itself made voluntarily by the parties. * * *

Local 93 and the United States also challenge the validity of the consent decree on the ground that it was entered without the consent of the Union. They take the position that because the Union was permitted to intervene as of right, its consent was required before the court could approve a consent decree. This argument misconceives the Union's rights in the litigation.

A consent decree is primarily a means by which parties settle their disputes without having to bear the financial and other costs of litigating. It has never been supposed that one party-whether an original party, a party that was joined later, or an intervenor-could preclude other parties from settling their own disputes and thereby withdrawing from litigation. * * * Accordingly, "the District Court gave the union all the process that it was due . . .". (Cit.Om.) * * * (T)he consent decree entered here does not bind Local 93 to do or not to do anything. It imposes no legal duties or obligations on the Union at all; only the parties to the decree can be held in contempt of court for failure to comply with its terms. * * * Indeed, despite the efforts of the District Judge to persuade it to do so, the Union failed to raise any substantial claims. Whether it is now too late to raise such claims, or-if not-whether the Union's claims have any merit must be presented in the first instance to the District Court, which has retained jurisdiction to hear such challenges. The only issue before us is whether § 706(g) barred the District Court from approving this consent decree. We hold that it did not. Therefore, the judgment of the Court of Appeals is affirmed.

The Civil Rights Act of 1991

Section 104. Prohibition Against Discriminatory Use of Test Scores

Section 703 of the Civil Rights Act of 1964 (42 U.S.C. 2000e-2) (as amended by Section 105) is further amended by adding at the end the following new subsection:

"(1) It shall be an unlawful employment practice for a respondent, in connection with the selection or referral of applicants or candidates for employment or promotion, to adjust the scores of, use different cutoff scores for, or otherwise alter the results of, employment related tests on the basis of race, color, religion, sex, or national origin."

Sexual Harassment

29 CFR Chapter XIV
Part 1604-GUIDELINES ON DISCRIMINATION BECAUSE OF SEX
1604.11 Sexual Harassment.

(1) Harassment on the basis of sex is a violation of Sec. 703 of Title VII. Unwelcome sexual advances, requests for sexual favors, and other verbal or physical conduct of a sexual nature constitutes sexual harassment when:

   (a) submission to such conduct is made either explicitly or implicitly a term or condition of an individual's employment;
   (b) submission to or rejection of such conduct by an individual is used as the basis for employment decisions affecting such individual; or
   (c) such conduct has the purpose or effect of unreasonably interfering with an individual's work performance or creating an intimidating, hostile or offensive working environment.

Ten years after the passage of the Civil Rights Act, Mechelle Vinson met Sidney Taylor; she was looking for work and Taylor was the manager of a branch office of Meritor Savings Bank. He gave her an application, which she returned the next day, and he later called to inform her that she had been hired.

She moved up her career ladder from teller-trainee, to teller, head teller, and finally assistant branch manager within four years. In September of 1978, she informed the bank that she was taking an indefinite sick leave, and the bank discharged her for excessive use of that sick leave in November.

She thereupon filed an action against the bank on the basis that she had been subjected to sexual harassment by Taylor for the four years she had been employed there; that following her probationary period (during which he acted as a "father figure", and had even lent her money to get an apartment), they had gone to dinner, and when Taylor suggested that they go to a motel afterward, she had at first refused, but then consented. Taylor made repeated demands for sexual favors thereafter, both on and off duty; she estimated that they had sexual intercourse over the following few years 40 or 50 times; also that he had fondled her in front of other employees, exposed himself to her, and even raped her on several occasions. These activities ended in 1977, when she started going with a steady boyfriend.

Taylor denied all the allegations, stating that she made the allegations after they had had a business dispute. Vinson stated that she had never used the bank's complaint procedure nor did she report the conduct to any of his supervisors, out of fear.

Vinson was advised by the court that she could bring in corroborating witnesses to rebut the defendant, but did not do so at trial. The district court found that she had not been a victim of sexual harassment and that the bank itself could not be liable if it had no knowledge of the conduct.

The Court of Appeals found that the district court had erred in not finding sexual harassment of the "hostile environment" type, that Taylor's making her submission a condition of her employment made the her voluntariness immaterial, and that the bank would be absolutely liable for sexual harassment which was practiced by its supervisors, regardless of whether it had actual knowledge or not.

The Supreme Court affirmed, but for different reasons.

MERITOR SAVINGS BANK v VINSON
United States Supreme Court (1986)
106 S.Ct. 2399

JUSTICE Renquist

(II) * * * Respondent argues, and the Court of Appeals held, that unwelcome sexual advances that create an offensive or hostile working environment violate Title VII. Without question, when a supervisor sexually harasses a subordinate because of the subordinate's sex, that supervisor discriminate(s) on the basis of sex. Petitioner apparently does not challenge this proposition. It contends instead that in prohibiting discrimination with respect to "compensation, terms, conditions or privileges" of employment, Congress was concerned with what petitioner describes as "tangible loss" of "an economic character," not "purely psychological aspects of the workplace environment." Brief for Petitioner 30-31, 34. In support of this claim petitioner observes that in both the legislative history of Title VII and this Court's Title VII decisions, the focus has been on tangible, economic barriers erected by discrimination.

We reject petitioner's view. First, the language of Title VII is not limited to "economic" or "tangible" discrimination. The phrase "terms, conditions or privileges of employment" evinces a congressional intent "'to strike at the entire spectrum of disparate treatment of men and women'" in employment. (Cit.Om.) Petitioner has pointed to nothing in the Act to suggest that Congress contemplated the limitation urged here.

Second, in 1980 the EEOC issued guidelines specifying that "sexual harassment" as therein defined, is a form of sex discrimination prohibited by Title VII. As an "administrative interpretation of the Act by the enforcing agency," *Griggs v Duke Power Co.*, 401 U.S. 424, 433-434 (1971), these guidelines, "while not controlling upon the courts by reason of their authority, do constitute a body of evidence and informed judgment to which courts and litigants may properly resort for guidance.'" (Cit.Om.) The EEOC guidelines fully support the view that harassment leading to non-economic injury can violate Title VII. * * * Relevant to the charges at issue in this case, the guidelines provide that such sexual misconduct constitutes prohibited "sexual harassment" whether or not it is directly linked to the grant or denial of an economic *quid pro quo* where "such conduct has the purpose or effect of unreasonably interfering with an individual's work performance or creating an intimidating, hostile or offensive working environment." § 1604.11 (a) (3)

* * * Of course, . . . not all workplace conduct that may be described as "harassment" affects a "term, condition, or privilege" of employment within the meaning of Title VII. (Cit.Om.) ("'mere utterance of a racial or ethnic epithet which engenders offensive feelings in an employee" would not affect the conditions of employment to sufficiently significant degree to violate Title VII); (Cit.Om.) For sexual harassment to be actionable, it must be sufficiently severe or pervasive "to alter the conditions of (the victim's) employment and create an abusive working environment." (Cit.Om.) Respondent's allegations in this case-which include not only pervasive harassment but also criminal conduct of the most serious nature-are plainly sufficient to state a claim for "hostile environment" sexual harassment.

The question remains, however, whether the District Court's ultimate finding that respondent "was not the victim of sexual harassment," 22 EPD ¶30708, at 14692-14693, 23 FEP Cases, at 43, effectively disposed of respondent's claim. The Court of Appeals recognized, we think correctly, that this ultimate finding was likely based on one or both of two erroneous views of the law. First, The District Court apparently believed that a claim for sexual harassment will not lie absent an economic effect on the complainant's employment. See *Ibid.* ("It is without question that sexual harassment of female employees in which they are asked or required to submit to sexual demands as a *condition to obtain employment or to maintain employment or to obtain promotions* falls within protection of Title VII.") (emphasis added). Since it appears that the District Court made its findings without ever considering the "hostile environment" theory of sexual harassment, the Court of Appeals decision to remand was correct.

Second, the District Court's conclusion that no actionable harassment occurred might have rested on its earlier "finding" that "(i)f (respondent) and Taylor did engage in an intimate or sexual relationship . . . , that relationship was a voluntary one." *Id.*, at 14692, 23 FEP cases, at 42. But the fact that sex-related conduct was "voluntary," in the sense that the complainant was not forced to participate against her will, is not a defense to a sexual harassment suit brought under Title VII. The gravamen of any sexual harassment claim is that the alleged sexual advances were "unwelcome." 29 CFR § 1604.11(a) (1985). While the question whether particular sexual conduct was indeed unwelcome presents difficult problems of proof and turns largely on creditabilty determinations committed to the trier of fact, the District Court in this case erroneously focused on the "voluntariness" of respondent's participation in the claimed sexual episodes. The correct inquiry is whether respondent by her conduct indicated that the alleged sexual advances were unwelcome, not whether her actual participation in sexual intercourse was voluntary. * * * While "voluntariness" in the sense of consent is not a defense to such a claim, it does not follow that a complainant's sexually provocative speech or dress is irrelevant as a matter of law in determining whether he or she found such sexual advances unwelcome. To the contrary, such evidence is obviously relevant. The EEOC guidelines emphasize that the trier of fact must determine the existence of sexual harassment in the light of "the record as a whole" and "the totality of circumstances, such as the nature of the sexual advances and the context in which the alleged incidents occurred." 29 CFR §1604.11(b) (1985). * * * While the District Court must carefully weigh the applicable considerations in deciding whether to admit evidence of this kind, there is no *per se* rule against its admissibility.

*   *   *

Although the District Court concluded that respondent had not proved a violation of Title VII, it nevertheless went on to consider the question of the bank's liability. Finding that "the bank was without notice" of Taylor's alleged conduct, and that notice to Taylor was not the equivalent of notice to the bank, the court concluded that the bank therefore could not be held liable for Taylor's alleged actions. The Court of Appeals took the opposite view, holding that an employer is strictly liable for a hostile environment created by a supervisor's sexual advances, even though the employer neither knew nor could have reasonably known of the alleged misconduct. The court held that a supervisor, whether or not he posesses the authority to hire, fire or promote, is necessarily an "agent" of his employer for all Title VII purposes, since "even the appearance" of such authority may enable him to impose himself on his subordinates.

* * * This debate over the appropriate standard for the employer liability has a rather abstract quality about it given the state of the record in this case. We do not know at this stage whether Taylor made any sexual advances toward respondent at all, let alone whether those advances were unwelcome, whether they were sufficiently pervasive to constitute a condition of employment, or whether they were "so pervasive and long continuing . . . that the employer must have become conscious of (them.)" (Cit.Om.)

We therefore decline the parties' invitation to issue a definitive rule on employer liability, but we do agree with the EEOC that Congress wanted courts to look at agency principles for guidance in this area. While such common law principles may not be transferrable in all their particulars to Title VII, Congress' decision to define "employer" to include any "agent" of an employer, 42 U.S.C. §2000e(b), surely evinces an intent to place some limits on the acts of employees for which employers under Title VII are to be held responsible. For this reason, we hold that the Court of Appeals erred in concluding that employers are always automatically liable for sexual harassment by their supervisors. See generally, Restatement (Second) of Agency §§219-237 (1958). For the same reason, absence of notice to an employer does not necessarily insulate that employer from liability. *Ibid.* Finally, we reject petitioner's view that the mere existence of a grievance procedure and a policy against discrimination, coupled with respondent's failure to invoke that procedure, must insulate the petitioner from liability. While those facts are plainly relevant, the situation before us demonstrates why they are not necessarily dispositive. Petitioner's general nondiscrimination policy did not address sexual harassment in particular, and thus did not alert their employees to employer's interest in correcting that form of discrimination. App. 25. Moreover, the bank's grievance procedure apparently required an employee to complain first to her supervisor, in this case, Taylor. Since Taylor was the alleged perpetrator, it is not altogether surprising that respondent failed to invoke the procedure and report her grievance to him. Petitioner's contention that respondent's failure should insulate it from liability might be substantially stronger if its procedures were better calculated to encourage victims of harassment to come forward.

In sum, we hold that a claim of "hostile environment" sex discrimination is actionable under Title VII, that the District Court's findings were insufficient to dispose of respondent's hostile environment claim, and that the District Court did not err in admitting testimony about respondent's sexually provocative speech and dress. As to employer liability, we conclude that the Court of Appeals was wrong to entirely, disregard agency principles and to impose absolute liability on employers for the acts of their supervisors, regardless of the circumstances of a particular case.

Accordingly, the judgment of the Court of Appeals reversing the judgment of the District Court is affirmed, and the case is remanded for further proceedings consistent with this opinion.

It is so ordered.

Teresa Harris was employed as a manager for Forklift Systems, Inc., from April 1985 to October 1987. The president of Forklift, Charles Hardy, often insulted her by reason of the following:

1) told her, on several occasions, in front of other employees, "You're a woman, what do you know"; and "We need a man as the rental manager"
2) at least once told her she was "a dumb ass woman";
3) in front of others suggested they "go to the Holiday Inn to negotiate (her) raise";
4) in front of female employees asked Harris to get coins from his front pants pocket, and asked her to pick up objects that he threw on the floor; and
5) made sexual innuendos about Harris' and other women employee's clothing.

Harris complained to Hardy in August of 1987, and Hardy expressed surprise at her complaint and apologized, stating that he was only joking and promised to stop such conduct. But the next month, in front of other employees as she was making a deal with a customer, he asked her: "What did you do, promise the guy some (sex) Saturday night?"

She quit October 1, and sued Forklift.

The District Court for Tennessee held that the conduct had not created an abusive work environment, even though the conduct would have offended a reasonable woman. The Court of Appeals for the Sixth Circuit affirmed.

HARRIS v FORKLIFT SYSTEMS, INC.
126 L Ed 2d 295 (1993)

JUSTICE O'Connor.

We granted certiorari . . . to resolve a conflict among the Circuits on whether conduct, to be actionable as "abusive work environment" harassment (no *quid pro quo* harassment issue is present here), must "seriously affect (an employee's) psychological well-being" or lead the plaintiff to 'suffe(r) injury."

As we made clear in *Meritor Savings Bank v Vinson* (Cit. Om.), this language "is not limited to 'economic' or 'tangible' discrimination. The phrase 'terms, conditions or privileges of employment' evinces a congressional intent 'to strike at the entire spectrum of disparate treatment of men and women' in employment,' which includes requiring people to work in a discriminatorily hostile or abusive environment. (Cit.Om.)

When the workplace is permeated with "discriminatory intimidation, ridicule, and insult," that is "sufficiently severe or pervasive to alter the conditions of the victim's employment and create an abusive working environment," Title VII is violated. (Cit.Om.)

This standard, which we reaffirm today, takes a middle path between making actionable any conduct that is merely offensive and requiring the conduct to cause a tangible psychological injury. As we pointed out in *Meritor*, "mere utterance of an . . . epithet which engenders offensive feelings in an employee," does not sufficiently affect the conditions of employment to implicate Title VII. Conduct that is not severe or pervasive enough to create an objectively hostile or abusive work environment-an environment that a reasonable person would find hostile or abusive-is beyond Title VII's purview. Likewise, if the victim does not subjectively perceive the environment to be abusive, the conduct has not actually altered the conditions of the victim's employment and there is no Title VII violation.

But Title VII comes into play before the harassing conduct leads to a nervous breakdown. A discriminatorily abusive work environment, even one that does not seriously affect employees' psychological well-being, can and often will detract from employees' job performance, discourage employees from remaining on the job, or keep them from advancing in their careers. Moreover, even without regard to these tangible effects, the very fact that the discriminatory conduct was so severe or pervasive that it created a work environment abusive to employees because of their race, gender, religion, or national origin offends Title VII's broad rule of workplace equality. The appalling conduct in *Meritor*, and the reference in that case to environments "'so heavily polluted with discrimination as to destroy completely the emotional and psychological stability of minority group workers,'" merely present some egregious examples of harassment. They do not mark the boundary of what is actionable. (Cit.Om.)

We therefore believe the District Court erred in relying on whether the conduct "seriously affect(ed) plaintiff's psychological well-being" or led her to "suffe(r) injury." Such an inquiry may needlessly focus the factfinder's attention on concrete psychological harm, an element Title VII does not require. Certainly Title VII bars conduct that would seriously affect a reasonable person's psychological well-being, but the statute is not limited to such conduct. So long as the environment would reasonably be perceived, and is perceived, as hostile or abusive, there is no need for it to be psychologically injurious.

This is not, and by its nature cannot be, a mathematically precise test. We need not answer today all the potential questions it raises, nor specifically address the EEOC's new regulations on this subject (Cit.Om.), (b)ut we can say that whether an environment is "hostile" or "abusive" can be determined only by looking at all the circumstances. These may include the frequency of the discriminatory conduct; its severity; whether it is physically threatening or humiliating, or a mere offensive utterance; and whether it unreasonably interferes with an employee's work performance. The effect on the employee's psychological well-being is, of course, relevant to determining whether the plaintiff actually found the environment abusive. But while psychological harm, like any other relevant factor, may be taken into account, no single factor is required.

Forklift, while conceding that a requirement that the conduct seriously affect psychological well-being is unfounded, argues that the District Court nonetheless correctly applied the *Meritor* standard. We disagree. Though the District Court did conclude that the work environment was not "intimidating or abusive to (Harris)," it did so only after finding that the conduct was not "so severe as to be expected to seriously affect plaintiff's psychological well-being," and that Harris was not "so subjectively offended that she suffered injury." (Cit.Om.) The District Court's application of these incorrect standards may well have influenced its ultimate conclusion, especially given that the Court found this to be a "close case."

We therefore reverse the judgment of the Court of Appeals, and remand this case for further proceedings consistent with this opinion.

So ordered.

Justice Scalia, concurring.

Today's opinion elaborates that the challenged conduct must be severe or pervasive enough "to create an objectively hostile or abusive work environment-an environment that a reasonable person would find hostile or abusive."

"Abusive" (or "hostile," which in this context I take to mean the same thing) does not to me seem a very clear standard-and I do not think clarity is at all increased by adding the adverb "objectively" or by appealing to a "reasonable person's" notion of what the vague word means. Today's opinion does list a number of factors that contribute to abusiveness, but since it neither says how much of each is necessary (an impossible task) nor identifies any single factor as determinative, it thereby adds little certitude. As a practical matter, today's holding lets virtually unguided juries decide whether sex-related conduct engaged in (or permitted by) an employer is egregious enough to warrant an award of damages. One might say that what constitutes "negligence" (a traditional jury question) is not much more clear than what constitutes "abusiveness." Perhaps so. But the class of plaintiffs seeking to recover for negligence is limited to those who have suffered harm, whereas under this statute, "abusiveness" is to be the test of whether legal harm has been suffered, opening more expansive vistas of litigation.

Be that as it may, I know of no alternative to the course that the Court today has taken. One of the factors in the Court's nonexhaustive list-whether the conduct unreasonably interferes with an employee's work performance-would, if it were made an absolute test, provide greater guidance to juries and employers. But I see no basis for such a limitation in the language of the statute. Accepting *Meritor's* interpretation of the term "conditions of employment" as the law, the test is not whether the work has been impaired, but whether working conditions have been discriminatorily altered. I know of no test more faithful to the inherently vague statutory language than the one the Court today adopts. For these reasons, I join the opinion of the Court.

In 1991, Joseph Oncale worked for Sundowner Offshore Services, Inc., as a roustabout on an oil platform in the Gulf of Mexico, and on numerous occasions, was forcibly subjected to sex-related humiliating actions by three of his co-workers workers in the presence of several of the other workers. Two of the eight man crew also physically assaulted Oncale in a sexual manner, and one threatened him with rape.

When he complained to his supervisors, there was no remedial action, and the Safety Compliance Clerk of the Company told Oncale that they "picked on him all the time too," even calling him a name that suggested that he was a homosexual.

When Oncale finally quit, he requested that his pink slip indicate that he "voluntarily left due to sexual harassment and physical abuse."

In his deposition thereafter, when asked why he left, he responded "I felt that if I didn't leave my job, I would be raped or forced to have sex."

The United States District Court for the Eastern District of Louisiana, held that "Mr. Oncale, a male, has no cause of action under Title VII for harassment by male co-workers." This was also affirmed upon appeal by the Fifth Circuit.

The Supreme Court granted certiorari.

ONCALE v. SUNDOWNER OFFSHORE SERVICES
118 S.Ct. 998 (1998)

JUSTICE Scalia.

Title VII's prohibition of discrimination "because of . . . sex" protects men as well as women, (Cit. Om.) and in the related context of racial discrimination in the workplace we have rejected any conclusive presumption that an employer will not discriminate against members of his own race. "Because of the many facets of human motivation, it would be unwise to presume as a matter of law that human beings of one definable group will not discriminate against other members of that group." (Cit. Om.) . . .

If our precedents leave any doubt on the question, we hold today that nothing in Title VII necessarily bars a claim of discrimination "because of . . . sex" merely because the plaintiff and the defendant (or the person charged with acting on behalf of the defendant) are of the same sex.

Courts have had little trouble with that principle . . . , where an employee claims to have been passed over for a job or promotion. But when the issue arises in the context of a "hostile environment" sexual harassment claim, the state and federal courts have taken a bewildering variety of stances. Some, like the Fifth Circuit in this case, have held that same-sex sexual harassment claims are never recognizable under Title VII. (Cit. Om.) Other decisions say that such claims are actionable only if the plaintiff can prove that the harasser is homosexual (and thus presumably motivated by sexual desire.) (Cit. Om.) Still others suggest that workplace harassment that is sexual in content is always actionable, regardless of the harasser's sex, sexual orientations, or motivations. (Cit. Om.)

We see no justification in the statutory language or our precedents for a categorical rule excluding same-sex harassment claims from the coverage of Title VII . . . . Title VII prohibits "discriminat(ion) . . . because of . . . sex" in the "terms" or "conditions" of employment. Our holding that this includes sexual harassment must extend to sexual harassment of any kind that meets the statutory requirements . . . . Courts and juries have found the inference of discrimination easy to draw in most male-female sexual harassment situations, because the challenged conduct typically involves explicit or implicit proposals of sexual activity; it is reasonable to assume those proposals would not have been made to someone of the same sex. The same chain of inference would be available to a plaintiff alleging same-sex harassment, if there were credible evidence that the harasser was homosexual. But harassing conduct need not be motivated by sexual desire to support an inference of discrimination on the basis of sex. A trier of fact might reasonably find such discrimination, for example, if a female victim is harassed in such sex-specific and derogatory terms by another woman to make it clear that the harasser is motivated by general hostility to the presence of women in the workplace.

. . . The prohibition of harassment on the basis of sex requires neither asexuality nor androgyny in the workplace; it forbids only behavior so objectively offensive as to alter the "conditions" of the victim's employment. "Conduct that is not severe or pervasive enough to create an objectively hostile or abusive work environment-an environment that a reasonable person would find hostile or abusive-is beyond Title VII's purview." (Cit. Om.) We have always regarded that requirement as crucial, and as sufficient to insure that courts and juries do not mistake ordinary socializing in the workplace-such as male-on-male horseplay or intersexual flirtation-for discriminatory "conditions of employment."

. . . In same-sex (as in all) harassment cases, that inquiry requires careful consideration of the social context in which particular behavior occurs and is experienced by its target. A professional football player's working environment is not severely or pervasively abusive, for example, if the coach smacks him on the buttocks as he heads onto the field-even if the same behavior would reasonably be experienced as abusive by the coach's secretary (male or female) back at the office. The real social impact of workplace behavior often depends on a constellation of surrounding circumstances, expectations, and relationships which are not fully captured by a simple recitation of the words used or the physical acts performed. Common sense, and an appropriate sensitivity to social context, will enable courts and juries to distinguish between simple teasing or roughhousing among members of the same sex, and conduct which a reasonable person in the plaintiff's position would find severely hostile or abusive.

Because we conclude that sex discrimination consisting of same-sex sexual harassment is actionable under Title VII, the judgment of the Court of Appeals for the Fifth Circuit is reversed, and the case is remanded for further proceedings consistent with this opinion.

It is so ordered.

Americans with Disabilities Act

Signed into law on July 26, 1990, The Americans With Disabilities Act (ADA) was passed as a comprehensive federal law designed to protect the over forty million Americans with disabilities from discrimination.

Its predecessor was The Rehabilitation Act of 1973, which forbid discrimination by the Federal Government, or by federal contractors receiving monies under federal contracts, from discriminating against handicapped persons, and was enforced by the Equal Employment Opportunity Commission (EEOC).

The ADA, as expanded Civil Rights legislation, strongly parallels the protections of the 1964 Civil Rights Act which prohibited discrimination based upon considerations of race, religion, and sex. Title I of the ADA, similar to Title VII, is concerned with discrimination in employment.

In 1992, the ADA applied to all employers and industries with 25 or more employees, and in 1994 was expanded to all employers with 15 or more employees.

In summary, the Act requires that reasonable accomodation be made by employers to qualified individuals with a disability to avoid committing discrimination.

Qualified Individual.

The person must be able to perform (with or without accomodation) the essential functions of the position. This means that such person can meet the requisite skills, experience and education that the employer has established for the position. It does NOT mean that the employer is required to train the unqualified disabled person.

Disabled.

A disability, under the Act, is defined as a physical or mental impairment that substantially limits one or more major life activities:

Physical Impairment: Includes physiological disorder, disfigurement, or anatomical loss;

Mental Impairment: Includes mental retardation, organic brain syndrome, emotional or mental illness, or specific learning disabilities;

Substantially limits: means that the person cannot perform an activity that an average person can perform;

Major Life Activity: Includes caring for oneself, performing manual tasks, walking, seeing, hearing, speaking, learning, working.

Disability also includes a person who has a record of such impairment or is regarded as having such impairment.

The EEOC issued a guidance memorandum in March of 1995 which requires that the determination of disability rests upon the consideration of three issues: 1) impairment, 2) major life activity and 3) substantial limitation; if any of the three are not present, then the individual is not afforded coverage under the ADA.

*Specifically **included** disabilities:*

> *Visual or hearing impairment*
> *Wheelchair restricted*
> *Lack of hand usage*
> *Loss of limb(s)*
> *Heart Disease*
> *Cancer*
> *Tuberculosis*
> *Diabetes*
> *Multiple Sclerosis*
> *Muscular Dystrophy*
> *Cerebral Palsy*
> *AIDS (HIV)*
> *Epilepsy*
> *Speech impediment*
> *Mental/Psychological Disorder/Impairment*
> *Mental Retardation*
> *Specific learning disabilities*
> *Alcoholism**

*Specifically **excluded** disabilities*

> *Temporary, non-chronic impairments:*
> > *broken bones, sprains, appendicitis, concussion, influenza*
> *Pnysical characteristics:*
> > *eye, hair color*
> > *left-handedness*

Predisposition to illness or disease
Obesity
Pregnancy
Kleptomania
Pyromania
Homosexuality, Bisexuality
Advanced age
Poor judgment, quick temper
Lack of education
Prison record
Compulsive gambling

Reasonable Accomodation

The employer is required, under the Act, to make reasonable accommodations to the individual unless it can be shown to cause an undue hardship. The purpose of the reasonable accommodation is to provide access to full and equal employment opportunities (and in other sections of the Act, services and facilities). Underlying the above issues is the question of defining the essential functions of the position and the employer will find the absence of well written job descriptions will make compliance difficult.

Age Discrimination in Employment Act (A.D.E.A.)

Originally, the Age Discrimination in Employment Act (ADEA) prohibited *private* employers from taking actions against employees based solely upon their age, and the range of ages which were protected by the Act was between 40 and 65, as amended. Later the range was extended to age 70, but the critical impact for fire service came when the Supreme Court, in a case involving a Forest Service employee who was mandatorily retired at age 55, pursuant the applicable federal statute, The Court held that the protections of the Act should properly apply to units of local governments as well as private employers.

The immediate effect of the judicial application of the Act to public employers was to negate municipal, state and federal agency budgets throughout the United States since those budgets were prepared in consideration of the replacement of those employees who would be mandatorily retired under their various statutes and ordinances.

The EEOC, in enforcing the ADEA as then interpreted by the Supreme Court, utilized the potential imposition of treble damages for "wilful" violations to assure good faith compliance in the form of amended statutes or ordinances, e.g., the city of Chicago amended their mandatory retirement ordinance to age 70. The EEOC thereupon limited potential back pay claims to 1981 for the city, still a sizeable amount in settlement.

Thereafter, municipalities and other agencies lobbied Congress for relief which came in the form of an exemption which permitted a return to previously existing mandatory retirements to allow these agencies to prepare to defend their particular age as a Bona Fide Occupational Qualification. Although studies were done to establish that the age restriction(s) were based upon the ability to fight fires, the results were not uniform, and a subsequent extension of the exemption through 1993 eliminated the impetus for the defense. Given that the exemption would span eight years, establishment of the bona fide qualification no longer was (at least a political) priority.

As 1993 drew to a close, another extension had already passed the House of Representatives, and by appending it to an Omnibus Crime Bill in an election year, its passage seemed certain. Retiring Senator Howard Metzenbaum (D-Ohio), long supported by the American Association of Retired Persons (AARP), had opposite views toward any age-based legislation, and he was the architect of severing that portion of the bill with the votes he could produce to pass (or defeat) the entire legislation.

As 1996 began, the bill to bring back mandatory retirement had again passed the House, and was held up in the Senate Committee. Its passage will probably depend upon the relative strength of the respective lobbies seeking its passage or defeat.

An interesting side note to the legislation was the fact that the city of Chicago, in restoring its age 63 mandatory retirement age, made it applicable to all its Career Service police and fire service employees, thereby creating a separate cause of action for the exempt rank (appointed) members who had been terminated at age 63.

ADMINISTRATIVE LAW

ADMINISTRATIVE LAW

The Fourth Branch of Government

While Administrative agencies of the government were created by the legislative branch, they contain the basic elements of all three.

These agencies have grown in power and breadth as a means of regulating specific areas of government since the creation of the Interstate Commerce Commission in 1887. Their duties and powers are defined by the statutes creating them, which uniformly grant broad discretionary power to determine and enforce compliance with the statutes over which they have authority. Thus, in their rule-making authority, similar to the legislative branch, they enact provisions which have the effect of law; in their decision-making authority, similar to the judiciary, they can conduct hearings and pass judgment on whether conduct or acts fall within the mandate of the statute; finally, their enforcement authority, most similar to the executive branch of government, they can enforce compliance by means of orders and sanctions (fines).

The Administrative Procedures Act of 1946 was passed by Congress to insure that the procedures utilized by the agencies also met with the due process concerns of basic fairness for those operating under the particular agency's authority.

Federal agencies, created by federal law, operate by either sharing authority with lower state agencies in a cooperative arrangement, or by preempting authority in a particular area.

The Federal Department of Labor's Occupational Safety and Health Administration (OSHA) shares its authority (and funding) with those states that adopt OSHA standards; the Equal Employment Opportunity Commission (EEOC) enforces Title VII in employment matters without a state EEOC (although many states, like Illinois, have a Department of Human Rights, as another forum for bringing claims of discrimination.

The vast majority of states enforce fire code regulations by means of a state fire marshal, who in turn, allows local governments to enforce their own codes with the requirement that they at least meet (they may exceed) regulations promulgated by the Office of The State Fire Marshal.

Thus a small village may enforce the state fire code regulations regarding the number of exits required in a public place, and a larger municipality might enforce a stricter standard requiring more, not less, number of exits, as a general example.

Fire Codes, in tandem with building codes, are the standards to ensure the prevention of fires and/or unsafe construction for the public good. It is the balancing of the common welfare against the rights of the individual that has always been the unique province of the courts, especially the Supreme Court.

In 1963, the Supreme Court had occasion to review the inspection procedures for fire code violations of the San Francisco Department of Public Health, to determine whether the procedures met with the command of the Fourth Amendment.

CAMARA v SAN FRANCISCO
United States Supreme Court (1967)
387 U.S. 523

WHITE, Justice.

* * * Though there were no judicial findings of fact in this prohibition proceeding, we shall set forth the parties' factual allegations. On November 6, 1963, an inspector of the Division of Housing Inspection of the San Francisco Department of Public Health entered an apartment building to make a routine annual inspection for possible violations of the city's Housing Code. The building's manager informed the inspector that appellant, lessee of the ground floor, was using the rear of his leasehold as a personal residence. Claiming that the building's occupancy permit did not allow residential use of the ground floor, the inspector confronted appellant and demanded that he permit an inspection of the premises. Appellant refused to allow the inspection because the inspector lacked a search warrant.

The inspector returned on November 8, again without a warrant, and appellant again refused to allow an inspection. A citation was then mailed ordering appellant to appear at the district attorney's office. When appellant failed to appear, two inspectors returned to his apartment on November 22. They informed appellant that he was required by law to permit an inspection under § 503 of the Housing Code:

> Sec. 503 RIGHT TO ENTER BUILDING. Authorized employees of
> the City departments or City agencies, so far as may be necessary
> for the performance of their duties, shall, upon presentation of proper

> credentials, have the right to enter, at reasonable times, any building,
> structure or premises in the City to perform any duty imposed upon
> them by the Municipal Code.

Appellant nevertheless refused the inspectors access to his apartment without a search warrant. Thereafter, a complaint was filed charging him with refusing to permit a lawful inspection in violation of § 507 of the Code. Appellant was arrested on December 2, and released on ball. When his demurrer to the criminal complaint was denied, appellant filed this petition for a writ of prohibition.

Appellant has argued throughout this litigation that § 503 is contrary to the Fourth and Fourteenth Amendments in that it authorizes municipal officials to enter a private dwelling without a search warrant and without probable cause to believe that a violation of the Housing Code exists therein . . . the District Court of Appeal held that § 503 does not violate Fourth Amendment rights because it "is part of a regulatory scheme which is essentially civil rather than criminal in nature, inasmuch as that section creates a right of inspection which is limited in scope and may not be exercised under unreasonable conditions." (Cit.Om.) Having concluded that *Frank v Maryland*, to the extent that it sanctioned such warrantless inspections, must be overruled, we reverse.

* * * To the *Frank* majority, municipal fire, health and housing inspection programs "touch at most upon the periphery of the important interests safeguarded by the Fourteenth Amendment's protection against official intrusion," 359 U.S. at 367, because the inspections are merely to determine whether physical conditions exist which do not compy with minimum standards prescribed in local regulatory ordinances. Since the inspector does not ask that the property owner open his doors to a search for "evidence of criminal action" which may be used to secure the owner's criminal conviction, historic interests of "self-protection" jointly protected by the Fourth and Fifth Amendments are said not to be involved, but only the less intense "right to be secure from intrusion into personal privacy." *Id.*, at 365.

We may agree that a routine inspection of the physical condition of private property is a less hostile intrusion than the typical policeman's search for fruits and instrumentalities of crime. For this reason alone, *Frank* differed from the great bulk of Fourth Amendment cases which have been considered by the Court. But we cannot agree that the Fourth Amendment interests at stake in these inspection cases are merely "peripheral." It is surely anomalous to say that the individual and his private property are fully protected by the Fourth Amendment only when the individual is suspected of criminal behavior. For instance, even the most law-abiding citizen has a very tangible interest in limiting the circumstances under which the sanctity of his home may be broken by offical authority, for the possibility of criminal entry under the guise of official sanction is a serious threat to personal and family security. And even accepting *Frank's* rather remarkable premise, inspections of the kind we are here considering do in fact jeopardize "self-protection" interests of the property owner. Like most regulatory laws, fire, health, and housing codes are enforced by criminal processes. In some cities, discovery of a violation by the inspector leads to a criminal complaint. Even in cities where discovery of a violation produces only an administrative compliance order, refusal to comply is a criminal offense, and the fact of compliance is verified by a second inspection, again without a warrant. Finally, as this case demonstrates, refusal to permit inspection is itself a crime, punishable by fine or even jail sentence.

The *Frank* majority suggested, and appellee reasserts, two other justifications for permitting administrative health and safety inspections without a warrant. First, it is argued that these inspections are "designed to make the least possible demand on the individual occupant." 359 U.S. at 367. The ordinances authorizing inspections are hedged with safeguards, and at any rate the inspector's particular decision to enter must comply with the constitutional standard of reasonableness even if he may enter without a warrant. In addition, the argument proceeds, the warrant process could not function effectively in this field. The decision to inspect an entire municipal area is based upon legislative or administrative assessment of broad factors such as the area's age and condition. Unless the magistrate is to review such policy matters, he must issue a "rubber stamp" warrant which provides no protection at all to the property owner.

In our opinion, these arguments unduly discount the purposes behind the warrant machinery contemplated by the Fourth Amendment. Under the present system, when the inspector demands entry, the occupant has no way of knowing whether enforcement of the municipal code involved requires inspection of his premises, no way of knowing the lawful limits of the inspector's power to search, and no way of knowing whether the inspector himself is acting under proper authorization. These are questions that may be reviewed by a neutral magistrate without any reassessment of the basic agency decision to canvass an area. Yet, only by refusing entry and risking a criminal conviction can the occupant at present challenge the inspector's decision to search * * *

The final justification suggested for warrantless administrative searches is that the public interest demands such a rule: it is vigorously argued that the health and safety of entire urban populations is dependent upon enforcement of minimum fire, housing and sanitation standards, and the only effective means of enforcing such codes is by routine systemized inspections of all physical structures. * * * In assessing whether the public interest demands creation of a general exception to the Fourth Amendment's warrant requirement, the question is not whether the public interest justifies the type of search in question, but whether the authority to search should be evidenced by a warrant, which in turn depends in part upon whether the burden of obtaining a warrant is likely to frustrate the government purpose behind the search. (Cit.Om.) It has nowhere been urged that fire, health, and housing code inspection programs could not achieve their goals within the confines of a reasonable search warrant requirement. Thus we do not find the public need argument dispositive.

In summary, we hold that administrative searches of the kind at issue here are significant intrusions upon the interests protected by the Fourth Amendment, that such searches when authorized and conducted without a warrant procedure lack the traditional safeguards which the Fourth Amendment guarantees to the individual, and that the reasons put forth in *Frank v Maryland* and other cases for upholding these warrantless searches are insufficient to justify so substantial a weakening of the Fourth Amendment's protections.

The judgment is vacated and the case remanded for further proceedings not inconsistent with this opinion.

On the same day, the Court ruled on the refusal of the owner of a commercial warehouse in Seattle to permit inspection of his locked facilities, holding that the Fourth Amendment protected the businessman who, "like the occupant of a residence, has a constitutional right to go about his business free from unreasonable offical entries upon his private commercial enterprise. "*See v City of Seattle*, 387 U.S. 541 (1967). Mr. Justice Clark, joined by Justices Harlan and Stewart, argued the powerfully worded dissent:

Eight years ago my Brother Frankfurter wisely wrote in *Frank v Maryland*, 359 U.S. 360 (1959):

> Time and experience have forcefully taught that the power to inspect dwelling places, either as a matter of systematic area-by-area search or, as here, to treat a specific problem, is of indispensable importance to the maintenance of community health; a power that would be greatly hobbled by the blanket requirement of the safeguards necessary for a search of evidence of criminal acts. The need for preventive action is great, and city after city has seen this need and granted the power of inspection to its health officals; and these inspections are apparently welcomed by all but an insignificant few.

Today the Court renders this municipal experience, which dates back to colonial days, for naught by overruling *Frank v Maryland* and by striking down hundreds of city ordinances throughout the country and jeopardizing thereby the health, welfare and safety of literally millions of people.

But this is not all. It prostitutes the command of the Fourth Amendment that "no Warrants shall issue, but upon probable cause" and sets up in the health and safety codes area inspection a newfangled "warrant" system that is entirely foreign to Fourth Amendment standards. It is regrettable that the Court wipes out such a long and widely accepted practice and creates in its place such enormous confusion in all of our towns and metropolitan cities in one fell swoop. I dissent. *
* * With due respect, inspections of this type have been made for over a century and a half without warrants and it is a little late to impose a death sentence on such procedures now. * * *

The great need for health and safety inspections is emphasized by the experience of San Francisco, a metropolitan area known for its cleanliness and safety ever since it suffered earthquake and fire back in 1906. For the fiscal year ending June 30, 1965, over 16,000 dwelling structures were inspected, of which over 5,600 required some type of compliance action . . .

In Seattle, . . . fire inspections of commercial and industrial buildings totalled over 85,000 in 1965. In Jacksonville, Florida, over 21,000 fire inspections were carried on in the same year, . . . In Boston, over 56,000 code violations were uncovered in 1966 . . . Los Angeles, over 300,000 inspections (health and fire) revealed over 28,000 hazardous violations. In Chicago during the period November 1965 to December 1966, over 18,000 buildings were found to be rodent-infested out of some 46,000 inspections. * * *

An even more disastrous effect will be suffered in plumbing violations. These are not only more frequent but also the more dangerous to the community. Defective plumbing causes back siphonage of sewage and other household wastes. Chicago's disastrous amoebic dysentery epidemic is an example. Over 100 deaths resulted. Fire code violations also often cause many conflagrations. Indeed, if the fire inspection attempted in *District of Columbia v Little*, 339 U.S. 1 (1950), had been permitted a two-year old child's death resulting from a fire that gutted the home involved there August 6, 1949, might well have been prevented.

Inspections also play a vital role in urban redevelopment and slum clearance. Statistics indicate that slums constitute 20% of the residential area of the average American city, still they produce 35% of the fires, 45% of the major crimes, and 50% of the disease. Today's decision will will play havoc with the many programs now designed to aid in the improvement of these areas. We should remember the admonition of MR. JUSTICE DOUGLAS in *Berman v Parker*, 348 U.S. 26, 32 (1954):

> Miserable and disreputable housing conditions may do more than spread disease and crime and immorality. The may also suffocate the spirit by reducing the people who live there to the status of cattle. They may indeed make living an almost insufferable burden.

* * * These boxcar warrants will be identical as to every dwelling in the area, save the street number itself. I daresay they will be printed up in pads of a thousand or more-with space for the street number to be inserted-and issued by magistrates in broadcast fashion as a matter of course.

The strong dissent and divided Court notwithstanding, the majority had held that the reach of the Fourth Amendment extended into administrative inspections, even where the inspections were under reasonably constructed schemes which insured minimal intrusion; the bare majority balanced individual privacy against the public welfare, and found the reasonable expectation of privacy to be the priority.

The only exceptions to the warrant procedure that the Court had permitted was for closely regulated businesses such as firearms (*United States v Biswell*, 406 U.S. 311 (1972) or liquor (*Colonnade Catering Corp. v. United States*, 397 U.S. 72 (1970).

It was these exceptions that the Department of Labor relied upon when it conducted inspections of workplaces for possible safety violations of the Occupational Safety and Health Act, which itself allowed its inspectors such authority.

The facts in the warehouse inspection case were very similar to the *Camara* and *See* cases: the inspector was refused entry to Barlow's Inc., in Pocatello, Idaho in September of 1975, followed by an order of the U.S. District Court of Idaho to permit the inspection, and a second refusal. Following this second refusal, however, the owner, Mr. Barlow, sought an injunction against the warrantless searches from the Court of Appeals, which granted his request. The Secretary of Labor (Ray Marshall) appealed to the United States Supreme Court to grant him the authority to conduct warrantless inspections of workplaces to carry out the federal mandate of the Act (OSHA) in making safer workplaces. The Court was once more divided, and Mr. Justice White again delivered the opinion of the majority, with the same result, federal law and commercial enterprise notwithstanding.

MARSHALL v BARLOW'S, INC.
United States Supreme Court (1978)
436 U.S. 307

WHITE, Justice:

* * *

The Secretary urges that warrantless inspections to enforce OSHA are reasonable within the meaning of the Fourth Amendment. Among other things, he relies on § 8 (a) of the Act, 29 U.S.C. § 657 (a), which authorizes inspection of business premises without a warrant and which the Secretary urges represents a congressional construction of the Fourth Amendment that the courts should not reject. Regretfully, we are unable to agree.

* * *

The Secretary urges that an exception from the search warrant requirement has been recognized for "pervasively regulated business(es)," *United States v Biswell*, 406 U.S. 311, 316 (1972), and for "closely regulated" industries "long subject to close supervision and inspection" *Colonnade Catering Corp., v United States*, 397 U.S. 72, 74, 77 (1970). These cases are indeed exceptions, but they represent responses to relatively unique circumstances. Certain industries have such a history of government oversight that no reasonable expectation of privacy, see *Katz v. United States*, 389 U.S. 347, 351-352 (1967), could exist for a proprietor over the stock of such an enterprise. Liquor (*Colonnade)* and firearms (*Biswell*) are industries of this type; when an entrepreneur embarks upon such a business, he has voluntarily chosen to subject himself to a full arsenal of governmental regulations. * * *

The clear import of our cases is that the closely regulated industry of the type involved in *Colonnade* and *Biswell* is the exception. The Secretary would make it the rule. Invoking the Walsh-Healy Act of 1936, 41 U.S.C. § 35, *et seq.*, the Secretary attempts to support a conclusion that all businesses involved in interstate commerce have long been subjected to close supervision of employee safety and health provisions. But the degree of federal involvement in employee working circumstances has never been of the order of specificity and pervasiveness that OSHA mandates. It is quite unconvincing to argue that the imposition of minimum wages and maximum hours on employers who contracted with the government under the Walsh-Healy Act prepared the entirety of American interstate commerce for regulation of working conditions to the minutest detail. Nor can any but the most fictional sense of voluntary consent be found in the single fact that one conducts a business affecting interstate commerce; under current practice and law, few businesses can be conducted without having some effect on interstate commerce. * * *

The critical fact in this case is that the entry over Mr. Barlow's objection is being sought by a government agent. Employees are not being prohibited from reporting OSHA violations. What they observe in their daily functions is undoubtedly beyond the employer's reasonable expectation of privacy. The Government inspector, however, is not an employee. Without a warrant, he stands in no better position than a member of the public. What is observable by the public is observable, without a warrant, by the Government inspector as well. The owner of a business has not, by the necessary utilization of employees in his operation, thrown open the areas where employees alone are permitted to the warrantless scrutiny of Government agents. That an employee is free to report, and the Government is free to use, any evidence of non-compliance with OSHA that the employee observes furnishes no justification for federal agents to enter a place of business from which the public is restricted and to conduct their own warrantless search. * * *

We conclude that the concerns expressed by the Secretary of State do not suffice to justify warrantless inspections under OSHA or vitiate the general constitutional requirement that for a search to be reasonable a warrant must be obtained.

GLOSSARY

accessory: a person who is involved with an offense, but not directly participating in the act; may be before, at or after the fact.

accomplice: a person who assists, aids or abets one in the commission of an offense.

actus reus: ("guilty act") the act or conduct prohibited by law which is part of the corpus delicti of a crime; the other required element is the mens rea ("guilty mind")

adjudication: the final disposition of a case by the court.

agency: the relationship wherein one party (the agent) acts on behalf of another (the principal).

affirmative action: court-imposed or self-initiated actions taken to remedy the effects of past discrimination by employers, or to assure non-discrimination in the present or future.

affirmative defense: a defense to an action which the court requires a party to plead before it will consider it; e.g., a statute of limitations bar to an action.

amicus curae: ("friend of the court") a non-party who wishes to address the court in some action in which they have an interest.

answer: in pleadings, a defendant's written response to plaintiff's allegations in complaint.

appeal: a complaint to a superior court that a lower court has issued an incorrect decision (the party making the appeal is the "appellant," the responding party the "appellee".

arson: the criminal offense of destruction of property by fire or explosive

assault: the criminal offense of placing another in fear of receiving bodily harm.

assumption of risk: a defense to an action in negligence based upon the fact that an injured party assumed the very risk which caused his injury

attempt: an inchoate offense which is one or more acts done in furtherance of the commission of a separate crime, but falling short of completion of the intended crime.

bail: security, usually money or a pledge of money, to insure the appearance of a party in court

battery: the unjustified contact with a person which, if intentional, is a crime; if unintentional, a tort.

best evidence rule: a procedural rule requiring the use of original documents in lieu of copies.

Bill of Rights: the first ten amendments to the Constitution which prohibit governmental intrusion on certain basic rights of citizens.

bona fide: "good faith" :reasonable, as in bona fide occupational qualification, legitimate, as in bona fide offer

breach of duty: failure to conform one's actions to meet a duty of care imposed by statute or the standard of reasonable care.

burden of proof: the requirement of going forward with the evidence to prove up a cause of action or to rebut it.

cause of action: a claim or right which a court will hear for adjudication.

certiorari: the common law writ used to gain appellate review of a decision.

circumstantial evidence: evidence which requires some inference to be probative

Common Law: the body of decisions which was transposed to America from England by the colonists forming the basis of early American law prior to the Revolution.

comparative negligence: the apportionment of responsibility by the court between the plaintiff and the defendant.

conspiracy: the criminal offense of agreeing to commit a crime.

Constitution: the written embodiment of the United States system of government and guarantee of certain basic human rights; the supreme law of the United States.

contributory negligence: negligence on the part of the plaintiff which may reduce or negate the liability of the defendant.

corpus delicti: ("the body of the crime") the elements necessary to prove a criminal offense

corroborate: to support with additional facts, testimony or evidence.

immunity: exemption from duty or penalty, via statute or as a grant from the prosecution

inchoate offense: an offense, complete in and of itself, which has as its design, the completion of another criminal act; e.g., conspiracy to commit arson.

independent contractor: a person employed by another, usually to perform a specific task, who retains control over the performance of said task, and whose negligence will not be imputed to the employing party.

indictment: the formal accusation of a party with the commission of a crime, usually via the Grand Jury procedure.

injunction: an order of the court to abstain from or to perform some act.

intentional infliction of mental distress: a tort based upon actions which are designed to cause psychological harm to another.

invitee: one who comes upon the property of another under express or implied consent.

jurisdiction: the authority of a court to enter a decision in a given matter before it

latent: hidden, as in a latent defect; as opposed to an obvious (patent) defect

licensee: a party who comes upon the land of another not by invitation, but by permission ("license")

malice: evil intent; a state of mind attributed to the doing of any unlawful act

manslaughter: the unpremeditated unjustifiable killing of another person

mens rea: ("guilty mind") the state of mind required for conviction of a crime.

misdemeanor: a criminal offense punishable by fine or imprisonment other than in a penitentiary.

municipal corporation: a political subdivision created by the state to perform some function of government

municipality: a unit of local government created by the action of the people directly for the purpose of self-government

negligence: a tort based upon the breach of a duty to another which proximately causes injury.

non obstante verdicto (n.o.v.): a judgment rendered by the court where the verdict of the jury is against the manifest weight of the evidence.

presumption of innocence: the basic doctrine of American criminal justice which provides that a person is innocent until proven guilty beyond a reasonable doubt of the acts alleged.

prima facie case: ("first look") all the elements of a cause of action which, if unchallenged by a defense, prove up a plaintiff's case.

proximate cause: that cause, uninterrupted by any intervening cause, which directly led to the injury of the plaintiff in a negligence action.

quasi-criminal: an offense against society, usually punishable by fine, less serious than a crime, such as a minor traffic offense.

quid pro quo: (something for something) the consideration for which another act was performed.

reasonable man: the standard in negligence actions which judges the foreseeability of harm from the negligent party's actions.

rescue: the legal doctrine that counters the defense of assumption of risk by interposing the defendant's negligence as the basis for the need for the plaintiff to respond to the situation.

res ipsa loquitur: ("the facts speak for themselves") a type of tort action of which the occurrence does not normally happen absent negligence.

respondeat superior: ("Let the Master answer") vicarious liability imposed upon the master or employer of a servant or employee for the negligence of that employee.

separation of powers: the division of authority in the Constitution between the legislative, executive and judicial branches of government

sexual harassment: the conditioning of terms of employment upon the submission to sexual favors or the creation of a hostile work environment based upon gender.

solicitation: the offense of requesting another to perform or assist in the performance of a criminal act.

sovereign immunity: a limitation on the liability of a governmental body for the negligence of its servants or employees, based on the Common Law doctrine that "the king could do no wrong".

stare decisis: "Let the decision stand" the doctrine of judicial precedence which should bind future decisions on similar matters

statute: a written law passed by the governing body of the state or federal government.

tort: an intentional or unintentional wrong committed against a person.

testimony: evidence in the form of statements made in court or by a deposition under oath.

trespass: entering upon the land or property of another without consent of the owner.

voir dire: the examination of prospective jurors by attorneys for either party to the action.

voluntary manslaughter: the intentional killing of another human being under circumstances which reduce the penalty from that of murder, e.g., under an irresistible impulse. This is compared to involuntary manslaughter, where the result was not intended to a specific victim, e.g., the killing of a party via the grossly negligent driving of an automobile.

WILLIAM J. WILKINSON is retired from many years of public service. A lifelong Chicagoan, he has been a teacher in its inner city schools, a Chicago Police Officer, and after a full career of 32 years of firefighting, he retired in late 2001 as a Battalion Chief from one of the busiest battalions (the 17th) in the city of Chicago. He was the Governmental Affairs Officer (Staff Counsel to the Fire Commissioner) for three successive commissioners in seven years, before returning to line service as a Fire Captain and then as Battalion Chief.

He has served as a trustee on the Chicago Firemen's Pension Board for nine of those years. As an Adjunct Professor for Southern Illinois University and Northwestern University, he continues to teach young firefighters and officers regarding the issues of management of Fire Service Operations and legal liability. He includes within his teaching some very practical skills in avoidance of fatal operational mistakes.

He serves as an arbitrator for the Cook County Municipal Court, and maintains a limited practice of law to spend maximum time with his grandchildren.

LaVergne, TN USA
31 December 2009
168674LV00003B/48/A